C   d Con   y oli

Other titles in

Gender and Community Policing

WALKING THE TALK

Susan L. Miller

NORTHEASTERN UNIVERSITY PRESS
Boston

Northeastern University Press
Copyright 1999 by Susan L. Miller

Library of Congress Cataloging-in-Publication Data
Miller, Susan L.
Gender and community policing : walking the talk / Susan L. Miller.
p. cm.—(Northeastern series on gender, crime, and law)
Includes bibliographical references.
ISBN 1-55553-414-7 (cloth : alk. paper).—ISBN 1-55553-413-9
(pbk. : alk. paper)
1. Community policing—Middle West. 2. Police—Middle West—
Social conditions. 3. Policewomen—Middle West—Social conditions.
4. Sex role in the work environment—Middle West. 5. Police
administration—Middle West. I. Title. II. Series.
HV7936.C83M6 1999
363.2'082'0977—dc21 99-25017

Designed by Gary Gore

Composed in Berkeley by Coghill Composition in Richmond, Virginia. Printed and bound
by Thomson-Shore, Inc., in Dexter, Michigan.
The paper is Glatfelter Supple Opaque Recycled, an acid-free sheet.

Manufactured in the United States of America
03 02 01 00 99   5 4 3 2 1

For my twin sister, Lisa,
who has always been there

Contents

Preface

This project began in serendipity. A friend of mine who is a sports sociologist invited me to observe the children's soccer program in Jackson City. (The name is fictitious.) The game was to be refereed by a female friend of hers who was a neighborhood police officer. Although I had been teaching an upper-level police seminar, my actual street experience with officers was limited to a number of "citizen ride-alongs" in a large East Coast city. On those occasions I had watched police kick suspects who were incapacitated by foot- and handcuffs and had heard them use many racist, misogynistic, and homophobic epithets to describe various residents. I was not impressed with their professionalism, their compassion, or their understanding of how their presence and behavior were linked to enduring social problems in the city. Even though I also saw some quality policing, the more troubling images stayed with me. Given this background, it was with some reluctance that I agreed to spend the day in Jackson City with the neighborhood officer. I wanted to see what was behind all the fuss about community policing, if only so that I would have new police stories to share with my students.

What I observed challenged my preconceptions and past experiences. During the afternoon, I saw residents greet "Officer Terry" with warm smiles, offering her lemonade and filling her in on events that had occurred while she was off duty. (The names of all persons mentioned in connection with Jackson City are fictitious.) She helped a teenaged boy retrieve his clothing from a Dumpster, where his mother had thrown all his things after kicking him out of the house. I found out later that he was a "gang-banger wanna-be," yet he lost his toughness around Officer Terry and was almost in tears. Since there were not enough players for a game, we also kicked the soccer ball around with some boys and girls who were African American, Southeast Asian, and white.

Among these uncommon sights, perhaps the most unusual event of all was the replaying of the neighborhood officer's answering machine. For about eight minutes, a male resident explained to Officer Terry why he had been arrested for domestic violence against his former wife the night before. He was not calling to shift the blame to his onetime spouse or to make excuses; he took full responsibility. But he wanted Officer Terry to know why he had done it, and how worried he was about his children, who had seen the entire episode. The man also wanted the policewoman's advice about what to do—not how to wriggle out of the arrest, but how to reduce the level of conflict in case his former wife came to his home again. This was something new to hear: a neighborhood resident "spilling his guts" to a police officer he saw as a confessor, therapist, strategist, and, yes, friend. Many patrol officers no doubt hear people's private stories, but the tone and wording of this message conveyed a different level of respect and connection. It was clear to me that this man *knew* that Officer Terry really did care about him, his children, and what had happened. And she did. In all of the community-police encounters I witnessed that day, my surprise only deepened.

When I decided to do research on community policing, I planned to explore the possible differences in response to domestic violence by neighborhood officers, who know the residents well, and traditional patrol officers in squad cars, who respond only after being dispatched by radio. But the more I spoke with Officer Terry and another friend on the force about the Jackson City Police Department and its community policing philosophy, the more I realized that I wanted to explore much more than domestic violence incidents. I was curious as to whether the interpersonal dynamics I observed with Officer Terry would be like those when a male neighborhood police officer (NPO) was involved. I wanted to delve into the heads and hearts of the NPOs, to see for myself what worked in community policing and to see what they felt did not. I wanted to examine how such a paradigm shift in the theory and practice of policing would affect the officers who desire street action, and how they would assess their new "walk and talk" colleagues. And so, with the continued help and support of my key contact people, the Jackson City Police Department opened its doors to me, and I began to explore the contested terrain of gender dynamics and community policing.

This book is the culmination of several years in the neighborhoods, watching, asking, tagging along, interviewing, and watching some more. I hope that my findings will speak to multiple audiences with various interests: criminal justice scholars, makers of public policy, students, and practitioners—among these both police and police administrators, as well as criminologists and sociologists who conduct research on gender and the professions. I also hope that this book will be of value to any reader who is engaged with our everyday world. Whether through informal encounters in our neighborhoods, as potential suspects, or as victims, we are all affected by the power and presence that police have in our lives. I know as a citizen that I now understand the social-control conundrum of community policing more clearly than I did when I began this project.

My data and analysis provide a foundation for exploring how community policing is accomplished across multiple styles, roles, practices, and personalities. The pages that follow indicate how the social constructs of masculinity and femininity interact with the organizational culture of the police, and the officers' sexuality, race, and gender, in many interesting ways. I hope that this book will contribute to the multidisciplinary literature that addresses gender and occupations, as well as to the police and criminal justice fields. As I worked and wrote, I was aware of the enormous debt of gratitude I owe to the talented scholarship of others, both inside and outside the criminal justice discipline, and I acknowledge the profound influence their work has had on my own thinking.

Acknowledgments

If it takes a village to raise a child, it also takes a village to write a book. I am delighted to formally thank the people of the village here. The work of data collection, analysis, writing, and thinking extended over several years. Many persons helped in this process by listening to my ideas, understanding my enthusiasm about the findings, making me take breaks for fun, and being patient when I disappeared socially.

I first thank my field observation research team: Kay Forest, Jann Thiel, Chris Kells, Michael Richardson, and Simon Newman. Celeste Hughes expertly transcribed many of the interviews. Michelle Meloy greatly assisted with the research, and Estralita Jones helped with the survey data. Nancy Quillen and Debby Hussnatter cheerfully organized express-mail deliveries and other crucial secretarial support. Barbara Lenes, the editorial assistant at Northeastern University Press, Emily McKeigue, the production editor, and Frank Austin, the copyeditor, helped the project through the course of production.

The manuscript was greatly improved by guidance and suggestions from my editor, Claire Renzetti, from Joanne Belknap, and from William Frohlich at Northeastern University Press. Claire and Bill urged me to avoid academic jargon, minimize citations, and get to the heart of the matter rather than provide too much theory and history and too many empirical findings. Of course, these suggestions are a social scientist's nightmare; in the end, though, I believe that the officers' stories and their meanings emerge with far greater clarity than they would have without this sage advice.

I also gratefully acknowledge summer research grants received from Northern Illinois University and from the University of Delaware, as well as aid from my colleagues and friends at these campuses. From the early days of planning the project through its completion, I have been fortunate to be connected to wonderful scholars and friends at both of these institutions.

My most constant and loving supporters are my parents, Marilyn and Ken Miller. Who I am has been profoundly shaped by their boundless love and support, and by their joy in reading and in exploring the world around them. My other supporters include my sister, Lisa, my brother-in-law, Joe DeRosa, and my wonderful, special nieces and nephew, Toni Anne, Samantha Lynn, and Joey. Their love and energies renew my spirit and my belief in a better world.

Authors in most academic fields tend to publish articles; therefore, we do not often get to thank all the persons who add meaning to our lives. Here, I am able to thank my family of friends who offered me diversions, support, laughter, and patience as sounding boards: Lisa Bartran; Janna Lambine; Donna and Bill Becker and their terrific children, Alex, Zachary, and Charlie; Patricia "Alpha" Stewart; Deb Mills; Helen Power and the entire "WWA"; Sue and Amanda Lawrence-Reeder; my four-legged friend Tasha; and Nick and Dune Scott. They have all made me realize, many times over, that I have many homes of the heart.

Reminding me about other important things in life, new friends and old friends have nurtured and inspired me with their wisdom, their politics, and their compassion, and in other ways they may not even know: a thank-you to Jessica Schiffman, Judy Schneider, Carol Post, Dan Atkins, Ronet Bachman, Mary Ruth Warner, Susan Caringella-MacDonald, Nancy Jurik, Ruth Triplett, Rosemary Barberet, Agent 99, and T.O. Special thanks to my running partner, Pete, with whom I ran my first (and probably only) half-marathon the week I finished writing this book.

Several close friends read drafts of earlier chapters, providing invaluable help and much support: LeeAnn Iovanni, Kimn Carlton-Smith, Chris Wilkinson, and Kay Forest. Their sense of humor—apparent even in the face of my dangling participles—and their intelligence made their feedback insightful. They helped tremendously to make this a better book.

The officers of the Jackson City Police Department deserve hearty applause for their openness, for their patience when being pestered and followed by me and different members of the research team on their shifts, and for their enthusiastic receptivity to being researched. Any resultant mistakes and misinterpretations are solely my responsibility. I am especially grateful to the chief and the inspector of the department, and to all of the current and former neighborhood police officers and patrol officers I interviewed; they gave me their time graciously and patiently and shared their experiences and feelings honestly and openly. Most especially, I thank my two friends who introduced me to the Jackson City Police Department, and in particular to two very special officers. I cannot name them for reasons of confidentiality, but their role in the project was vital. I hope that this book makes them proud.

Gender and Community Policing

Background

The Research Goals, Methods, and Site

Introduction

In the first century of policing in the United States, beginning around 1850, women were excluded from the "male" world of policework because they were thought of as too soft to be crimefighters on patrol.[1] The early policewomen were presented as mother figures who dispensed care and guidance (see Schulz 1995; Appier 1998). Women's job responsibilities reflected social assumptions about their emotional, compassionate, and cooperative temperaments. Thus, the policewomen's domain included helping runaway, lost, or abused children, along with prostitutes, because policewomen were believed to have higher moral standards of behavior than did men. Policewomen also performed stereotypically female clerical roles. Women's perceived physical deficiencies, such as their lack of strength or the aggressiveness needed to intimidate crooks or to fight, as well as their "fragile" emotional composition, kept policewomen from moving out of prescribed roles focusing on children, fallen women, and typewriters (Milton 1972).

While women were being excluded from policing, policemen were being celebrated as masculine crimefighters who were brave, suspicious, aloof, objective, cynical, physically intimidating, and willing to use force and even brutality. Women's femininity, by contrast, suggested a less masterful, more submissive style: partiality, subjectivity, gentleness, conciliation, and a focus on affective connections.

Traditional policing, masculine and paramilitary, has rejected "feminine" traits and skills, banishing them to the periphery of the organization so as not to contaminate the preferred image of the aloof professional or the macho crimefighter. In fact, many observers view the criminal justice and legal system overall as operating with a uniquely masculine voice, a detached and impersonal one that emphasizes the rational at the expense of the relational. Others maintain, however, that a feminine voice could also be present, particularly when decisions are made based on contextual or affiliational factors. Given the ideological preoccupation with masculinity in policing, though, any behavior that appears tied to femininity, weakness, or subjectivity is suspect and denigrated. Those who express care and connection beyond superficial niceties have been mocked or dismissed as too emotional to be proper police officers. In particular, such beliefs have been used historically to justify excluding women from the profession. With the advent of the "new" genre of community policing, however, such "feminine" constructs as cooperation and the maintenance of connections have been reintroduced.

Community policing emerged in the early 1980s as a result of the growing tension between police and citizens (Kelling and Moore 1991). This "new" approach—actually, the most recent in a series of such reforms—emphasizes building closer ties between police and members of the community. It is hypothesized that by increasing community members' contact with police, suspicion and distrust between the two groups would decrease, citizen satisfaction with police would increase, quality of community life would be improved, and levels of fear would be reduced. One predicted outgrowth of community policing is that residents (as witnesses or victims) would also be more willing to come forward with information about crimes and become more involved with prevention activities because police officers would be more familiar and less intimidating.

The promises of community policing are vast. They include "an emphasis on improving the number and quality of police-citizen contacts, a broader definition of 'legitimate' police work, decentralization of the police bureaucracy, and a greater emphasis on proactive problem-solving" (Rosenbaum 1988, 334). In addition, this approach encourages the police to be "responsive to citizen demands" and committed to "helping neighborhoods help themselves" (Skogan 1990, 92) and to fully know the district they serve—its residents, its habits, its trouble spots, and its strengths. Community policing introduces major role reorientation among the officers themselves; if successful, it relies on the ability to implement both philosophical and organizational change within an institution that is characterized by "rigid bureaucratic procedures [and] fear of change among employees" and hypermasculinity (Rosenbaum and Lurigio 1994, 303).

Officers on foot patrol, one of the most popular forms of community policing and that most heavily supported by federal funds, are challenged to do more than duplicate earlier police reforms. Today, they are expected to interact with community members, not just respond to merchants and political leaders, and to move beyond the traditional functions of surveillance and arrest (Rosenbaum and Lurigio 1994). There is an expectation that foot patrol officers will engage in more nontraditional activities, such as participating in community meetings, and that community police officers in general will identify neighborhood problems and design strategies to fix them. Officers are encouraged to organize community initiatives, resolve disputes among residents, establish connections, and make referrals to appropriate social service agencies (Trojanowicz 1986).

This image of the ideal community police officer has a social-work orientation, a style that traditionally has been beyond the purview of acceptable policing. These new activities are expected to come about through a process of decentralization, which brings police closer to the neighborhoods in ministations or storefront offices within the community, particularly in the more troubled areas. Decentralization particularly increases community police officers' independence from the larger organization. At the same time, though, it may exacerbate the negative feelings held toward neighborhood officers by routine patrol officers, who misunderstand the new approach and see these efforts as "*social work* rather than real policework" (emphasis in original, Rosenbaum and Lurigio 1994, 306; see also Skolnick and Bayley 1986). Making these sorts of changes will not be easy. Success depends upon the receptivity of the officers who carry out the new programs. In order to be accepted by the rank and file, the "feminine" traits involved in community policing may need to be appropriated as masculine ones and reshaped to appear powerful and desirable.[2] Hence, in what follows I explore the various contradictions that emerge when a recalcitrant institution is challenged to change and expand its ideology and practice.

In particular, this book investigates how women and men negotiate gendered skills and knowledge within a proactive and dynamic community context. It also examines the ambiguities that surround "feminine" skills and their enthusiastic appropriation by community policing, in contrast to their rejection in traditional policing. The pages that follow represent the first steps in constructing a feminist conceptual framework of community policing, which also introduces related policing questions and empirically explores the ideas contained herein. Community policing offers the potential of forging closer connections and deeper trust between police and citizens. To realize this potential, however, images and structures of the police organization must accommodate such changes. Altering the masculinist bias, for example, requires a shift in policing paradigms to which many officers remain resistant. Without such a change, however, the potential of community policing may not be realized.

Administrators and officers need to do far more than just "talk the talk";

they need to put new goals into practice, to truly "walk the talk." The questions raised by this ideological concern are varied. How can policing be transformed to honor the values of care, connection, empathy, and informality (the "female" voice) within the traditions of a paramilitary, masculinist organization? What changes must occur to reconcile the contradictions between "masculine" and "feminine" activities and to attract officers to community policing positions? What matters more, the gender of the officers, or that those of *either* gender actively integrate the "ethic of care" within their social control and policing ideology? Under a community model, will policing still be gendered by *who* is seen as the "expert"? Are there other characteristics of officers besides gender, such as race and sexual orientation, that increase the effectiveness of community policing? These questions are explored in this book. Throughout, gender is a key variable; when relevant, race and sexual orientation are also introduced and analyzed.

There are several parts to this first chapter. I begin by introducing the research setting and the city itself. I then outline the structure and demographics of the police department. (Additional details regarding the research design and methodology can be found in the Appendix.) Next, I trace the development of the city's community policing program, exploring the motivations of the first wave of officers who were drawn to the new neighborhood positions and how their motivations resembled or differed from those of later neighborhood officers. Finally, I present the difficulties members of the department faced in making the transition from patrol to neighborhood officer status, including their treatment by the established police subculture. I end by describing the progression of the subsequent chapters.

Important Points about the Book

Before I describe the research setting, two matters need to be made clear. First, I refer to *neighborhood police officers* as NPOs. These women and men are assigned to a designated neighborhood for three years and thus spend much of their time on foot. They are not required to answer radio dispatch calls to their neighborhoods; rather, they are permanently stationed there to respond to local needs, which could include prevention and program development as well as crimefighting. *Patrol officers* drive police squad cars; their function is reactive, waiting for instructions from the radio dispatcher. They are assigned to different sections of the city; the patrol officers interviewed and observed in this study work the same neighborhoods as the NPOs, with the difference that they patrol by car.

Second, although the chief and the individual officers I interviewed and observed were forthcoming with their information, and gave me permission to quote them and reveal the identity of the city and of particular assignments, I have come to believe that their anonymity should be preserved. Accordingly, the names used here for the city, the designated neighborhoods, and the individual officers are all fictitious. When we talked, I encouraged the respondents to be as frank and open as possible, and I do not want anyone compromised by my analysis. Whenever it is relevant, I identify the officers' race, gender, and status (current or former, NPO or patrol officer), and I occasionally note sexual orientation. In general, though, I chose not to reveal particular identities or statuses when I thought that the quotation could be traced and easily attributed to an individual. Given the openness of the department, several researchers have published their work without disguising the name of the city. For the reasons described above, I have decided not to name these research articles and monographs, although I do draw information from them. I indicate the location of this material in the text, and I urge readers who need additional information to contact me directly at the University of Delaware.

Research Setting

Jackson City lies in the Midwest and is home to about two hundred thousand persons. Unlike the case in many larger cities, the Jackson City Police Department is not under fire for its bad practices; rather, it enjoys a solid reputation with the citizens, many of whom indicate an overall satisfaction with the treatment they receive from police. In many ways, the project site is a researcher's dream. Although the city has had its share of problems, it has not been ravaged by the disintegration wrought by poverty, homelessness, and drug use that has plagued most larger American cities. Jackson City has a reputation for liberal politics, cultural diversity, and progressive urban planning and programs. Lakes and parks surround the major thoroughfares. The center of the city hosts the state capitol; the police department lies at one end of a pedestrian street lined with trendy bookstores, art galleries, clothing shops, and coffee shops, and the leading state university lies at the other. The city is frequently rated among the top places in the country to live. The police department, run by one chief for twenty-two years, has warmly embraced partnerships with university and government researchers. The current chief, who took over in 1994, is an African American man who strongly supported the community approach in his former police department; he maintains this interest, as well as his connection with researchers. At one point during an interview with me, the current chief said on tape, "If you find anything negative about our department, go ahead and print it; it will only make us improve our policing."

Demographics of the Police Department

The commitments to diversity and to hiring highly qualified officers are reflected in the composition of the department. The force in Jackson City boasts a high percentage of college graduates, and many officers remain engaged in postgraduate work (1988 statistics indicate about half of the force has achieved a college degree or more). Diversity in hiring has flourished; although most top-level executives are white men, several Hispanic Americans and African Americans are in higher supervisory ranks, and several women are in the detective bureau and above. In 1988, women constituted 19 percent of the department, whereas by 1995 the figure had risen to 26.27 percent. This percentage is well above the national average; indeed, it may be one of the highest in the country.

In 1995, the Jackson City Police Department had 335 commissioned officers, including patrol personnel, supervisors, and detectives. African Americans made up 9.25 percent of the force; Hispanic Americans, 3.88 percent; Asian Americans, 1.49 percent; and Native Americans, 1.19 percent. The numerical breakdown was as follows:

Men:	White	205
	African American	25
	Hispanic	10
	Asian	4
	Native American	3
	Total	247
Women:	White	77
	African American	6
	Hispanic	3
	Asian	1
	Native American	1
	Total	88

Of the 216 patrol officers, including the NPOs, the numerical breakdown was as follows:

Men:	White	119
	African American	18
	Hispanic	6
	Asian	4
	Native American	3
	Total	150

Women:	White	58
	African American	3
	Hispanic	3
	Asian	1
	Native American	1
	Total	66

Departmental records revealed that 22 women, as compared with 97 men, held ranks above patrol officer.

At the time of the research project, there were forty-five former and current neighborhood police officers. Eighteen (40 percent) of them were women and twenty-seven (60 percent) were men; a significant number of the women were "out" lesbians. (I am deliberately not providing detailed information about individual gay or lesbian officers in order to preserve their anonymity. Even in the most enlightened groups or places, backlash can occur and hurt one's career.) When most of the interviews and fieldwork was done, the officers assigned to the neighborhoods numbered ten men (four of whom were African Americans) and three white women.

The diversity of the neighborhood officers in race, gender, and sexual orientation may simply reflect the overall diversity of the force. The former chief was deeply committed to creating a department that mirrored the community it served. Many of the officers told me about this philosophy with obvious pride. On the surface, at least, there did not seem to be any cleavages between officers of different races, genders, or sexual orientations. The following statement by a white heterosexual male neighborhood officer was typical:

> Our department has been very understanding, very open, to people with different lifestyles, different sexual lifestyles. If you get an officer in there who's homophobic, you can create a very big problem if you're in a neighborhood that has residents that have a different lifestyle. And Jackson City is known for having more women per capita, or per authorized strength, than any other department in the United States . . . we have a high population of lesbian officers. And to me, I think it's great. But if you go to some of these other police activities around the state, such as state bowling tournaments, state golf tournaments, or to other schools like some of these small departments like up north, and they say, where you from? Jackson City. You know, right away it's, oh ya, you got all those lesbians.

Another officer declared the diversity to be a strength:

That's what makes our department so good is that we have, I mean, you can't expect me as a white male to go into a domestic dispute between two males who are involved in a relationship, and if I'm heterosexual and they're homosexual, to go in there and be able to understand everything there is to understand about their relationship and their problems, I can't do it. But by having me on this department with other people that have a similar lifestyle to theirs, there's a sense of education that takes place within the department. By my associating with, supervising, talking, doing things away from the department with these people, I learn about their lifestyles. They learn about mine and I can take that with me to this call.

Several lesbian officers stated that they would not consider working elsewhere: "There are very few departments that have been as good to women and gays and lesbians and minorities as this department" (Pam, white lesbian, former NPO). Garth, a white male heterosexual former NPO, explained:

It doesn't matter if you're gay or black or white or female, doesn't mean you can't do the job . . . and we get quality people and not the traditional cookie-cutter model of a police officer. . . . [N]onwhite males do a good if not better job than a typical white male would because they bring different understandings and life experience to the job, and a lot of white males' understanding they learn from nontraditional cops.

These remarks illustrate the positive features of diversity within the Jackson City department: educating other officers about cultural differences within the force itself, and improving officers' responsiveness to the diverse communities in which they serve.

History of the Community Policing Program

Jackson City is a city that's built by neighborhoods. —Former police chief, architect of the city's community policing program

Someone's always criticizing foot patrol; it's easy to be a Monday morning quarterback. —Lisa, white lesbian, former NPO

Under the leadership of the former chief, in the 1980s the Jackson City Police Department began to transform its traditional philosophy. The goal was to change the internal organizational design, following the Quality Leadership model developed by W. Edwards Deming, along with other models, to facilitate achieving the external goal of improved service to the community. Using Quality Leadership principles, the department sought to create a supportive leadership style, bring about physical decentralization, and support community- and problem-oriented policing. The department's mission statement reflects these sentiments:

> We believe in the dignity and worth of all people. We are committed to:
> Providing high-quality, community-oriented police services with sensitivity; Protecting constitutional rights; Problem solving; Teamwork;
> Openness; Planning for the future; Providing leadership to the police profession. We are proud of the diversity of our work force which permits us to grow and which respects each of us as individuals, and we strive for a healthful workplace.

The proposed changes within the police department gained momentum in 1985 when the then-mayor introduced the concepts of Quality Leadership to the city in a four-day workshop led by Deming himself. The police department thus adopted a management philosophy that followed Quality Leadership principles, along with other management goals; the principles emphasized teamwork, goal setting, data-based problem solving, a customer orientation, employee input in decision making, establishing a supportive environment for creativity and risk taking, and tolerance for mistakes, among other things. (The source here is not named to protect the anonymity of the department; please contact the author for additional information.)

The chief strongly believed that Quality Leadership was the key to implementing effective community policing. The motto of the department reflected this philosophy—Closer to the People: Quality from the Inside, Out. Citizens were viewed as "customers," and police were committed to learning about and to handling their needs. The hope was that encouraging greater interest by citizens in crime control would lead them to play a greater role in providing information to solve crimes because they would come to respect and trust the police more. Jackson City's philosophy was in line with the trend in national policing policy to stimulate greater citizen involvement in crime control efforts, particularly in some communities whose inhabitants felt estranged from the police, a tension exacerbated for marginalized residents, usually poor, people of color, or both. Thus, a high value was put on establishing closer ties with the community, particularly since the majority of requests for police services involved, not "crimefighting," but assistance in other situations.

These changes transpired at a moment that was fortuitous for the department. The then-chief was young (thirty-four years old), dynamic, and open to new ideas. His background included liberal political activity in college; he had actively criticized police and their handling of students protesting the Vietnam War. Many of those interviewed talked about the turmoil facing him in the first ten of his twenty-two years as chief. The following account was confirmed in multiple subsequent interviews with officers of all ranks:

> [T]he chief was very close to getting fired for alleged rumors of [trouble] and all this kind of stuff, which he probably was doing, given the crowd of people that he ran with at the time . . . he was young, he wore sandals and was pretty much out there. He promoted all rising young people obviously close to his age, that's why most all of the current captains and lieutenants are so young, they are people who were so close to the chief. That whole group got him through his first ten years or so . . . he created the Officer Advisory Council because there was so much unrest in the department. The chief saw this as a way to make the decision-making process a little more democratic in the organization. But, there was definitely an A-Team/B-Team dichotomy. (Bill, white man, former NPO)

The chief made promotions from the "A-Team," mostly men who were his inner circle of confidants, a group other officers referred to as the "chief's disciples." Those who were devotees of Total Quality Management and in the chief's inner circle (or aspired to be) even laminated Deming's ten principles to put in their wallets. Using these loyal friends as troubleshooters and ambassadors, the chief instituted new programs that have had a lasting impact on the Jackson City police force. First, he transformed selection and hiring with his commitment to diversity; women, people of color, and older officers were actively recruited. For example, Katie, one of the first NPOs (a black woman who has been on the force since 1975), recalled:

> We had the most unique class in the history of the Jackson City Police Department, because we had several women, several people of color, and a variety of ages, and we just covered the gamut of who normally wasn't hired. So it was real nice, and very, very reflective of what affirmative action wanted and the diversity within our community.

This attention to diversity in hiring continued throughout the chief's tenure. Moreover, he used the principles of Quality Leadership and explicitly anchored them to the new model of community policing. Anecdotal stories and research about community policing were just beginning to find their way into police magazines and academic journals. The chief, described by many as a visionary, was committed to trying the new methods in Jackson City to enhance traditional policing efforts.

When community policing was introduced in the early 1980s, Jackson City was experiencing neither a serious crime problem nor excessively divisive racial tensions. The chief's progressivism reflected the tenor of political and community sentiment in the mayor's office and throughout the government structure. Money and resources were not that difficult to secure; not only did the chief learn how to garner external funds (the department became nationally known for its support of research and willingness to be innovative), but he also had an excellent rapport with the mayor. Both men, in fact, separately published articles about the city and the police department. Male and female candidates who were drawn to the force often had interesting educational and career backgrounds, with many degrees earned in a variety of subjects outside criminal justice; earlier careers in nursing, social work, and teaching were common.

By 1996, the department had practiced community policing for over a decade. The initial project had been proposed in 1983, and foot patrolling began in the first six neighborhoods in 1986. The path to a bona fide community policing program in Jackson City was bumpy. The following description of its beginnings is based on interviews with five of the original six neighborhood officers, interviews with their (male) supervisors, and subsequent interviews with other current and former neighborhood officers that confirmed key events. One of the original NPOs was no longer with the department, three remained on active duty, another had retired, and one had retired on disability.

A unit called Special Operations had been created, consisting of six to eight officers who were reassigned from the streets to work on select projects. In 1983, one of the female members of the group wrote a proposal to the chief about designing a foot patrol program in Jackson City. She was motivated by dissatisfaction with her encounters with citizens. She felt there was something missing; she sought a style or approach that blended greater intimacy with deterrence. Citizens seemed hesitant to talk to her unless they specifically needed something, and people of color and poorer residents were particularly reticent. She missed the "old" style of police contact in the days before squad cars, so she began reading about new programs springing up across the country. Accompanied by her two supervising officers, she attended one of the first foot patrol conferences in an adjoining state. Hearing about the community policing innovations developed in other departments inspired her to rewrite the initial proposal to include a small storefront office, like a ministation, modeled after what seemed to work in another state. The hope behind these ministations was to offer a less formal, alternative environment to the main police station, in order to encourage more men and women from lower socioeconomic classes to come to the police with their neighborhood problems. Another new strategy was to post "wanted" lists in local bars that described residents who had warrants outstanding. These lists gave offenders an opportunity to turn themselves in and avoid confrontations or arrests in front of their families or neighbors. They also freed the police from having to "bust down doors." The chief accepted the proposal, and the officer remained in her neighborhood on full-time foot patrol while looking for a separate office. It took a year to arrange donated space, but businesses and residents responded warmly to the idea of having a foot patrol officer of their very own. Overall, the community policing program received very good coverage in the local papers, which reflected well on the department.

Interestingly, over time, community policing in Jackson City became a top-down program, meaning that the chief set policy and requested the administrators and rank and file to carry it out. But the idea was born out of bottom-up efforts, meaning that several lower-ranking patrol officers championed the concept and captured the chief's attention. Seizing an opportune moment, he introduced community policing to Jackson City at a time when police innovations were coming to be widely embraced and starting to be financially supported by the federal government and by various research communities.

The chief decided to expand the program to several additional targeted neighborhoods that had been experiencing a large volume of police activity and seemed in need of increased support. Lisa, the officer quoted at the beginning of this section, helped to shape the initial applicants into the first group of NPOs. In addition to their high volume of calls, neighborhoods were selected based on demographics and the types of crimes experienced within, some of which—for example, family violence and incidents involving guns and fights—were seen as being more amenable to community policing. The poorest districts, which were often populated mostly by members of minority groups, made up most of the areas designated for NPOs.

Difficulties Facing Neighborhood Officers

Despite the enthusiasm of the six original officers, the department as a whole did not embrace the community policing program. This resistance stemmed from two major factors. First, community policing was viewed as "just another wild plan" from the chief. Although he was often lauded as a visionary and an innovator by many of his officers and by academic researchers, the chief's single-mindedness and exuberance when introducing new ideas often met with skepticism. At the same time, however, these "wild ideas" attracted the interest of external funders and of researchers eager to evaluate the department's efforts. Thus, money poured in to the city, much to the delight of the mayor's office.

The second reason for skepticism was that the community approach represented a brand-new idea in policing. Most officers did not know what it meant or what it would eventually mean to the department. Research findings have suggested that as officers become accustomed to tradition, to "how it's always been done," they increasingly resent change and innovations. As some police scholars contend, it is difficult to "bend granite" (Guyot 1979). Ironically, the old guard's general resistance to change may have inadvertently eased the way for the first wave of neighborhood officers. Women, people of color, or both all had been selected from lower-level patrol ranks, and they were relatively powerless in the organization. There was no competition for such positions. In fact, most of the other officers were either unaware of these new assignments or had absolutely no interest in pursuing them.

It might seem strange that in the beginning only women and people of color desired the neighborhood policing positions. Kelly, a former (and the only) female supervisor of the neighborhood officers, believed:

> More women and minorities were attracted to the neighborhood position initially because they were newcomers to the profession. In the old days of white males, certain white males have a certain mentality on how that job was supposed to be done. Then, other men started hiring people who didn't necessarily think that was how the job needed to be done, that one could accomplish a lot in other ways. This may be somewhat of a generational thing, but gender might be a significant factor. Women have a different approach because we're not raised in as much of an environment where competitiveness and physical strength and force and control are used as ways to accomplish things. It's a whole different mindset . . . it is a lot like social work, although old-time officers and some still today don't like to think that social work is part of the job.

Every officer interviewed mentioned how unpopular the neighborhood policing program was when it began. The comments of a former NPO, a white man, were typical:

> Since the initial NPOs were all women and two black men, everyone thought they would just go off and just basically hide away and do nothing, in a policing sense, nothing would be done. Politically, it was an attractive thing to do [to get recognition and external grant money]. The

management team didn't really have a clue what they were doing, but since the chief wanted it done, he convinced the managers to go for it. (Bill)

In talking with the former neighborhood police officers, several consistent themes emerged that characterized the difficulties the early NPOs faced: lack of clear guidelines; lack of understanding and cooperation from patrol; practical difficulties, such as inflexible schedules; no patrol cars; and isolation. At the same time, however, these officers were highly motivated and eager to be in their new positions.

The first dilemma the NPOs encountered was the dearth of guidelines. Previously, as patrol officers, they had typically driven around in their squad cars and awaited calls for service from the radio dispatcher. Now things were not so clear. There were no specific objectives or duties because neighborhood policing models involve a radical departure from the call-driven, rapid response models of patrol policing. Although the first group of NPOs spent a lot of time reading about the philosophical objectives of community policing and about how departments in other jurisdictions across the country tried to accomplish them, they did not know how to link these objectives to Jackson City. The new NPOs persevered, however, and established their own goals for each district. All of the early neighborhood officers expressed the strong desire to get closer to the community and to avoid call-driven policing. These desires steered their efforts. As Francine, one of the first NPOs, remarked, "We're an antibiotic, while patrol is a Band-Aid." They wanted to be seen as part of the solution, not part of the problem. Many of the neighborhood activities begun by the earliest officers reflected their personal motivations for becoming NPOs. For instance, the first African American woman to join the unit explained her interest in community policing this way:

We had some concerns about drugs coming into the city and some activities that we didn't want started. In 1980 or 1981, there was a period of time when three of us who worked on Special Operations . . . saw a need to have a police presence in the community and develop a storefront station. At that time the department was adamantly opposed to having us there because it would have meant [to others] there were some concerns and problems. But as street officers, we really saw and heard about it and knew that it exists. It takes someone who has an investment in the community. . . . I'm from here . . . but even if you are not from here, if you've got some ideas and some things you want to do yourself as a person to help, that works. Policing in general is about helping people, even if we end up arresting. If they are interested in helping, then I think they can give of themselves. And I think you have to be a giving person to be able to be really daring. Community policing lets you give of yourself more. When you give of yourself more, you can get a lot. They get a lot, and you get something. You are part of the solution. (Katie)

Other officers selected neighborhoods for other reasons. A second early female NPO, Francine, was attracted to the Water Lane area because she had lived in different countries and was interested in different cultures, particularly that of the Hmong people of Laos. Water Lane had a large immigrant population and Francine knew several languages. Both she and another female NPO (Lisa) believed that being a woman was an advantage in working with the Hmong immigrants, because they had a deathly fear of police.

They had come from a war zone, and a uniform was associated with death. But a woman in a uniform was a curiosity, so it was kind of really an advantage working with them. My first meeting with the Hmong association, there were about seventy-five or eighty male Asians and one blonde, blue-eyed female police officer!

Francine felt her gender loosened up some of the distrust the residents felt for police in general.

In addition, many persons from the first and subsequent waves of NPOs had strong ties to neighborhoods: often, they had grown up there and their children went to school there. The officers exuded a sense of pride in the police force and a strong commitment to the city and its various residential areas.

Since the new NPOs did not have any guidelines to follow, each of them had to negotiate her or his position in the neighborhood and figure out how best to introduce the new and constant police presence in the lives of the residents. By 1995, of course, citizens were far more familiar with the sight of permanent foot patrol officers assigned to their neighborhood. But in the beginning, this presence was misunderstood and viewed with suspicion. Citizens felt they were constantly being watched. Most NPOs went door-to-door to introduce themselves, often providing pictures or short write-ups giving their phone numbers. (Many officers still follow this practice, and now they also give out their pager and cell phone numbers.) The NPOs stressed that it was not their primary role to handle emergencies ("We weren't there for them to leave messages on a machine that they can't breathe!"), but to be a resource for other kinds of concerns. After time, many residents relaxed and grew accustomed to the daily sight of the same officer on foot, walking around their community. As

Lisa described it, once the NPOs' identities became known and local people trusted them more, "the residents became so used to you, let alone the fact that they would deal with you on the street, I had to take my phone number out of the book because I would get people calling me at home, often wondering why I wasn't in the neighborhood!" Many citizens grew to feel a certain "ownership" of their neighborhood officer, calling with minor problems or even just to gossip.

Along with the lack of clear guidelines, another difficulty encountered by the early NPOs was a lack of cooperation and understanding on the part of patrol officers. Since the concept and activities of community policing were so different from those of traditional policing, patrol officers had difficulty appreciating the new NPO positions and understanding their purpose, and there was a great deal of incomprehension and even derision from them. (Again, "patrol officers" are based in squad cars, are assigned to a set beat, and are primarily call-driven, responding to messages from radio dispatchers.) Patrol officers felt as if they were still responding to *all* the calls in the neighborhood, which did not make sense to them if the area had been given a permanently assigned officer of its own. Therefore, patrol felt the new positions did not decrease their workload, but rather increased it. One of the reasons was structural: the first wave of NPOs did not have "a red light and siren on our heads, nor did we have squad cars" (Pam). Community officers simply could not physically respond to calls as quickly as patrol could because they were on foot. There was also an assumption by patrol that NPOs were not "real" police officers because they were too busy acting as social workers to be fighting crime.

> Some of the discrimination that was thrown at us by patrol officers reflects the 1980s. The early part of our career as foot patrol officers was very difficult. They didn't like that we were human, since then we weren't the *real* police. When in actuality, communicating is the gift we all need to use with each other. Women and men in policing today are being sent to school to learn better interpersonal communication skills, and we women already valued and practiced this. Maybe women need to learn more assertiveness, while men need to learn how to better open up and communicate. (Lisa, white lesbian, former NPO)

The neighborhood officers were defensive about the criticism they received, feeling that, more so than patrol, they really *knew* their neighborhoods: "We know every apartment, who lived where, how many aunties and uncles there were, how many children, doors, past arrests, and the layout of the apartment"

(Katie). The NPOs felt unduly criticized by patrol, especially since they all worked many extra unpaid hours.

Conversations with former neighborhood police officers revealed extensive and deep-seated feelings of alienation and segregation. They no longer felt welcome to "hang out" with patrol in squad cars, or swap greetings or information over the police radio. The former NPOs repeatedly described how tough it was for them to fit into the existing police subculture once they left traditional patrol duties. As one officer recalled,

> In the first ten years of foot patrol, the rank and file did not accept foot patrol officers. And it was a tough battle. But you know, that's why it took strong women to do this, and one man initially, because you were more or less ostracized by a great majority of people. You'd call, you needed backup, they wouldn't even come for a long time. You know, they didn't agree with change, but by now, it has turned around.

Other first-wave NPOs described how this isolation from patrol exacerbated their own fear of residents' revenge. Local persons could now *easily* identify the NPOs—police officers were no longer anonymous uniforms in squad cars.

> At first it was really hard because you didn't know how they'd feel about it and you didn't know about citizens' retaliation. We are out there alone, we didn't have a car, people didn't often know where we were because we moved around so much. With traditional policing, you go to an address, you tell [the] dispatcher where you are so people know where you are. So if you need help, they know where to send help. As a walker, you go all over the place and unless you specifically are going inside or get into something where you can radio ahead that there might be trouble, people don't know where you are. So, consequently, you have to worry about people who might come after you because, you know, a lot of people don't like the police. (Katie)

The NPOs felt isolated from the patrol officers and strove to keep up contact with them. They welcomed their colleagues into the ministations to talk, use the phone, or have a cup of coffee. Although the NPOs felt it would be helpful for patrol officers to walk around the neighborhood with them, this was difficult to encourage because of the demands for service. The NPOs also felt stigmatized by their colleagues, but they still believed that if only patrol officers would increase their knowledge through hands-on experience the exposure might minimize this stigma.

The early neighborhood officers faced additional structural problems that impeded their work. One of these was that NPOs were expected to follow an inflexible schedule; they were told to work set hours, from noon till eight in the evening. Neighborhood officers thought this plan was crazy:

> Almost nothing goes on at noon . . . I mean the place is quiet. The kids are already off to school. . . . [T]his may not be very sensitive to say, but a lot of adults hadn't even raised their head up off the bed, and there just wasn't a lot of movement out there. Things didn't happen until afternoon, when the kids got home, in the evenings, and then later on the weekends, particularly in the summer, you wondered whether anybody goes to bed.

The NPOs felt that the period from noon until eight was not always the time when residents needed them, and it defeated the purpose of being responsive to their needs. For instance, if something happened after eight o'clock the residents would not benefit from knowing who "their" officer was because an anonymous patrol officer would respond. Also, NPOs did not want total scheduling predictability: "I didn't want people to be able to predict a time clock, that, she punches in at this time and she punches out at that time, because then all you gotta do is wait for me to leave and then carry on with whatever." The early neighborhood officers fought to alter the policy of set hours; once the change was approved, after a couple of years of fighting, the NPOs began to vary their schedules. They often arranged to meet another officer at night to walk the streets together, both for safety and because there was a lot of "cross traffic" between two neighborhoods, allowing them to check out familiar faces and exchange information.

Yet another obstacle was that the early NPOs did not have police cars and often had to drive their own vehicles into the neighborhood. Using personal cars, however, compromised officers' personal anonymity, especially in the case of those who lived relatively close to their assigned neighborhoods. Often, NPOs would use the car or truck of a husband, wife, or partner and park far enough away from the district's ministation to throw residents off their track.

Despite the complaints about the lack of guidelines for the new NPOs, there was also an advantage to having an open-ended agenda. Officers were told to use their creativity to develop activities that fit the neighborhood's needs and their own interests. These activities were designed to bring about greater personal contact with the community. The first wave of NPOs repeatedly indicated that they were given no clear goals except to respond to "whatever the neighborhood needed." Since many of the officers had clear reasons for seeking the NPO position, this flexibility provided many opportunities to set their own agenda and priorities. The following short discussion revealed one neighborhood officer's emphases and spirit:

> I came in with the assumption that there were a lot of people in the neighborhood who just wanted to live next to an elementary school and have a place for their kids to grow up and they just wanted to do those things and go about their daily lives, but there were a lot of pretty classic bad guys there too so I needed to hook into the good types and let them know that I was willing to listen to them and let their agenda drive what I was going to do in the long run. (Linc, white man, former NPO)

When asked about the residents' response to a different type of police officer, Linc recalled how his arrival was marked by a homicide in the second or third week:

> People's attention [was] pretty well focused [on] the question of personal safety [there had been some drive-by shootings and people with drugs and guns running around] so one of the ways we dealt with the aftermath was to have meetings, and there were so many people we had to have them in the elementary school gym.

He felt his job was made easier because he already knew some of the people from having done patrol duty in the same neighborhood. Linc believed "it was do-able; I don't like to take on projects that I believe are a failure to start or too big and aren't planned properly so I thought that was a do-able thing."

The NPOs developed different ways of keeping track of the residents of their neighborhoods. Terry kept card files and cross-referenced all relatives and relationships, present and former. Andrea kept a spiral notebook and made family trees with extended diagrams; since there were sometimes four generations in the same household, it was a useful tool for subsequent NPOs. Neighborhood officers typically took note of frequent visitors and vehicles. They ran license plate checks when unfamiliar faces appeared or something seemed not quite right. Many NPOs created newsletters and distributed them door-to-door, using the publications as their introduction to the residents. Keith printed flyers bearing his name, phone number, and picture, then posted them on the front doors of all apartment houses and on telephone poles. He also walked the neighborhood three times a day, first in his uniform and then wearing civilian clothes, in order to break down barriers.

All of the neighborhood officers detailed the incredible amount of time they took getting to know children and teenagers and how they tried to win their trust. Some NPOs created programs based on suggestions from other social service agents, such as a computer-mentoring program. Theresa (white, current NPO) began a computer program after meeting with a technologies outreach worker for the school district. It had a dual purpose: to reach out to young persons with nothing to do after school, and to create a good opportunity for her, and other police officers, to learn computer skills. Other efforts included a Christmas for Kids program (with help from a local radio station) to coordinate donations of presents so that parents without money could ask for gifts for their children; working with probation and parole officers as a unit; coordinating building inspections, especially when an absentee or uncaring landlord was involved; developing a merchant committee to oversee vendors; enforcing parking and landlord codes (for example, when slumlords let empty apartment buildings become drug houses, trying to close the structures down by citing building-code violations); dealing with bars not just by writing tickets for serving under-aged drinkers, but also by trying to develop activities for older teens that did not involve drinking; and keeping files of the medical conditions of residents (among them heart problems, mental illness, and cancer, as well as domestic violence), along with a referral bank for resources in the community.

The motivations of the NPOs from the second and third waves contrasted with those of the pioneers. When the newer officers sought the NPO position, it had become a more established job on the force, and the chief supported a community policing mindset for all of the department. Three reasons in particular were mentioned as accounting for second- and third-wave officers' interest: (1) the officer was feeling burned out from patrol duties and needed a change; (2) personal-scheduling reasons, such as going to night school or family obligations; and (3) the officer saw the NPO position as a stepping-stone to promotion.

For instance, one third-wave NPO was attracted to a particular neighborhood because of its location and because the apartment houses were run as a "tight ship." He had been a patrol officer for only five years at the time, but "in the early years, NPO positions weren't that desired because it strayed away from traditional policing, and you lost a lot of things, you lost overtime, holiday pay. But you also gained a lot of things, you got to set your own schedule, if you preferred, you had your holidays off" (Keith, black man, the third NPO in Crestview). Both current and former neighborhood officers who are African American often selected a position in their own neighborhood. One current African American NPO was in patrol for seven years before taking his new posting. For the immediately preceding five years he had been in the Safety Education unit, working with children in school. He acknowledged that in this capacity he saw the good side of things and did not really deal with people's problems, such as poor living conditions or drug crimes. He put in for the NPO job in his childhood neighborhood.

William, another African American and former NPO, also selected a district in which he resided. He had been on the force for only three years before he became a neighborhood officer. He explained that before taking the NPO position he was thinking of quitting. "Even though this is a more open, more liberal department, it was still too confining. Everything was all mapped out. Everything to how you respond to a call, the way to come in, and the repetition of doing that. I was still learning, but I could see maybe another five years down the road, it was going to be old hat for me real quick." He credits neighborhood policing with teaching him more about himself and how to deal with people. Once an introvert, while in the neighborhood position William had to force himself to speak to people, not just "command" them to do certain things. Now he is very comfortable in interactions with residents, an ease he credited to his time as an NPO. He said this is a long way from his youth in a troubled city in the 1960s, where he watched his parents being carted away by police at demonstrations and marches:

> I spelled police P-I-G. And when I was in patrol, I still looked at myself as outside the profession. I separated the two. I always separated the two, and when I became an NPO, I could finally say that this is something worthwhile, this is something that has benefit to not just protecting certain individuals in society, but the entire society. It has value to me, this profession, and so now instead of separating the two, I think I am connecting the two and how I value this profession. I had despised the human side of policing because I had always been harassed before. Now I see a different side and how it works with people.

Personal reasons and family concerns sometimes influenced an officer's selection of a particular area. A black former NPO, Barbara, said that she picked the Crestview neighborhood because she was a parent and needed flexibility and it was close to her house. Three postings were open at the time, but one was close to her child's school and she did not want to ever arrest a relative of one of her child's schoolmates or use the same grocery store as persons she had arrested or their family members. Many college students lived in another district, and she thought that she lacked the patience needed to deal with them. She also believed that the remaining neighborhood had the most resources; this was an incentive because she would not have to start from scratch.

On occasion, the enthusiasm and satisfaction of the first wave of NPOs influenced other patrol officers to want to try the new position themselves. Andrea, for instance, was drawn to neighborhood work after having been on patrol for about seven years. She began to feel herself

> getting an edge . . . getting kind of crusty around the edges, that you kind of maybe feel coming on with age, and the fact that you don't always get a lot of positive contacts, most of your day during your shift, these tend to be not positive, mostly negative, and I was getting kinda cynical. . . . I was looking for something more interesting, and I obviously got a lot of encouragement and a certain amount of—I hate to use the word—propaganda from Lisa, who encouraged me to put in for it because she thought that I had a good personality for that position.

Since Andrea had worked the same part of the city while on patrol, she had already seen a lot of neighborhood policing done by the three original female NPOs. Also, she had domestic considerations: "I have family, my children were much younger, and I thought this was something that would still work well with my family schedule because that's normally my primary consideration in just about any assignment that I take."

By the time the second wave of NPOs was assigned, a few additional neighborhood positions had been created. Training was still haphazard and informal. New officers learned from other NPOs or on their own, not from their sergeant or captain in charge. The administration was seen as still "working on promoting the theory." This lack of expectations had a positive side, though: it gave NPOs great leeway in devising their own plans for their time and energy spent in the neighborhoods. As one second-wave former NPO (a black man) declared:

> You are blind when you go in there. . . . [E]verybody has a different style . . . the former NPO will give you an idea of who and what you need to watch, but you focus on what you like. . . . [E]veryone's different, some people like to work with kids, and that's a project for them, some want to improve or take down the crime level, some people want to concentrate on getting drugs off the street. Everyone has their own pet peeve they want to work on. Whatever your strengths are, and what you like, that's what you can go for. . . . I wanted to deal with juveniles and drugs. (Keith)

After the first round of promotions following the inauguration of the neighborhood policing program, other officers began to notice that many NPOs were being promoted. In fact, *all* of the second- and third-wave NPOs mentioned the belief among the rank and file that promotion was tied to experience in neighborhood policing. One white officer, Tony, said he chose to be an NPO after eight and a half years on patrol because he needed a change and he felt that his career was not going anywhere. He admitted:

> And I also needed something for career advancement. I'd be lying to anybody if I said I didn't take this position without some thought to whether or what could happen to my career. . . . [T]he percentage of NPOs getting promoted is real high, and I think this might be the push that I need to put me up over the edge there and make sergeant.

Tony inherited a posting in which the previous NPO did not have a good reputation for really caring about the neighborhood and working hard. He described the officer this way:

> Matt just wanted to avoid a lot of the extraneous stuff that I've gotten myself wrapped up in. He was focusing on sitting up in the car out here and watching for people. He was finishing law school, and he put in for a training position and he didn't get it. And I noticed there was a noticeable difference in Matt's attitude from that point forward. He just didn't give a shit. Matt was out here doing the cop stuff that he needed to do, but it was like he was just biding his time.

One of the most recent (third-wave) NPOs, a white woman, expressed very similar motivations for putting in for the NPO position:

> I would like to say all the buzzwords about getting closer to the community, and all the things that NPOs are supposed to be wanting to say, but I pretty much have a lot of my own agenda. (Carol)

This same officer also expressed some disappointment that she had not yet been promoted. Carol explained that she had been on the list for sergeant, and the department made a number of promotions, all persons she felt were well qualified and had more experience than she (at least two NPOs were promoted). Carol selected the Eastville neighborhood since she was already socially connected to the other (male) NPO already in place (they played on the same hockey team). Nonetheless, "Neighborhood officers have this reputation, and I am getting ribbed about this: Oh sure, you've been on the sergeant's list for two years, and you didn't get promoted, now you're going to the neighborhood just because you want to get promoted."

Another current NPO had a similar opinion on his and others' motivation for taking on their new positions:

> I don't think everyone that puts in for neighborhood positions gives a shit about the neighborhood. . . . [A]nd it's not just that they want to be promoted but that there's not a lot of accountability, nobody's telling you what to do every day, like responding to calls, you can make your own hours, if you want a day off, you can take a day off. There are a lot of advantages just to the schedules and through the workload. The accountability in patrol is there, you are sent to a call and you better go. In the neighborhood, you are told to do some possible work, and they don't tell you how to do it. (Stewart, black man, current NPO)

To summarize, this chapter has provided relevant background information that followed the development of the community policing program in Jackson City. From the beginning, those who sought the neighborhood positions faced stigmatization, ostracism, and lack of support from patrol officers. After the program became a key feature of the department, more officers were eager to pursue these positions, albeit for different reasons than the first wave of NPOs. Such occupational factors as career motivation, policing philosophy, and type of work, as well as such social status characteristics as gender, sexual orientation, and race, may play direct or indirect roles in various decisions: desire to become an NPO, selection of neighborhood, and activity planning and goal setting for the work conducted in the neighborhood. How and why these decisions take shape will be revealed by the data presented and analyzed in subsequent chapters.

This book offers a fresh examination of the issues related to community policing, gender, race, sexuality, work, and the social constructions of masculinity and femininity within the police subculture. As such, it asks a number of questions. How do male and female officers "reconcile" incompatible images of masculinity and femininity? How does this reconciliation differ between NPOs and traditional rapid response patrol officers? How do community police officers renegotiate, or impression-manage, their positions, given the rejection of feminine qualities in a masculinist organization that resists community policing? How do gender and gender-role expectations shape police activities and the evaluation of the new skills?

The remainder of the book proceeds as follows. Chapter 2 describes what neighborhood officers *do* and how their activities vary across districts. In this chapter, I provide in-depth profiles of three different neighborhoods and six different NPOs. Chapter 3 moves away from the specific workings of the Jackson City Police Department to explore gender theories that are relevant to my research on community policing. This chapter also examines the historical development of policing as an institution, as well as women's entrance into this male world. Using these foundations, I demonstrate how community policing models of the 1990s borrow from early-twentieth-century police models. In the process, I consider the transforming of "women's work" that was previously considered to be meritless into the showpiece of community policing today.

Chapter 4 explores identity and image issues that develop for neighborhood police officers and how these issues shape policework. I also look at whether relationships between NPOs and patrol officers are supportive or antagonistic, and at how officers' race, gender, and sexual orientation may affect the negotiations of police image and practices. Chapter 5 further investigates the interactions that neighborhood police officers have with community members, how NPOs adjust to their new roles, the types of activities that develop in the neighborhoods, and how these vary by individual officer and policing style. Chapter 6 examines the world of patrol officers and how they perceive themselves as being similar to and different from NPOs. Domestic violence and the role that community policing plays in relation to this offense are also examined. Finally, Chapter 7 summarizes the major findings of the analysis of neighborhood policing and their policy implications.

Notes

1. Some of this chapter draws upon Miller 1998.
2. Relevant studies about femininity constructs and occupations include Hunt 1990, Young 1991, Jurik 1988, Cockburn 1991, Martin and Jurik 1996, and Myers and Chiang 1993.

A Day in the Life
of an NPO

In-Depth Profiles of
Six Officers

This chapter documents the daily activities of a half dozen community police officers. These profiles illustrate the three very different kinds of neighborhoods that exist in Jackson City, as well as the variety in officers' policing styles. I selected two NPOs to represent each type of neighborhood (criminally active, program development, and maintenance). Thus, the descriptions provide a representative sampling of the various residential districts.

Different neighborhoods attract different kinds of officers. Procedurally, he or she has to have seniority in order to request and get the desired position, since other officers may have competed with him or her for the posting. A number of officers who are natives of Jackson City are interested in being an NPO in the part of town where they grew up or went to school. Identifying with the neighborhood, they are nostalgic about "how it used to be" and want to take part in bringing it back around. Two areas are largely the province of their current NPOs. Both have been on the force for almost twenty years and are thus unlikely to be displaced because of their seniority.

Certain neighborhoods develop certain reputations, which may influence the willingness or lack thereof to serve in them as NPOs. Eastville, for example, is located on the side of town that has a rough reputation, whereas the Davis Street area seems so stable that many on the force did not believe it still needed a neighborhood police officer. In fact, Linc, a former NPO (white male), said during an interview that "expecting one officer to be in one given spot forever isn't the right way to think about things." He added, somewhat jokingly, that in one of the richer communities with an NPO "the officers are rumored to walk people's dogs when they go on vacation, so I don't know if that is community policing."

The areas designated for neighborhood officers need different kinds of police presence. It would be ideal if residents and officers agreed on problems and approaches to solving them, but often there are conflicting and competing demands that short-circuit such a match. Essentially, there are three ways to describe the neighborhoods. Eastville and Taylor, the first pair, are *criminally active*. This term indicates a district where lawbreaking is routine, residents' fear is high (as is anomie), there are obvious breakdowns in informal controls (by families, by landlords), there are many problems involving delinquency, and many residents face outstanding warrants. It seems generally accepted that this kind of neighborhood attracts (or tries to attract) officers desirous of traditional enforcement action and crimefighting.

The second pair, Westend and Crestview, exemplify another kind of district, which I call the *program development* neighborhood. The area has passed its crisis point and is moving toward stability. Community programs, initiated or augmented by the neighborhood officer, help maintain the growing calm and work to reestablish informal controls, with the NPO acting as a catalyst for this change. Often, such districts are seen as needing an officer who is creative, innovative, highly motivated, and enthusiastic. She or he should be able to look beyond crime control measures toward a more holistic approach to rebuilding a healthy neighborhood.

Fairlawn and Davis Street, the final pair, represent the *maintenance* neighborhood. If an area has achieved this status, it generally means that the NPO is performing routine, minor tasks relating to service and maintaining order. The rates of crime and fear have significantly decreased, and residents strongly support community programs, which are operating smoothly and consistently. This stability may also mean that it is time for the NPO to move on to assist a more troubled neighborhood. Community members usually resist such a change, however; they have become accustomed to having an NPO at their disposal and fear what might transpire should he or she be reassigned. It is widely believed in the department that maintenance neighborhoods tend to draw officers who are not, or are not any longer, seeking challenging positions. Hence, such districts may be particularly attractive to some officers close to retirement age, who are not looking for a lot of action near the end of their careers.

Although each description that follows of the neighborhood activity chronicles one day of fieldwork, the observations of communications between police and community members and the researchers' impressions are consistent across months of fieldwork observations in the same neighborhoods by different researchers, both male and female. In fact, it is striking how consistent the experiences and the interpersonal dynamics between neighborhood police officers and community residents were throughout the summer of fieldwork, regardless of the time or day of observation or the gender of the researcher.

What is most obvious in the descriptions are the varied approaches that the NPOs use in their neighborhoods, as well as the officers' distinct personalities. Although some variation in behavior may be dictated by the NPOs' perceptions and assessments of each area's needs, different policing styles may also be explained by each officer's unique personality and comfort level in the role of NPO in her or his particular neighborhood.

In the summer when most of the fieldwork was conducted, there were thirteen NPOs assigned to twelve designated neighborhoods (one district was assigned two officers). Ten of the thirteen NPOs were men. All of the women were white. Four of the men were African Americans (one black man was temporarily assigned to light duty at the main station downtown while recovering from knee surgery).

The descriptions provided in this chapter raise multiple questions related to gender, race, masculine and feminine roles and images, and policing. What is an average shift like? Are activities concentrated around social work, law enforcement, or some combination of the two? How do citizens respond to NPOs? Can any police-citizen interactions be attributed to the race or gender of the officer? How do NPOs' personal styles affect interactions with residents? How do such styles influence what officers *do* in the 'hoods? What connections do neighborhood officers have with other members of the force, such as patrol officers? How do NPOs see their role in the neighborhood? Do they conduct themselves or select activities in ways that reinforce traditional gender roles? Can we observe how NPOs might negotiate masculinity while downplaying femininity, or vice versa? I will explore and analyze these and other issues in subsequent chapters. My aim here is simply to present the daily lives of NPOs at work.

PAIR ONE

Eastville—Criminally Active Neighborhood

It is another hot, humid July afternoon, with the kind of mugginess that makes foot patrol officers yearn for their former positions in air-conditioned squad cars. Last night, a near riot had broken out in Eastville, stemming from an undercover buy-bust drug operation that culminated in the arrest of a well-known dealer. Several officers needed to physically restrain the suspect; he fought them until he was subdued by Mace. Tempers remained high among the residents, who thought that the officers' use of the disabling spray was gratuitous since there were so many of them fighting only one man. Thus, "damage control" was on today's agenda for Patrick, the neighborhood officer on foot patrol assigned to the Eastville community. A high-energy, gregarious white man in his early thirties, Patrick had been in the neighborhood position for only about seven months. Earlier, he had worked under cover for seven years with the drug and gang task force. Before that, he had been a police officer in another state.

Although Patrick typically rode a mountain bicycle around the neighborhood in the summer, his shift today began in a squad car. He drove downtown to the new jail to connect with Justin, another resident arrested in the previous evening's melee. The jail, located across the street from the building housing the Jackson City Police Department, had opened the previous fall, with four hundred beds. The facility was very high-tech; fingerprints, for example, were taken via a computer monitor screen. Patrick was well known, and without any questions asked he was escorted to Justin's cell. When the door opened, Justin, a black man in his early twenties, greeted Patrick warmly. Patrick told Justin that he was not there to talk about last night's events, just to see if he was okay; Justin replied that he was. However, he wanted to make sure that Patrick knew that he had only sunflower seeds in his mouth, not any crack cocaine. Justin said this several times, and he seemed relieved that Patrick assured him that he knew it was not crack, only sunflower seeds. Patrick slapped him lightly on the back, saying "Hang in there," asked if he had any questions, and clarified something on the citation that Justin had received. He also said that he was counting on Justin's help in calming things down in Eastville once he was released. The entire exchange was respectful and lighthearted. "It's important," Patrick explained later, "to follow through, kind of public relations, so that things will be smoother later on when Justin gets home. Justin is well liked in the neighborhood, and basically a nice guy, so his arrest made some people angry." In fact, later that night Justin *was* back home, and when he saw Patrick he called him over and asked if they could speak privately. Again, their tones conveyed mutual respect and trust, and the camaraderie exhibited during their exchanges suggested that Patrick was an older brother giving advice.

En route back to Eastville from the jail, two different reports of officers engaged in foot chases came over the radio. Since Patrick personally knew one of the suspects from his undercover days, he decided to help. He put on the cruiser's police lights and sped to the street where the man was last sighted; he passed several other squad cars, some sitting and waiting, some driving around other blocks. Children waved at the cars. Then a report came over the radio that patrol officers had pulled over a suspicious car and believed one of the persons they were looking for was an occupant. Patrick jumped from his car, ran over to help, and was easily able to identify the man. Meanwhile, two other officers patting down another suspect found a crack pipe made from a broken piece of hollow car antenna.

Situated in the roughest quadrant of Jackson City, Eastville has a reputation for toughness. Although spacious middle-income homes and a beautiful lake lie along the perimeter, police concentrate their efforts in the poor area of eight or nine blocks, where the majority of calls for service originate. Because of the high volume of crime-related calls, two neighborhood officers are assigned to Eastville. Three-quarters of the residents are African American; the rest of the inhabitants are mostly white, with a few Hispanics and very few Asians. The area experiences high residential mobility, and it is seen as a drug gateway from a major city in an adjacent state. Many families have been attracted to the neighborhood by what are seen as generous state government assistance policies. But given the size of Jackson City, police operate on a smaller scale. Residents quickly discover that small-time drug dealing that police would have ignored in a bigger city does *not* get ignored here. Once they find that the officers actively pursue misdemeanors and minor felonies, newer residents often go back home.

A small park sits in the center of the neighborhood; it is flanked by an array of brick buildings, all two or three stories high. One building is federally operated, and the Department of Housing and Urban Development hires armed security guards to augment local police power by walking around the property. Several buildings have remained privately owned, with slimy absentee landlords who do not care about their buildings or their tenants. In one of the most dilapidated blocks, there are three eight-unit buildings collectively known as the "hole" because of their bad reputation, poor upkeep, and virtually nonexistent management. In fact, evicted tenants from all over the city ultimately end up here because the private management company does not screen rental applicants.

The "hole" was also the site of the near riot Wednesday night. As young people and adults, all African Americans, recognized Patrick in the car, they waved. He yelled out warm hellos, calling people by their names and nicknames. Patrick parked at the central apartment building, which housed the offices of the neighborhood's social worker and parole-probation officer, as well as providing meeting space for the neighborhood officers. This is not where the NPOs spend most of their time; the other neighborhood office, located in another apartment building, has the only computer. Patrick exchanged pleasantries with Sandra, the social service coordinator, and several resident women with their young children. They seemed quite comfortable and welcoming, and easily returned his greetings. Patrick checked his answering machine for messages after one of the women outside told him she had left one. On his way out, the social worker suggested to Patrick that he might want to organize a neighborhood meeting to explain what had happened Wednesday night and reassure the residents. He told her that NPOs *always* do that, but he would wait for a couple of days until tensions calmed down. Later, out of earshot, Patrick remarked:

> Sandra has a heart of gold, but is a classic social service worker in that she believes everybody and lets them have many chances, and never thinks of the law enforcement aspect. She never believes that women can do anything violent; if they get caught, it is because some man had put them up to it. Yet, I've seen some of the women's records on the computer, and they have done some bad things and for many years. Sandra also thinks that one male resident hangs the moon, but he is the same guy who had some crack packaging stuff on him last week. So, someone other than a social worker has to look objectively at the law enforcement aspect. That's *our* job.

Several patrol officers in squad cars drove over to "shoot the shit" with Patrick. They exchanged information, and all of the patrol officers seemed to have a general sense of who a lot of the residents were and what crime problems existed.

Patrick exuded warmth and irrepressible energy. All during his shift, he immediately waded right in to any situation. He greeted everyone with a smile, slapping backs or "high-fiving" children and teenagers. Patrick used the names of both adults and young people when he knew them, and he asked them to refresh his memory if he had forgotten. He answered questions, writing down any complaints or things to look into. The residents were open and unguarded, with no sign of distrust, even in light of the previous night's events. Patrick connected with the people in the truest sense of the word. He was always very respectful and open; despite his white skin, his presence did not seem to threaten residents or to suggest invasion or surveillance. Patrick's pager went off throughout his shift, and he would call residents back from his cellular phone. He was glad that many local persons did appreciate the NPOs' presence and tell them so, and that they gave the officers information about criminal activities in the neighborhood.

A black man approached Patrick, the same man who, several weeks ago, he had found with crack-packaging bags. The man wanted to explain that he had taken his son to the hospital following last night's incident because the boy was experiencing symptoms that seemed related to Mace exposure (they live in the apartment above where the chemical had been sprayed). He also wanted to assure Patrick that he deliberately did not mention the word "Mace" at the hospital because he did not want the staff or the media to blame the cops. Although their conversational tone was warm and respectful and Patrick thanked him, he did not engage in dialogue about the matter or seem overly appreciative. When the man left, Patrick explained that he did not think there was any way that his son could have breathed in any Mace, but he did not want to respond and perhaps fuel speculation that might be inaccurate.

While these conversations were taking place, many persons, all African Americans, passed by saying hello or exchanging some taunting, almost flirtatiously friendly words. Residents frequently joked with Patrick about his appearance. He was wearing black shorts, a black police department T-shirt, black socks, and tennis shoes. People kept referring to his shorts—"Are you gonna wear those all winter?"—and joking around about seeing his legs. It was getting windy and cool that night, which made them poke a little more fun at him. Patrick joked back a lot, and the exchanges were super-friendly.

It was now time for the Fishing Club to meet. The local group was part of a national organization, Fishing Has No Boundaries, developed to encourage handicapped children to participate in out-of-doors events. The chapter in Eastville was started last year by a group of six or eight fathers and grandfathers between the ages of twenty-four and seventy-six, several of whom owned boats. This year, they received eighteen hundred dollars in grant money to pay for hot dogs, soda, bait, and transportation. Patrick has a platoon boat, which they have used for girls and boys in wheelchairs. Besides the trip planned for the handicapped children, the Fishing Club also sponsored events for other youngsters in the neighborhood. The members were extremely comfortable with Patrick, and clearly saw themselves as a team working together. They all expressed ideas and each listened attentively to the other. The youngest member, aged twenty-four, kept bringing up interesting ideas, such as having the young people pass a "no-brainer" safety test as a screen for picking the first group to go on the fishing and boating trip. The men talked about their lack of experience in working with handicapped persons. They decided to each be responsible for only one or two children, and not to bring their own sons and daughters along. This way, they would be able to direct all their attention to the handicapped boys and girls. At one point, the leader said that fishing was just the vehicle, and the real reason they were involved was to act as mentors and role models. The members seemed very concerned that residents of the "hole" would be ignored, and that the appearance of favoritism would create problems when selecting the youngsters. They came up with the following solution: each neighborhood association, social worker, and other community group would pick one child; the members would each pick one child; and Patrick and David (the other NPO) would pick one child apiece from the "hole." It was clear the club members really liked Patrick and thought of him as integral to the group.

The leader pointed out that Patrick had left his cooler at his house; obviously, they had done things together before and had a real relationship.

It was getting close to seven o'clock, the designated time to meet the Drug Task Force officers to plan a "show of force" in the neighborhood that evening. On the way, Patrick took a spin through the "hole" and pulled up alongside a brand-new white sports car with rap music blaring from the radio. An African American man (wearing an extremely expensive gold watch) was surrounded by black teenagers, who scattered, nonchalantly, as the squad car pulled in. Patrick greeted the man and joked around about his new car. The man was good-natured and asked Patrick why he was always picking on him. Patrick replied, "Because you are so much fun." As Patrick was looking at the car, the man said, "Go ahead, look inside. You know you want to; there's nothing in there, and the liquor bottle on the floor is unopened." Patrick joked around some more, checked out the music, and then said good-bye. There seemed to be a little tension in the air; although young boys kept coming by to see what was going on, the teenagers stayed away. Once Patrick was back in the car, he explained that the man, Duke, was the biggest drug dealer in the city. But police could not get to him because there were so many layers of people between Duke and the drugs. Patrick was concerned because lately Duke had been hanging out on the block more and more. He drew in many children and teenagers, like the Pied Piper of Eastville.

The NPOs and the patrol officers made plans to walk around the "hole" to make their presence highly visible. Patrick also wanted to search some of the basements for drugs. Several officers commented that Duke had been seen hanging around more frequently than usual. Patrick left and drove toward the "hole"; when he was a block away he verified that everybody was ready, and in they went. Patrick parked by the other neighborhood police office so he could get sodas later for officers who wanted them. He noticed that its windows had been broken, probably by rocks. A white woman from the apartment immediately across from the neighborhood police office said that it had happened the night before. It was not clear if the damage preceded or followed the incident, or even if the events were related. Patrick felt sure there was a connection, since the vandals hit only the windows in the police apartment. Nearby, two little boys were playing; they stopped to watch as a police cruiser pulled over a resident's car. The younger boy, probably around five, started crying when he realized that it was his mother who had been stopped. It turned out she did not have any license plates on her car. By this time there were several other officers around, and they soothed the little boy and asked him his mom's name. Patrick told the child to wait there and walked over to the car to verify that the driver was indeed his mother. He had her wave to her son to show that she was okay.

Patrick and another officer began walking around a couple of the buildings. Children and teenagers often came up to them to greet Patrick. He frequently stopped to ask adults how they were doing and how things were since last night. Everyone seemed to know him and they answered his questions, some persons volunteering more information than others. Patrick knew many of them by name, and he asked about family members. Very often, the citizens initiated the hellos.

Then, Patrick and several of the armed private security guards went into the basement of one building to see what might be there. At each of the three buildings, Patrick would start with a knock on the door of a ground-floor apartment to ask for a basement key. The women who answered were always friendly and cooperative, and they would complain to Patrick about their absentee landlords. By the time Patrick had got the key and walked to the basement door, a security guard would have already opened it with a knife. It was clear from all the cuttings and markings by the door that this was a standard method of entry. In fact, upon seeing this the women complained to Patrick that everyone got inside that way. One woman (unless noted otherwise, all residents were African American) ran after Patrick, asking him to get the landlord to fix the lock on the basement door because the landlord ignored her calls. He whipped out his cellular phone and dialed right there in front of her. After leaving the basement, Patrick told the woman that the landlord did not answer; he promised to try later and get back to her. (He did call later from the ministation, but again got no answer.)

In the basements, officers poked at the insulation where the walls met the ceilings. They often found stashes of drugs there, and last week they had found a gun. The police also looked in the garbage cans and washing machines. The search uncovered two different baggies full of "jackets" (tiny bags of crack) and also a bag of marijuana. In some empty laundry detergent bottles, Patrick also found more than forty empty corners of baggies used to sell crack in twenty-dollar quantities on the street. He documented all this in his pocket notebook to show the absentee landlord later.

Back outside, several officers were surrounded by a bunch of onlookers from the neighborhood as they frisked three young men, two black, one white. They had been spotted going from their car into an apartment house in which they did not live; it was a known shooting gallery for heroin. John, one of the police officers conducting the frisk, had been the arresting officer in the incident the night before. At one point, someone yelled from the window of the apartment facing the officers, "Fuck you, John!" One of the young men had a rock of cocaine on him; another admitted to having had a marijuana cigarette laced with crack, but said he threw this out the window of the car, around the corner. Patrick went off on foot to look for the crack-laced cigarette.

His search was briefly interrupted when a black woman in an unmarked squad car came by; a detective assigned to the drug unit, she is also Patrick's wife's best friend. She wanted to tell him that she was going to watch his child tomorrow. The detective also let him know that something big was going down with the drug unit tonight, but that he should keep it to himself until she told the supervising sergeant. She left. Patrick nonchalantly mentioned that her female romantic partner was also a detective, and that many cops are in relationships with other cops. He then received a call over the radio saying the young man had remembered that he did not throw out the doctored cigarette, but that it was still in his back pocket. So, with the search called off, Patrick went back to the ministation to do some paperwork.

Taylor—Criminally Active Neighborhood

Across town, in an equally dilapidated, high-crime residential area, the neighborhood officer was halfway through his day. Like Patrick, Matt is a white man in his thirties; however, he is admittedly less motivated or influenced by community policing rhetoric than is his counterpart. Matt's interest in the NPO position arose because he thought the scheduling flexibility would help him to arrange the study time he needed for law school. Whereas Patrick was gregarious, Matt was taciturn, his spirits and energy much lower.

The Taylor neighborhood appears neglected, with litter strewn around, brown, untended grass, and no flowers or gardens visible. Taylor is made up of ten or twelve two-story apartment houses of four to six units, a couple of blocks of somewhat run-down single-family homes in the contiguous area, a city-owned housing development consisting of about five more buildings, and a big park with volleyball and basketball courts. Three years ago, this neighborhood hosted the biggest open-air crack cocaine market in the city. Men and women drove in at all hours of the day and night to make purchases. Children and young teenagers were routinely used as lookouts; as juveniles, if they got caught they would receive hardly any punishment. Youngsters could easily earn several hundreds of dollars a day or week. Most of the apartments are home to single mothers with children, along with assorted relatives or else fictive kin, who show up and stay temporarily. Except for the city-owned complex, which primarily housed Asian families, the neighborhood was almost completely African American in the apartment buildings, with some poor white and black families living in the run-down tract housing nearby. One-quarter to one-half mile outside the neighborhood's perimeter lay some much nicer middle-class, single-family homes, but these did not fall within the NPO's responsibility.

Matt worked at a slower pace than Patrick, and he did not look for proactive policing opportunities. Matt felt his neighborhood was a slum, the result of years of neglect. Apartments had been managed by a terrible company, so tenants were never screened or evicted. Then, about a year ago, a new group bought the complex and vowed to establish a stable (and ultimately profitable) community. The company planned to evict undesirable tenants, refurbish apartments, and discourage "bad people" from hanging around the neighborhood. The new managers worked with the city and the police to post huge ordinance signs on the buildings that faced the parking lots where the drug sales were going on. As Matt pointed out, the signs were very prominent: NO PARKING, NO TRESPASSING, NO LOITERING, and NO STANDING were among their messages. The police followed up with rigorous enforcement action, ticketing like crazy (with hefty fines—from $65 to over $200), conveying the message that they were serious about enforcing ordinances. The new management company also hired armed security officers to augment the police presence. These young, mostly white men patrolled from nine in the morning until midnight.

Smack in the middle of the neighborhood, in a donated building, is the Salvation Army's community center. The group provides space for the neighborhood police officer, a social worker, and a community nurse. The building has a huge parking lot, which is frequently used by patrol officers and the NPO to "shoot the breeze" during their shifts. The parking lot, and thus the police cars, were plainly visible from many of the apartments.

Matt always arranged to bring a squad car to Taylor. He kept up a running conversation about the duties of NPOs. Matt kept stressing that although the neighborhood officers were involved with issuing tickets and enforcing the law, it was the active and aggressive stance of the new property manager that seems to have made the most difference in taking back the streets. Nevertheless, he said he would never walk alone at night in Taylor, and he would always wear a bullet-proof vest for safety.

Matt complained that he felt unwelcome in the 'hood when he responded to calls from residents; either no one admits to calling, or he is challenged about being there by citizens who insist that it is he who has the problem. Matt said that most of policing is just "game playing, both us and them," with no one wanting to lose face. Moreover, there are so many times that he sees adults teaching children to think poorly of police, even though the officers are trying to walk around and establish some rapport with citizens. He repeatedly hears African American adults tell children, "If you see the police, run; if the police want to talk to you, shut up."

Matt pulled the squad car into an empty parking lot near a vacant apartment building. Immediately, five girls and boys approached. Although his windows were rolled down, the air conditioner was going full blast. The children kept remarking how nice it felt and asked if they could come in, or even sleep in the car. A female member of the research team was in the front passenger seat, which intrigued the children. They kept wondering who she was, asking if she was Matt's girlfriend or maybe a police officer. They kept pestering him for baseball cards. Neighborhood officers carry them around, and they give out rookie cards all summer long to children. The cards are used as a tactic to reach out to youngsters and create relationships or interrupt suspicious or hostile ones. They help to break the ice and to provide ongoing opportunities to talk with young people and soften their impression that police are only around to investigate trouble. Matt had no cards with him. The boys and girls kept reaching inside the squad car to play with the power locks and window controls, and they opened the back door. Although they surrounded the passenger side, where the researcher sat, not one was over at Matt's side of the car. He did not seem to be able to get them to stop playing with the electric openers and the back door. He kept telling them to stop, and they ignored him. At one point the oldest child, a girl of about eight, said she knew of some people selling drugs, and asked if he wanted her to show him who they were. Matt ignored her. She kept asking until he just repeated what she had said. It was obvious he did not take her seriously. Several times she remarked, "You just don't care about us." Matt continued to ignore her and made no attempt to reassure her. Then he decided to drive away, without ever exchanging any pleasantries with the children. They kept hanging onto the car, yelling that they were going to jump on the back and ride on the trunk. He told them no, and kept inching the cruiser forward. It seemed as though he was going too fast and would run over their feet. After, in his words, the car "got away," he explained that "those kinds of kids" just do not listen. The subject was dropped. Matt continued to patrol the streets, driving very, very slowly.

During the entire shift, very few adults except for an occasional woman were around the neighborhood. Mostly young children were outside; there were also some surly teenagers, who stared and acted defiant when we walked or drove around them. Matt said this was typical.

He parked at the community center and went in for a few minutes to pick something up. His office was very tidy and businesslike, with nothing around to personalize it. In contrast to the rest of the center, it was drab. In the center, there were three computers for young people, a TV and VCR, school tutoring in the basement, lots of modern furniture, evidence of programs and activities run by the Salvation Army for youngsters, a social worker's cluttered desk, and a community nurse's office. Board games for children, hockey games, and Ping-Pong tables completed the picture.

Matt grunted hello to the residential social worker, explaining later that he had a lot of difficulty with her. He did not like to, or even want to, work closely with her because they saw things differently. For example, as a law enforcer, Matt wants to clean things up and get the bad people out. As a social worker, she wants to give them more chances and points out how so-and-so is going through some kind of rehab program and should be cut some slack. Matt resents that; it interferes with what he sees as his responsibilities. Overall, Matt could not generate much enthusiasm for the center, or for the potential of more cooperation between the NPO and the social worker. A couple of boys and girls, and two groups of mothers with children, were in the center, but he virtually ignored them, not even saying hello. Matt pointed out that he had taken over the position from another NPO, who seemed quite popular. He said that his own name had not caught on yet. He remarked that "Officer Garth" was easier for children to say, or more appealing since it had a better ring to it, than "Officer Matt." He seemed disappointed that children still asked for the former NPO and did not seem to accept him.

In contrast to his feelings about the social worker, Matt thought that having a probation-parole officer in the community center was a very good idea, particularly for deterrence. He believed that mothers often ignored advice from police or social workers, such as getting their children free immunizations at the neighborhood center. But a mere suggestion from a probation-parole officer was another story. Since the officer can hold the threat of revocation—and incarceration—over the parolees' heads (whether the women themselves, their partners, or their older children are on parole or probation), then that suggestion could be seen as more of a threat and they would take it seriously.

Matt turned on his answering machine, and as the messages played back he complained about the endless requests for his presence at meetings.

> If an officer wants to be hooked into the community, he could spend his entire shift at meetings, and that's not why we are here. Every single group wants me to be on their committee, and hence, go to their meetings, even if it has *nothing* to do with police issues. For example, a community group called Families First really wants me at their meetings. I had worked till midnight the night before, and their meeting began at 8 A.M. the next day. So I got up at 6:30 A.M. and then went to the meeting. It was a waste of time. They spent the initial fifteen minutes talking about some fifteen-year-old boy who was having school problems because of dyslexia, and they hammered out a program for the school to follow helping him. I couldn't believe I was there. Why was I needed?

What a waste of time. Yet everybody wants me to be present at their meeting. It gets in the way of law enforcement.

Matt decided to check on what was happening outside, since he did not want to be outdoors later, when rain was forecast. He walked toward the cluster of apartment buildings near the community center. Matt kept his head thrust forward, rarely initiating any contact with residents, not even saying hello. He did respond if anyone greeted him first, which happened several times. In each case the women involved uttered an exaggerated "hello," as if they were mocking him. Their expressions and body language conveyed that he was an unwelcome presence. As Matt walked, some young children raced up to him and asked for baseball cards. When he felt like it, Matt gave them to the boys and girls; mostly, though, he told them he did not have any. There were no other conversations.

Matt joined up with four armed guards from the private security company (all in their early twenties, all white). The five of them moaned about how quiet the evening was, with not much to do. They bragged about their past successes in getting rid of "problem people," and they speculated about the upcoming evictions. Despite the flow of residents coming and going between the parking lot and the apartments, the officers never exchanged any pleasantries with them to break the ice. All five men, in uniform and armed, stood and talked loudly. Not a single adult came near them, even though they were smack in the middle of a yard in front of several occupied buildings. Yet all of those who lived nearby could not help but notice the law enforcement presence, the officers surveilling the ghetto, almost as in a police state. The racial difference between the armed men and the residents was stark. The female researcher finally asked if they felt any tension or any resistance from the community. This led to a lot of mock groaning and showing off: "Hey, we are the thin blue line in action! We are the *reason* why things haven't exploded!" said one. "The residents should be thankful for us!" said another. According to a third, "There is no racial tension; there is only tension because there are so many officers here and they know they can not get away with something because so many of us would give chase." One of the guards said, "Yeah, if something happened and an officer gave chase, miraculously, more residents would materialize out of nowhere, . . . not necessarily to help the police but to follow what was transpiring. So, they're just looking for action." Matt explained that it was good to have so many colleagues available as backups; handling incidents would be dangerous for only one officer. The men talked as though, if not for their presence, the neighborhood would fall to a siege by criminals. No concern was expressed for the residents, nor were any ideas put forward on how things got this way (e.g., unemployment, poverty) or on how to encourage neighborhood empowerment. The five officers told some more stories about crimefighting. The security guards strutted a little and tried to emphasize their importance to Matt.

Meanwhile, the athletic courts were filling up, in segregated fashion. The black residents, mostly boys and young men, were using the basketball courts or playing football, while entire Asian families played volleyball.

As they talked, the officers identified problem people by name and updated each other. Matt told the security guards stories involving law enforcement or crimefighting. For instance, one-way bus tickets had been purchased for some residents who were wanted in other cities across the country, but not so badly as to have them extradited. He told the story of one officer, who could sell anything to anybody, who convinced a wanted man from New York City to leave town on a bus and promise to turn himself in. The officer then called Chicago; when the bus made a connecting stop, police there picked the man up, eventually sending him on to New York under guard. He also was able to reclaim the man's welfare check before he left, saving the state six hundred dollars. They all got a big, big laugh from this story and told each other, with lots of winks, that *this* illustrated problem-oriented or problem-solving policing.

A patrol car arrived and the driver, Dan, another young white man, joined the "jawing" session. He and Matt together related a story (which would be told twice more in the next two hours) about an incident that had occurred the week before. Dan was with Matt as they chased a fifteen-year-old who had been challenging them. The teenager had given them grounds for arrest: waiting until they came by, he deliberately got into a car and drove it around the block; then, smiling, he parked it next to the squad car; finally, he got out and walked into his house. The officers had been watching the youth because they knew he was dealing drugs or serving as a runner or lookout, and because he was continually and conspicuously driving cars around underage. So, Dan kicked down the door and made the arrest; they found five hundred dollars in his pocket. In the next couple of days they chased down another teenager; he was carrying five thousand dollars. The story was always told with pride, especially the part about chasing the juvenile and kicking in the door, ending with disgust being expressed at how much money these "punks" have in their pockets.

The officers had been standing outside in the same circle a good half hour. No residents came near them, and they did not initiate any contact with the residents. Finally, the men split up, walking off in different directions. Matt planned to go back to the community center to check for phone messages, and then maybe grab something to eat. This triggered a round of jokes about getting the required daily dosage of fat and cholesterol. Off he went. Again, Matt rarely initiated contact with anyone as he walked; he just was not very friendly. He also seemed very suspicious and impersonal. At one point, however, Matt stopped to talk to a woman who drove up with several children in her car. He appeared to be very friendly, laughing with her and paying her the compliment that "you are a working mother, and thus, a good resident." She had kicked out a "no-good" husband, and Matt believes she is better off without him. He told her that she was a good person, and he wanted her to know that he had seen a fifteen-year-old boy from the complex driving her car the other night. She thanked him, seeming friendly and relaxed.

Matt said there was a big problem with teenagers driving underage. He used to handle such issues by holding the suspect and spending the time to issue a ticket on the spot. But, out of nowhere, a crowd of onlookers would materialize and mouth off, and he "didn't need that hassle." Consequently, Matt now writes citations in his office and gives them to the persons the next time he sees them. In his view,

> The residents' communications, the informal grapevine, are very developed. You could think and see no one around, but as soon as something happens, everyone knows and is there to watch. So, I like to do a pro-active surveillance and watch the apartment dwellers' activities while I am hiding inside another apartment. So I can gather probable cause for drug selling or something. You can watch the mannerisms and activity levels change, depending on if the residents see a police officer or not.

Matt then decided to deliver two citations, since it was easier to do it after the fact than "in the moment." Then, there would be a lot of people around, only one officer present, and the potential to lose control of the situation.

Matt apologized a couple of times about how slow the shift was; he did not receive any calls the entire night. He said that was unusual, because a lot of children had been flagging him down over the last couple of days to complain about their bikes being stolen.

It started pouring rain, and he said, "That's the end of foot patrol tonight." Matt drove to a fast-food restaurant for a carryout supper. He was bored. And he did not feel close to the people: "Frankly, I would rather *not* get to know them really well; I prefer not to be known as Officer Matt, so that I can more easily be a law enforcer."

PAIR TWO

Westend—Program Development Neighborhood

Helen was dressed in street clothes. She had promised one of her residents that she would come to a meeting as her advocate, wearing civilian dress to avoid stigma, in a hearing that might end with the Department of Children and Family Services taking the woman's children. Although Helen did not know the DCFS side of the story, she did believe that the woman was making progress and should get a chance to prove herself. Helen, white and in her mid-forties, grew up in Westend, which is why she likes this assignment. She has been with the Jackson City police for twenty-five years, the first sixteen of them as a civilian employee. Helen is married to a sergeant, and they have a young child.

The Westend neighborhood is made up of mostly single-family apartments, typically home to a woman and her children. The majority of the buildings house two-bedroom apartments; there is also a row of four- and five-bedroom townhouses. Other features are a playground and a community center, which has been active for twenty years; a bus stop is two blocks away. The campus of a community college, with rolling green lawns and tennis courts, borders the neighborhood. The racial composition is 30 percent each for whites, blacks, and Asians (mostly Hmong); most of the remaining population is Hispanic.

Helen was busy organizing the self-esteem workshop for female residents of Westend. She devised this program because of the high number of domestic violence incidents in the neighborhood. She felt that women's low self-esteem was a big contributing factor, so she became involved in a long-term project to address the issue. A woman's club was established; it meets for two hours once a week, and speakers are invited to discuss battering and other topics related to self-esteem. Guests had included someone from the battered-women's shelter to talk about its policies, someone from the court to explain legal options, someone to do massage, and someone to talk about hair and skin care. The women are also given a light lunch, and childcare is provided. In addition, those who attended all of the workshops could earn a small amount of credit from the local community college. Since many of the women had not finished high school, this gave them a sense of empowerment and accomplishment. The self-esteem group was ongoing.

Helen has access to all police reports from her neighborhood of incidents that occur when she is not there, and she has identified domestic violence as the biggest recurring problem. She believes that being the NPO allows her to be absolutely tenacious about immediately following up such reports. Part of her quick response is to let the victim know that she cares and can help; the other part is to recognize that an abused woman is typically more willing to talk to her if her batterer is away in jail, out of earshot. She finds it helpful if a different officer makes the arrest, because then she is not seen as the "bad guy." This allows her to sit down over coffee and really talk strategy with the victim. Helen is able to explain what a restraining order is, and to offer to bring the woman down to the courthouse and help her apply for one. She also volunteers to tell the apartment managers about abusive situations so they can help with restraining orders. Helen proudly remarked that not one of the battered women she knows can say that she could not do something because she did not have a car, information, or knowledge—Helen provides them all. She is concerned, however, that there are many very isolated battered women; they do not reach out for help, so people do not know about them.

Helen pulled into the parking lot, then slowed to talk to a middle-aged black man on the right-hand sidewalk. She was driving her personal car, but she could control the automatic window on the passenger side, a feature officers use a lot. The man was collecting cans, and she told him to come by the office because she had some more to give him. (She explained, out of his hearing, that he was a nice guy who drank too much and then got in trouble. One of the conditions of his probation is to pick up trash. So, he collects cans for the deposit money.) He came inside, and Helen asked how he was doing and if he was staying out of trouble; he assured her that he was. She also asked about his wife, and they exchanged basic chitchat.

Helen's office is in a two-bedroom unit in one of the apartment buildings. The room is sparsely furnished, but her walls are adorned with newspaper clippings highlighting neighborhood youngsters and children's drawings of her made to welcome her to the new office when she moved out of the community center. The other bedroom is occupied by the private security officer permanently assigned to the neighborhood. On his wall are letters from the management showing which residents were evicted and why, along with their mug shots. Helen did not want the material in her office, both for reasons of confidentiality and because it could make some of the residents feel uncomfortable. Yet, the letters and pictures provide good information and a visual display of "bad guys" who could be immediately cited for trespassing (which carries a $247 fine) by the patrol officers. Helen's closets are overflowing with toys and basketballs. The toys occupy children while she is interviewing their mothers. She uses the basketballs to "reward" boys and girls for giving her information about domestic violence. Helen feels that the children want to speak up but are afraid that their mothers or fathers (or some other adult) will retaliate. She also believes that they are afraid to be seen with her. So, she ignores them to preserve their anonymity; in a couple of days, she gives them a new basketball to stress how very important their help was.

Helen next went downstairs to meet with the management people. She is extremely pleased that the police, private security guard, and residential management are all so close that they can exchange information smoothly and easily. Helen told them about a Pakistani family with big problems. She had just arrested the son, aged sixteen, for beating on some ten-year-old boys. The father, who rules the household, drinks and beats his wife. She asked that Helen never stop over, because he would become suspicious and beat her more. Helen can only call and use inquiring about the children as a cover. But whenever the man gets locked up, the woman comes to the neighborhood office and talks. Helen thinks the boy is taking out his own anger on the little children because it would be too risky for him to challenge his father's behavior.

A walk around the neighborhood was next on the agenda. Helen greeted people by name, and they conversed easily and with great familiarity. Her first stop was to check the progress of repairs on an apartment that had caught fire. It was nothing special, but there were new appliances, and everything had been repainted and cleaned. The white painter–maintenance man was a little cynical: Helen said, "They look nice when they're all new"; he replied, "Not for long; they'll ruin it." A black man, probably in his forties, was hanging around outside. Helen asked if he was staying out of trouble, and he assured her that he was. She said later that he was a major drug dealer, but she knew he did not deal here, only in a different, high-crime neighborhood. She could easily cite him for trespassing, or have the management company obtain a restraining order, but she was torn. His wife and three children live in a townhouse next door. Since he is not dealing there, she thought it better for the young children to have their father about; moreover, they were too young to understand what he did. She thinks he respects her position and the feelings of his wife, which may explain why he does not deal drugs close to home. Helen knows he has a court date in a few weeks, so she will wait and hope the situation will be taken care of. The man is facing several drug charges, and she thinks he will get prison time.

Whenever people drove into the parking lots, they waved to Helen or returned her wave. She stopped to talk to the children and teenagers at the playground, specifically following up on some boys who had been hit earlier by an older bully. She told them what she had done with the bully and encouraged them to talk to her if anything else happened. They wanted to know if he was "in jail"; Helen demystified this for them, saying that children do not get put in jail but still need to know that they cannot do certain things. She also greeted a little girl who is bilingual, and talked a bit about her family background. Helen seemed to know a lot, both good and bad, about family backgrounds. She said she wished her presence was so commonplace that no one would think twice if she stopped in any apartment to chat or have a cup of coffee. She believes that residents still wonder "what happened there" whenever she stops in at an apartment. But local people call her answering machine all the time, especially the ones who do not want her to drop in.

At this point a patrol car drove by. Garth, a former NPO in an adjacent neighborhood, and another officer were looking for a suspect. Helen and Garth knew each other very well and they joked around. When he had been an NPO, they planned joint neighborhood activities with the boys and girls. She teased him about the Easter Bunny costume he had worn at a party for the children. Helen had driven him to the gathering in her squad car, which was a big hit with the children.

The officers drove on, and Helen next wandered by the neighborhood garden. A hand-painted sign listed the rules: "Everybody has to tend their own turf; you can't grow anything illegal; you can't grow anything to sell." The management company donated chicken wire for fencing, local businesses donated seeds, and an Asian family volunteered to teach their neighbors, particularly teenagers, to garden. Residents gathered every afternoon to learn about gardening and work on their crops. When Helen walked by, some twelve-year-old Asian girls were watering their plots.

As we walked around, everyone seemed to know Helen and waved or said hello. She seemed surprised, because she was in civilian dress. She likes to wear her uniform for visibility and so that people know she enforces the law. Citizens initiated conversations and the tones were casual and friendly.

Helen also stopped by the community center to check on some programs' attendance: older teens mentored younger children, helping them with homework and earning hours that would entitle them to a free field trip at the end of the year; teenagers had a drop-in center; HUD had provided money for a van to transport residents to a grocery store, since none is within walking distance; and a parents' outreach group relieves stressed or cooped-up parents for a couple of hours if they need a break from their children. There were also enthusiastically supported plans to revive the residents' association committee. The previous organization was run by a bossy woman; she angered too many people, and it became her exclusive club. The woman was transferred (with her consent) to another HUD housing unit in the city, and now the residents wanted to restart the program. It had been supported with HUD money, and elected building captains were paid a nominal amount to sweep up, keep the laundry room clean, handle concerns of residents from their building, and represent them at the main meetings. The shopping van was provided through this group's efforts, since they pointed out that mothers with toddlers have a difficult time managing both their children and bags of groceries on a regular bus. Helen spends about an hour every day at the community center. Following this afternoon's visit, she walked back to her office to do paperwork.

Crestview—Program Development Neighborhood

Theresa, a tall white woman aged about thirty, a former college basketball star, is walking the beat. Married to another police officer, Theresa has been an

NPO for a little over a year, after serving for ten years as a patrol officer and a member of the Drug Task Force. Crestview was at one point considered a very criminally active neighborhood, but it has been cleaned up and is now seen as a success. People are eager to move in; there is currently a nine-month waiting list to get into the neighborhood. The apartment management is very good at taking care of problems, and the neighborhood association is active. This group has been able to help out with a lot of things that a brand-new NPO might encounter, such as arranging public meetings and getting sports programs started. All in all, Crestview is close to the final stages of the neighborhood program, moving toward being designated a maintenance neighborhood. Theresa's full-time work here is winding down, and she spends some of her time in a new district. The resident association (the Round Table) and the apartment managers have not objected, so they realize, perhaps, that they can continue the NPO's effort on their own. Theresa was quick to say that Crestview is not trouble free, but it is doing well overall. She laughs about this, however, saying that she does not want to talk herself out of a job.

The neighborhood is geographically isolated from businesses and stores; it is one of just two residential areas on its side of town, and Parkside is a good ten minutes away by car. Crestview is surrounded by fairly affluent neighborhoods, making it unique in that respect, too. The other districts are closer together. About a third of its residents are African American, a third white, and a third Asian or Hispanic.

A walk around Crestview reveals two long roads lined by three-story apartment houses, each with six to eight units. The properties are nicely tended, with no trash or graffiti in sight. The manager is also a landscaper, so he does a lot of work on the grounds. One of the women who works for the property manager also lives there and plants bulbs all over the place; in the spring, the area is in full bloom. There are some isolated drug problems, but no open-air dealing for the most part. Theresa believes the biggest problem is interpersonal conflict—neighbors just do not always get along. She is sometimes asked to mediate verbal fights, and she often arranges mediation services from a group of lawyers in training who volunteer their time. At this point, she gestures around and says, "Yeah, this is my neighborhood." Her tone of voice indicates a sense of proud ownership.

Earlier in the morning, Theresa had begun her shift by checking on some children to see if they made it to school. Since the girls and boys are smart and have a lot of potential, verifying that the mother gets them off to school has become a pet project of hers. Theresa knows the family well. She believes the mother is a very good manipulator, who lets you think that she is 100 percent behind you when she is really just a lot of hot air and empty promises. Theresa has learned that, even if she is of a different race than a group of residents, once enough time and energy are spent getting to know them the NPO will make an intimate connection regardless of racial background. On the walk around the neighborhood, Theresa talked about her Cops on Computers project. Initially, Theresa met with residents about school-related issues, and one participant was a "lady" who was the technologies outreach worker for the school district; she suggested it might be "neat" to get the police involved. (Theresa always referred to women as ladies.) Although she had no idea exactly what she was letting herself in for, Theresa thought it would be a lot of fun, despite the huge time commitment required of both officers and young people. (She believes programs are always worthwhile if youngsters get involved.) Theresa admitted that the sessions would also provide the opportunity for officers to learn computer skills beyond whatever fundamentals they had picked up in the department. Children and teenagers love to use the machines, so the officers could learn themselves as well as being good role models.

Despite her overall enthusiasm, Theresa said there were some days she wished she were still in a squad car and not emotionally involved with people. On patrol she could just sit back, do her work, not have any emotional attachments, and go home after her shift with no lingering tugs. At the same time, however, she now likes to go from one family to another and check in on persons to whom she has become really, really close. Theresa believes her job is a lot easier if she knows what members of the community are going through, and this knowledge pushes her to look for alternatives beyond the traditional methods. Moreover, even on crisis calls, she knows individuals' histories in greater depth. So instead of just going in and being judgmental about their lifestyles, she is able to understand that they are good people involved in bad situations, making it easier to maintain at least some empathy.

Theresa says hello to a middle-aged African American resident who is outside washing his car. He cheerfully returns her greeting. When asked if she still attended briefings, and how connected she felt with the rest of the department, Theresa said she did not feel too isolated. Although, because of her hours, she attends fewer patrol meetings, she does get to task force and detective briefings. But she tries to attend patrol meetings every couple of weeks or so just to stay in touch with the other officers, and she calls them to see what is going on. Theresa regularly types up an information sheet of addresses to watch in the neighborhood, and it goes out to patrol officers who work the area around Crestview. She encourages them to walk the neighborhood with her, but their work prevents them from leaving their squad cars too much.

Next, Theresa has a long discussion with a black social worker about jobs programs. Persons who are receiving Aid to Families with Dependent Children are being recruited. There is some concern that if they do not show up for their appointments, or do not participate in the program, their AFDC benefits are cut. Every time persons do not attend, the AFDC benefits (around $425) are reduced, beginning by taking out the equivalent of an hour's pay and by cutting food stamps. Theresa and the social worker are trying to figure out a way to post job information for residents. They are particularly concerned that although mothers who have a child under the age of one are exempt, once that child turns one year and one day the mother is required to seek work. Theresa tells the social worker about phone calls she made the other day to see if the city can send out job openings to post. She also called the governor's office for job information and to see what documents had been translated for the Hmong.

A number of boys and girls are playing around, many at the playground. Theresa knows a lot about youth programs. For instance, there is a summer camp every year for the elementary school, and she wants to encourage a new resident who just had a baby to be one of the teachers. As another way of connecting with youngsters, Theresa keeps a lot of stuffed animals in her office. She gives them out to children who are sick, who do well in school, or who are celebrating birthdays.

After leaving the office, Theresa speaks to another black man working on his car; they joke around easily. She offers to give him a jump, but he needs a tow and a new battery. A white patrol officer joins her, explaining that he had to get out of the car for a while. Theresa asks him what was going on in the 'hood that morning before she got in. He said not much, they just talked to a bunch of children, which is always fun; they flock around the cars, what is that, what is this, what does that do? Theresa says she has to drop some stuff off at the management office, and he says he'll walk with us to get the lay of the land. When this policeman was asked if he would ever want to be a neighborhood officer, he said: "I'd give it some thought. I'm not sure if I have the energy to do it. I'm a little bit in awe of people like Theresa and Patrick and David. This is a very demanding position, to be a neighborhood officer, and I don't know if I'd have the stamina to keep up with it." It seemed unusual that he got out of his squad car to actually observe, since our research team has talked with patrol officers who do not know what NPOs do. His response:

> Well, look, you have to get out of the cruiser every so often, that's the whole crux of it, this community policing concept, and it would be nice if I could do it more often than I do, the problem being that I generally have such a sprawling beat area to cover that being on foot is simply impossible. I do what I can, I take a little walk through the mall and talk to mall security during lunch hours, that sort of thing, but as things

stand now, I don't have as many opportunities as Theresa does to simply get out and talk to people, which I regret.

The patrol officer believes the best consequence of neighborhood work was to personalize the police; everyone knows them and calls them by their first name. This helps make all officers seem more approachable, especially to young people, who get a highly distorted image of policework from television and movies. The officer admits that the only time he had to "crank off a round from Old Bessie" in eight years was to kill a wounded deer. By and large this was true for most of his colleagues, who did not ever shoot at anyone in the field. It is not dramatic to be checking out a four-car accident or rounding up an old person with Alzheimer's disease who wandered away from a nursing home. Naturally, screenwriters concentrate on all the sexy stuff—car chases and shootouts—and people come away with a misconception.

Meanwhile, Theresa was talking with two residents (one African American and one Latino), and she apologizes to the patrol officer for not having introduced them. They are doing maintenance in the new development. Now she starts talking with the children who are playing all around, loosely supervised by adults. She asks the girls and boys how they are. The patrol officer remarks that the nice thing about the neighborhood program is that Theresa does not just show up when there is a problem—she is part of the community.

One adult resident tells Theresa he won fifty dollars in the lottery. She jokes around, saying he is the luckiest man, and they share lots of laughter and funny stories about good and bad luck. Next, she calls the school to see if the children she checked on earlier had shown up. Theresa had devised a plan with the social worker to get them to classes: the two of them will stop by every day, the mother is going to be up and have them ready, and everybody will work to ensure they make it to school. She explains that this morning the girls missed the bus, but she gave them a ride so they arrived on time; although the boys were reluctant to go with her because they were embarrassed to ride in the squad car, Theresa said she would drop them off a block away from the building.

But when she came by this morning to be sure they were ready for school, the two boys were making excuses so they could remain at home and play Nintendo. Their mother backed them up, promising Theresa that her sons would attend school for the rest of the year. Theresa did not believe her, and she called the social worker to tell him what was going on. Together, they decided to hook the family up with local resources to help with the boys. If the mother will not cooperate, she may be arrested. Theresa, disgusted and frustrated, said, "The kids are the ones who are suffering, and we need to stop giving the mom so many chances. She is not helping."

The patrol officer involved with the situation came by to make sure he knew the name of the mother and children with the school problem. Theresa moves on to talk with two residents, a white man and a black man, about the paint job in the apartment building. She seemed proud of the neighborhood's stability and said there was no need to use private security guards. In fact, Theresa picked Crestview because she had been assigned here as a patrol officer; she knew some of the residents and knew the neighborhood could be made to work.

Theresa goes to the apartment management office to call the school and check on the boys. One of them went, the other did not. She explains the plan she has devised with the social worker and leaves her beeper number with the school.

Back outside, Theresa talks to residents about the resident association meeting that was held last night. She had been there and felt it was a really good session. They discussed neighborhood conflict, noise complaints, and people hanging around. The residents maintained that since it was *their* neighborhood, and the NPO cannot be there all the time, it is up to them to set the standards for what is acceptable. They devised a plan to submit to the full neighborhood association to vote on. Theresa then mentions walking through the parking lot last week and seeing a car with a broken window, the owner standing beside it. "When did that happen?" she asked. The man said it happened a couple of weeks ago. Theresa then asked why he had not called her about it. "Oh, this is Crestview, you gotta expect that," he replied. "No you don't," Theresa told him. She went on to say that any broken glass in the parking lot gets cleaned up. She reminds the residents to tell her about it; then, even if she cannot find out who did it, at least she would know that this parking lot is having a problem, to watch that, or to let all the residents know about the problem.

Another local woman told Theresa that her particular concern is with men sitting in their cars drinking beer and blasting the radio. Legally, they can drink on their patios, but they also drink when there are basketball games going on. When there was drinking in the summer in the parking lots, little children could overhear all kinds of foul language and adult stories.

The apartment manager joins the group, and they talk about inspections. Theresa learns that word is spreading among the residents and they are cleaning their apartments, as evidenced by the full Dumpsters. She moves on and walks around. Theresa says she rarely walks alone at night since there are some people she is not comfortable being around; also, night patrol is not that necessary since it is quiet after sundown. At the playground, girls and boys start yelling greetings. Some of the children ask for baseball cards, but they accept her answer that she will not have any for a couple of weeks. The youngsters ask Theresa about her uniform, gun, radio, badge, and so on. She answers each question carefully and with a lot of warmth. She puts one little girl's shoes back on for her. A boy asks Theresa to put her handcuffs on him. "No," she says, "you're too good of a kid, I couldn't put you in handcuffs." This banter continues for more than fifteen minutes. Theresa tells one child to let her mom know that she will be by later to see her. On to the community center, where one of the resident-workers says a patrol officer with a child in the back of his car came by to find Theresa. She calls him and finds the child is an uncontrollable five-year-old whose mother is not home. Theresa begins phoning around to find another relative.

The next incident involves the manager of the community center and an irate resident who is insisting on taking chairs out of the building. For the next half hour, there is a major discussion about the insurance policy for furniture in the center and strategies for letting residents borrow items. Theresa helps to solve the problem, suggesting alternative ideas on how to handle this concern in a fair manner.

Theresa also discussed the perception that patrol officers have of NPOs. She suggested that some see the benefits, whereas others see them as social workers who can play basketball whenever they want. She said that people have different personalities and different ways of doing this job; 95 percent of them are good ways, 5 percent are not. Theresa believes her own style is totally different from that of her husband, a patrol officer, even though they see eye to eye on a lot of things. He is more militaristic. He likes to do things by the book and is more ready to make arrests. For her part, Theresa is more ready to sit down and talk about a situation.

Theresa begins to return phone calls. She informs one man that a couple of officers from the Drug Task Force are looking for someone he knows, in case he has any contact with him. Her tone is very friendly. Theresa then calls the community college to see if there are any job openings she can post for her residents. Then, she listens to a message left the night before by an upset female resident:

> Theresa, this is Joannie, last night. I want to tell you that, as you can see, my husband is very much in pain about what I've gone and done. I don't want Ricky really pressured because the thing [is] I don't want him to run, I don't want him to leave town. At least right now, we knows he's in town, we know he's okay. Because he feels like he's closed in and he may up and run. He's gotten unstable. He . . . , he's not calling, he's not medicated. So, there's never ever telling what he's going to do or how he's thinking. . . . I think what he really needs is communication. I don't think my husband actually does believe that Ricky wants to come back

home and live, but . . . Theresa, I just wanted you to know what's going on.

Theresa exhales deeply and writes the information down, deciding to return the phone call later that day.

PAIR THREE

Fairview—Maintenance Neighborhood

In another section of the city, Curtis was doing his own version of community policing. He describes his office as "the Cadillac of all neighborhood offices" since it is a two-bedroom carpeted apartment, provided solely for his use by the building's management. He proudly points out his well-stocked refrigerator, microwave, and two televisions, as well as the decorations on the wall that were his own contribution to the decor. (One was a photocopied paper saying that senior citizens are the biggest carriers of AIDS: bandAIDS, hearingAIDS, and walkingAIDS. Another sheet was a takeoff on the serenity prayer of Alcoholics Anonymous; the last line read "and let God grant me enough guns so I can kill the ones who piss me off.")

Curtis, an African American aged fifty-seven, started in the department when he was thirty-nine years old. He has been the neighborhood police officer in Fairview for five and a half years. Before becoming the NPO, Curtis was a patrol officer here too, so he feels he knows the area quite well. Curtis also owns a house in the neighborhood, and his children attended local schools. He acknowledges that his shifts are relatively quiet, since Fairview has changed greatly over the years. Katie, the first NPO, really cleaned things up and got things organized; she was here for three or four years. She was followed by Tom, who served for about five years. So, Curtis does not do much proactive policing, but waits for folks to come to him for help. In fact, Curtis says (with some pride) that he does most of his work just sitting in his office, observing through the slats of the venetian blinds. From this vantage point he can see everything, especially with binoculars, but because of his black face (his words) no one can see him. (The entire time researchers were with him, however, he never once looked out the window.)

And so Curtis waits in his office-apartment for residents to seek his help. For instance, a mother asked him yesterday to come and talk to her children, who had been caught shoplifting. He informally warned the boys about what could happen to them. He tells people to ignore the uniform and just talk to him, because he is a person, too. Curtis is a self-described "people person" and he believes that no one can be an effective NPO without being such.

Contained in his file cabinet is a copy of the schedule of talks for the community policing panel he had helped to organize, along with the well-known policy book for community police officers, Herman Goldstein's *Problem-Oriented Policing*. However, Curtis claimed that the book had absolutely no relevance to the Jackson City neighborhood policing program. Officers should take the trouble to read it only if they were interested in looking good at promotion time. He also said the book teaches you how to do things you already do as a police officer. Then he went on to speculate at great length about how much money Goldstein makes, not just as a law professor, but from all the consulting work he does around the country. Curtis turned to the sheets that detail the expectations and roles of the NPO and pointed out that one guest speaker was a police chief from a small town in North Carolina; he speculated that the chief probably earned a lot of money doing consulting. Then Curtis went on, again at great length, about how he might retire in anywhere from six to eighteen months and have a very lucrative career on the consultant circuit, just talking about his experience with the Jackson City department. He suggested that anyone could do it; since departments all over were willing to pay, then why not? He feels ready to retire anyway.

Curtis stayed away from discussing his neighborhood duties, preferring to talk about his "other" jobs. These were private security tasks that he often did in the morning on his way into the neighborhood office. So, he tended to be in Fairview from noon to 8 P.M. or from 10 A.M. to 6 P.M. Today, he intended to work till 7:30 P.M., then go home and have catfish for dinner. Curtis speculated about how it helped to have an NPO in the neighborhood. He said people knew him; they called when they needed help. He remarked that he was not an aggressive person; he believes in talking first and issuing warnings, with aggressive action being the very last option. Curtis explained that he sees the same people every day, day in and day out, but that they are with different friends all the time. So, the advantage for NPOs who know their neighborhood is being able to spot who is out of place, who does not belong. He recognizes strangers and unfamiliar cars in the parking lot, and he keeps an eye on that. There are about 290 residential units in Fairview, although some are for senior citizens, who give him no trouble. Curtis thinks about 40 percent of the housing is occupied by Asians, but he says we will not see them around much because they keep to themselves.

Curtis believed that his neighborhood was stable for two unique reasons. First, the apartments have only one owner, the local Baptist church. All potential residents are screened (for a fee of five dollars), which involves credit and criminal history checks in cooperation with the police department downtown; this eliminates the need to hire private security guards. All kinds of subsidies for housing are plentiful; some persons are paid to live in the units, some are charged five dollars, and others are charged full rent. The main problem at other buildings is that landlords let people stay; here, they are evicted. Curtis pointed out a difficulty, though: residents let others stay with them. If an eighteen-year-old girl with a baby gets evicted, she just moves back in with her momma. Accordingly, the apartment owners expect him to enforce the trespassing ordinance vigorously, believing that arrests will send out a deterrent message. Curtis said he used to "paper" quite heavily, but now people have got the message and know that the police are serious. For instance, he has issued none of the trespassing citations this year, and he issued only about five last year. Each carries a hefty $270 fine. Curtis also indicated that because there is only one owner, the owner is on the ball, and got $300,000 or so from the government to build two different community centers. Local taxpayers complain that their money is being wasted, but none of this outlay came from city funds. The managers have offices in the community centers, along with the social coordinators and the nurse, so they work on site.

The second unique feature of the neighborhood is that it includes a shopping center. This is convenient for the residents, but it also means that Curtis answers a lot of calls for retail theft and shoplifting. He goes on to say that he avoids meetings, explaining that although NPOs are invited to a lot of them, they do not have to go.

> You could spend your whole day in meetings, and there's no point. I
> have it so that I only attend about one meeting a month, and never go to
> department briefings downtown. That's a plus. . . . About twice a year, I
> go to the mayor's meeting, and every other month there is a meeting
> with the elderly. But, I am not going to any old meeting. There is no
> tenant association, so no meetings with residents. The NPOs who go
> to meetings all the time just don't know how to say no; I know how to
> say no.

Curtis had a lot of time to chat. He said that he had no pressing business, although he did want to stop at home for lunch. Talking about programs in his neighborhood made him angry. He emphatically stated that he will *not* do youth programs; soccer and fishing are not part of his job. In fact, Curtis got into a fight once with a resident who called and said, "You don't spend any time with the kids. How are they supposed to grow up to trust you?" But playing with children is not his job, and he had to set the man straight so he would understand Curtis's position.

Curtis was gregarious, with a warm smile for all he met. He explained that he likes talking to folks, not aggressively going after them in a squad car. He does not even like to "go lights and sirens" anymore, because it creates too much potential risk of harm from traffic accidents. Drivers keep their windows rolled up and do not hear the sirens, and they ignore the lights. He does not want that kind of excitement anymore. It is too unhealthy and the adrenalin is bad for your heart; he'll stick to cigarettes.

Then Curtis switched subjects and said that Asians make up 40 percent of the minority population in Jackson City. At first, they had no trouble getting apartments because they were just off the boat, had no bad credit, and could waltz in anywhere with no problem. But now, many landlords are requiring years of good rental history. So, what happens is that a woman in her late teens with a baby gets her own apartment (required by law if her mother lives in the apartment complex, too), and then her boyfriend moves in the next day. If she is evicted, she and the baby go back to her mother, at least for a while.

At this point, a female dispatcher asked Curtis across the police radio if he was available for calls. "Only in my area," he said. She apologized. In fact, the call was from an adjoining complex; Curtis drove by there several times during the afternoon. He explained that he handled his area only, especially since he did not have a squad car. He said he was *not* a call-driven police officer anymore and he was not going to act like one. He also explained that he could get a squad car at the downtown police station, but he does not bother because he only lives two blocks away.

Curtis continued to relax in his chair as he offered more details about his routine. He tries to spot things from his window, and then pass the information on to a patrol officer so that he does not have to get involved. This prevents him from becoming a "bad guy" and allows him to maintain a rapport with the residents. If the arrested resident says "Did you know?" Curtis can say he knew, but the resident can also see that he was not the arresting officer. (This approach also meant he would not have to work as much.) Curtis also complained about how separated NPOs were from the rest of the force, causing feelings of isolation and problems with communication. He believed all officers, new and old, may now go through training to learn the expectations for NPOs. Curtis felt this was important because neighborhood officers do not receive "hot sheets" alerting them about what to keep an eye on. (The other officers get them during briefing. Curtis makes a deliberate choice not to attend briefing.) Curtis said that he could get E-mail through his computer; in fact, he has a computer specifically for hooking up and getting the information. He went through hours of computer training, but he cannot even get the thing to turn on. Curtis expects that he will figure it out at some point. He reiterated his view that training sessions involving all officers would be good because most patrol officers have no clue what NPOs are doing. In fact, some of his colleagues have not seen Curtis for over a year.

He mentioned that two social workers did get involved in community groups and organized activities, one at each center. Also, a probation-parole officer came in once a month. (The schedule used to be once a week; he has no idea why it changed.) He feels these professionals should handle the community activities.

Curtis remarked that the most important issues for him at Fairview were domestic violence and drugs. Then, he changed his mind and listed his priorities as making the parking areas safe, getting rid of drug markets so children can play, and keeping the district safe for those who come home late at night from work, especially women. He said that crime is way down in Fairview. As he sees it, this was only partially because of the NPO position; the truth is, he said, that the drop is due to the new property managers, who now screen potential residents. However, he also recalled what he said about crime rates to the last researcher who spent the day with him in Fairview: "It's like squeezing a balloon; it just pops out somewhere else."

Dispatch called again, asking for his help with answering a call. Curtis reminded her that the call was not in his beat and he did not have a car. She apologized once more.

Curtis next decided to go around the neighborhood and then downtown to photocopy some papers. But he did not go on foot. Although he had told the dispatcher twice that he did not have a car, and had also explained that was why he did not go to briefing, he climbed into an unmarked police car, complete with light and siren; he said it was the lieutenant's car, and he parked it there.

Curtis drove around Fairview and some contiguous areas, moving slowly through parking lots while he looked around (and keeping his windows up although it was nearly a hundred degrees). No one was about. He then moved on to the adjoining housing complex, Northglen, which he considered the worst; there was no screening of tenants. It seemed fairly well kept and middle class, but Curtis said that was because "you don't know the people living inside." He recognized a white man, around fifty years old, and joked around with him, asking why he still lived here. The man said this was where he would retire. Curtis told me later that the man was a sheriff, had an extensive gun collection, probably felt pretty safe, and had always lived there. He also told the man that his son was moving into Northglen and asked him which was the best building.

Curtis showed his house to the researcher, then drove to his old house, about ten blocks away. He pointed out the aluminum siding he had put on and the garage he had built. He went by the grade school that most of his children had attended. Curtis also kept up a running monologue about growing up in North Carolina under segregation, how difficult it was for him when his family moved here (he could not find the colored toilets or water fountains) and how strange it was to be the only black child in his class. His white schoolmates were used to black girls and boys in their classes, but he had never gone to school with white children before.

Next, Curtis crossed the street and drove around the perimeter of the parking lot of the shopping center; he cruised one of the parking areas of the other complex in his district on that side of the road. Then on to Greenwood, an adjoining neighborhood with another NPO. On the way, while still in his own neighborhood, Curtis stopped the car to talk and joke with a black woman in her early twenties. He had grown up with her parents. Once in Greenwood, Curtis stopped and leaned out the window to ask a black man in his early twenties what he was doing in this neighborhood, since he lived in Fairlawn. The young man explained that he had heard there was a block party going on today (there was) and he was taking his daughter to it (she was not in sight). They exchanged a few more words and we moved on. Curtis said he was a minor dealer, a nice guy, had shot a woman with a BB gun several times, and was on probation. The woman was not a girlfriend or former girlfriend; the assault probably involved drugs. Curtis never got out of the car during this drive. At the corner, he stopped again and yelled out the window at a black man in his twenties walking with a white woman and a baby. Curtis said, "I thought you were dead!" The young man explained that he had been down in Myrtle Beach, visiting family, but he was on probation and had to move back here. They talked a bit more, and Curtis moved on. He explained that the man had sickle-cell anemia and that he was serious when he mentioned death because he had not seen him in a year or two.

This day, only African American residents seemed to be around, which opened up the opportunity for Curtis to reflect on how citizens perceived him. He said they saw a uniform, not a race. He recalled that when he was working as a patrol officer on the city's south side, three black policemen were trying to restrain and handcuff a black male suspect. He was yelling, "Get your fucking white hands off me, you fucking cops!" But there was no white officer around. Curtis said that young men who are unemployed and often in legal trouble, usually for drugs, frequently see him as selling out to the white man, earning a huge salary, and being disloyal to the race. So, he asks them why they are in trouble; they reply, " 'Cuz of the white man." He responds, "There's no white man here; what did he do?" They say, " 'Cuz I didn't get no education." Whose fault is that? Curtis asks. I got some college, I did not choose a drug lifestyle. They say, "I ain't gonna flip burgers for four bucks an hour." To which Curtis replies, "Well, with you sitting under a tree, do you really think some business-man is gonna come by and offer you a twenty-dollar-an-hour job?"

Curtis loved to talk about how he dealt with conflict among citizens. He went on at great length about how the first thing to do in talking to African American residents is to get on their level, but in a way that does not demean them. For instance, Curtis knows speaking to black people is different from speaking to whites or more educated folks. He has to mumble because "black people mumble at each other," so he "aims to speak their language or dialect." Curtis believes that mumbling diffuses his image of power and authority and breaks down the barriers between him and the people. He tells them to forget he wears a badge; he is a person, too, with blood and guts and everything.

Curtis arrived at the station around four-thirty to do some photocopying. There were big hellos for the secretaries and chitchat with others, but no one seemed to know him really well. He drove the scenic (long) way back to Fairview to show that Jackson City is situated between two lakes. He also drove by the airport, pointing out where the future police district station for that side of town might be built, which was very close to his neighborhood. Curtis said if it were built it would probably mean the end of the neighborhood policing office in the complex. He then began driving back to his office.

Curtis circled the shopping center parking lot again and spotted a woman, Shirley, who was on the cleaning staff for the property. He chatted briefly with her, and asked her to open the community center, which was locked. Meanwhile, he never stopped saying hi and waving to people. Their faces lit up when they saw him and they teased him about "working." It appeared that many of the residents he encountered today were somewhat surprised to see him around and about. They seemed genuinely happy to see him and they clearly liked him, but the encounter looked like a rare occasion.

No one was in the community center, but the tour was impressive. There were a number of creative things for girls and boys to do, original children's artwork on the walls, computers downstairs, offices, and places where Head Start met, with everything new and shiny. It was apparent that Shirley was proud of it. Curtis said he likes this center the best; he does not ever go over to the other one, even though it is closer to his office.

He then went for another spin around the parking lot and spotted two women and a bunch of children. One of the women was his cousin-in-law, and Curtis pulled over for some banter and chat. They were off to a picnic, and he teased them about food and drinking too much. Curtis said later that his in-law had a drug problem, so he liked to encourage her to do some entertaining things with her children.

Then, even though they were out of his neighborhood, Curtis drove up to a new development of condominiums. He wanted to visit one of his sons. At this point, he received a message that a patrol officer would be coming to get the researcher. The female officer pulled up just as one of her colleagues nearby was requesting backup. Since she was in the middle of clearing off the front seat, Curtis (with much hesitation) said he would go. Quickly, the patrol officer said she would take the call. She told the researcher to hop in, now, and they sped off.

Davis Street—Maintenance Neighborhood

Just blocks from the Jackson City Police Department building is another designated residential district with a foot patrol officer. The NPO's office is in a corner of the general office at the Davis Street fire department station. It is not personalized at all, there are no bulletin boards, and it is clear this is not a meeting place. Frank, fifty-one years old and white, has twenty-nine years of experience on the force. He is friendly and laid-back, a little reserved in his communication style. He waited until the Davis Street NPO position opened, then put in for it. He was interested in Davis Street because it is *not* a disorganized, poor neighborhood. He said he did not want to have that much work. Also, he knows the area quite well. He lived there until moving in with his girlfriend recently, owns several rental properties in the district, grew up in the neighborhood (as did his mother), and went to the schools there. His biggest frustrations with Davis Street and being an NPO are, as he puts it, the "politically correct institutions" and how to negotiate through all the "politically correct crap." He believes Davis Street could easily give up its NPO and rely on regular patrolling, but the local community activists would never allow it.

Frank spent some time on the phone, returning a couple of calls that had come in on his voice mail. He also tried to get a computer program to work, with no success. He next decided to walk around the neighborhood. Frank pointed out different houses with problems, among them drug dealing, loud music, bad landlords, and bad tenants. It was very clear who owned their houses and who rented, which landlords kept up their properties and which did not. On Davis Street, there were a number of "yuppie" alternative establishments, such as some healthy lifestyle businesses, a pet store, and restaurants, as well as rental properties. Frank's first stop was at a small new Jamaican restaurant where the car of an employee (the chef) had been damaged and he had forgotten to take down the license plate number. She was white, young, and not Jamaican; they had an easygoing, almost flirtatious rapport. The next destination was the neighborhood middle school, with an enrollment of 550 students between the ages of eleven and fourteen. Frank had received a report about graffiti while he was away on vacation, so he wanted to follow up. There was some graffiti on the walls, but it had already been covered with a coat of paint. Frank talked and joked around with the secretary while waiting for the principal. They spoke of how bad youngsters were nowadays, how their parents established no rules, and how even the parents themselves got into fights. The two agreed that the girls were the worst, it was all about saving face and being tough in front of peers, and there were no rules at home. They complained that nowadays juveniles would report their parents as child abusers for spanking them.

The principal (also white) came out and talked with Frank briefly, and he and the secretary complained about the lack of security guards or police assigned to the school for the hallways. Frank said that he had tried to apply for some of the America Corps young people, particularly for "rumor control" since things were so out of hand, but had not heard anything yet. They all talked about the "good ol' days" when children respected their elders and were more easily managed. Again, the three used a very familiar conversational style.

Frank confided that the former NPO, Tina, had spent 95 percent of her time in the schools, being a friend to the teenagers, particularly the younger black girls. Frank thought they had the hardest time, because the black boys wanted fat white girls, not them. He said Tina had received a lot of complaints for neglecting the rest of the neighborhood, so Frank was trying to balance the various and competing needs in the community.

In the middle of the neighborhood was a park, which was the next stop. Frank told a rambling story about his actions and frustrations related to neighbors' complaints about juveniles playing basketball at night in the park. The court faced expensive residential homes. The complaining residents were all white, and the teens playing ball were black. The matter became a huge question of political correctness, with any rules about when to play, who could play, or how to play (full- or half-court) being seen as discriminatory. The alderwoman for the area could not control a meeting on the issue. Everybody seemed unhappy with whatever compromises were suggested. Frank talked about his big role, but it was not clear exactly what he did, especially since this story was recounted with much sarcasm. The city did end up installing wooden backboards and nylon nets in place of the louder metal ones. Frank immediately went to the new police chief (an African American) to tell him what was going on and to report that he *knew* the residents would "play the race card." The chief came down and sat in the bleachers during one of the games and heard the bad language and observed the bad behavior. He told Frank he would back him if the "race card" were played. Frank went to check on whether the new sign with the new rules had been posted. It had not.

Meanwhile, Frank continued to indicate homes that were owned by slumlords or good landlords, or that had bad tenants. He also pointed out where he grew up, and where his mother was raised. He did say hello to all the children and adults we passed, but there were not a lot of conversations.

Next on his rounds was a visit to the community center to catch up with the director, a young white woman. On the way we passed Spring Street, which borders the lake. There is a nice public beach there; two men (one black, one white) knew Frank and came up to chat a bit. He kept introducing the researcher as a professor who was with him to watch what he did on the job. Everybody seemed to get a kick out of that, almost as though he did not do much worth observing. At the same time, Frank did tell stories about drug busts and other arrests he had made.

At the community center, the director came out to talk to Frank and to ask if a little white girl had come by to see him the day before. She had lost the key to her bike lock and was afraid to go home without the bike because she thought she would get in trouble. The director had urged her to get Frank, since his tools could cut the bike wire. He had not seen her. The girl then came out and showed him the bike; it was attached to the bicycle stand and another bike. The director and Frank wondered whose bike it was (a black girl said it was hers, but they did not quite believe her). He promised that he could cut the wire after he got his tools at the station. (His shift ended at three o'clock. Frank never did anything about the bike, nor did he mention it again.)

The community center had just received a lot of money for remodeling, and everyone was waiting impatiently for air conditioners to be installed. It is a big, nice center, in an old church. It has space for food pantries, youth camps, tutoring when school is in session, and many activities for senior citizens. There was a room full of elderly persons, all white, playing cards or bingo, as well as a racially mixed group of young people. Frank told the director that he was taking part in a research project on community policing, and she said they loved having a neighborhood officer. The director felt comfortable knowing he was there for them, even though, she said confidentially, they probably did not need one anymore. Frank agreed that Davis Street was one of the best neighborhoods, and probably did not need its own NPO. The director said she would never make her real feelings public because the residents did not want Frank to be taken away. Plus, she believed that neighborhoods could change quickly.

This comment sparked a lengthy conversation justifying the need for an NPO. The director of the community center contends that some families kicked out of other areas may be moving to Davis Street. For his part, Frank believes there are some drug dealers in the neighborhood who should be evicted. But the director kept insisting that when one person is evicted the whole family usually moves as well. The concern is that many of the bad landlords in the Davis Street neighborhood do not screen their tenants. They both concluded that the presence of an NPO is justified.

Frank contends that the problem with the landlords is that they do not screen. It is politically incorrect, and people might think they are racist. Or else they have never screened before, so they think themselves (falsely, he adds) to be very good judges of people. Meanwhile, in his view, the potential tenants lie easily to the landlords. Frank laughed about their ignorance and unwillingness to ask the right questions for fear of being politically incorrect.

When asked if he did any follow-ups, or was able to provide more information or referrals to victims, Frank said that he did not. He expressed some disdain for "social work" activities or interventions. Then, Frank flagged down a young white man on a motorcycle. They had a long chat about spark plugs and various cycles they owned or had sold. The man left, with the promise to bring some motorcycle parts to Frank soon.

The next stop was a neighborhood biker bar owned by Tiny, a huge man with a huge beard. Everybody was white. The patrons and staff clearly knew Frank very well; he owns at least one motorcycle, and he hangs out there a lot. We sat at the bar and got sodas. Frank was very familiar with other patrons, the female bartender, and even the two workmen who came in to fix a broken window. He also knew where the napkins were kept behind the bar and helped to get them.

Frank left and walked slowly toward the station. Right outside the bar, one of the workmen asked him about a ticket (for sixty-seven dollars) his son had received for parking his car on school property while he and some friends played catch. Frank told the man he could not remember the actual citation by number or what it was about, but he could look it up. He thought it concerned trespassing on school property, a citation usually directed at suspended young people hanging out on the grounds or at suspected dealers. Frank was very sympathetic with the workman. He told him he probably should have fought the ticket because school was not in session.

As he walked, a young black boy followed Frank for a little while, imitating animals. Frank joked with him and tried to guess the kind of animal he was acting out. When Frank was ready to move along, the boy left quickly. Frank next stopped to say hello to several black men sitting on their front porches. After an exchange of pleasantries, he would ask them about noise, activity, or the house next door or across the street. The residents seemed comfortable telling him anything they saw or did not see; there was some familiarity and rapport between them.

Back at the station, Frank put some of his stuff together and a patrol officer in a squad car picked him up. His shift was over for the day.

I now turn to an examination of theoretical, historical, and empirical issues, followed by several chapters of data analysis.

Intersecting Gender with Community Policing

A Review of the History, Existing Theories, and Research

> The policeman's culture is that of the masculine working man. It is of the docks, the barracks, the battlefields.
> —Jerome H. Skolnick

> Street cops see community relations as "Mickey Mouse bullshit."
> —Elizabeth Reuss-Ianni

This chapter differs from the others in that it does not directly address research data. Rather, it provides a theoretical and historical framework with which to anchor my analysis of community policing in Jackson City. Thus, it may speak more to academics than to practitioners. The chapter documents several things. I begin by examining the gendered culture of policing and the ways in which this masculinist culture manifests itself in the everyday reality of policework. In so doing, I explore how stereotypically "feminine" traits once used to exclude women from participating on patrol, or to separate the "real" crimefighters from the "office cops," have now been resurrected and elevated to the pinnacle of community policing agendas and practice. The success of this resurrection, however, depends on reshaping unacceptable traits, associated with femininity, into acceptable ones associated with masculinity, or "real" policework. Next, I describe the historical background of policing and women's entrance into this occupation. The historical framework is important in understanding the development of "male" and "female" police roles. Past writings reveal that women followed patterns of work distinctly different from those of men, reflecting ideological assumptions that law enforcement was a masculine endeavor. This initial division was reinforced by gender socialization that prepared women to accept prevailing cultural standards of femininity and dictated appropriate roles for them. In this section, I also examine how the institution of policing experienced several major transformations of both ideology and practice during a century of existence. Finally, I illustrate the similarities between "women's work" accomplished by early policewomen and contemporary community policing ideology and context. It remains a struggle for the masculinist police institution to re-shape the "feminine" foundations of women's policework into a more modern and attractive ideology of community policing. One way to accomplish this is for the "new" ideology to emphasize the law enforcement duties that are part of community policing, thus attracting "masculine" men. Accordingly, I begin by looking at how gender has shaped the assumptions made about policework.

Policing as a "Male" Institution and Site of Gendered Action

Feminist researchers, among them Martin and Jurik (1996), Messerschmidt (1993), Connell (1987), Acker (1990), and West and Zimmerman (1987), frequently write about the gendered nature of organizations and how these structures shape the behavior of men and women so that their responses and the responses to them by others are also conditioned by gender role expectations.[1] The sociological term "doing gender" describes the activity of practicing such behavior. It characterizes an interactive social process through which assumptions about power, sexuality, and role expectations shape reactions to men and women (see Martin and Jurik 1996). "Doing gender" goes far beyond the social identity of being a man or a woman; it involves "the activity of managing situated conduct in light of normative conceptions, attitudes, and activities appropriate to one's sex category" (West and Zimmerman 1987, 127). "Doing gender" reflects differences in how persons are treated and overseen within organizations, such that "advantage and disadvantage, exploitation and control, action and emotion, meaning and identity, are patterned through and in terms of a distinction between male and female, masculine and feminine" (Acker 1990, 146). Policing, as a masculine organization, assumes that there are "socially gendered perceptual, interactional, and micro-political activities that cast particular pursuits as expressions of masculine and feminine 'natures' " (West and Zimmerman 1987, 126). The issue is not one of *not* all women possessing these traits (or of all men *not* having at least some of them), but that these entrenched gender-role stereotypes and assumptions have been used to exclude women from becoming fully participating, vested police officers with job roles and responsibilities similar to those of their male counterparts.

In his theoretical treatment of structured action and the construction of masculinity, James Messerschmidt uses the police to illustrate "how gender, specifically masculinity, is socially constructed and resultingly institutionalized" (Messerschmidt 1993, 174). He discusses the male-dominated nature of the police work force: despite inroads made since the 1970s in assigning women police officers to routine patrol activities, the division of labor within the force remains segregated. For instance, in 1989 only 10 percent of police officers in this country were women (Martin 1989). More recent statistics reveal that although women made up only 8.8 percent of sworn police officers in departments of all sizes, they made up 14.6 percent of the force in departments serving populations of 1 million or more, 12.4 percent in departments serving populations of 500,000 to 999,999, and 11.9 percent in departments serving populations of 250,000 to 499,999 (Maquire and Pastore 1997). Despite their significant numbers, female police officers remain "virtually excluded from upper-level management . . . just as they are in corporate boardrooms and law partnerships" (Martin 1989, 6), thus reproducing the gendered power relations that exist in society at large. Messerschmidt (1993, 175) contends that

> [w]ithin police agencies, men's power is deemed an authentic and acceptable part of social relations. This legitimacy of the power by men in police work adorns them with greater authority. Indeed, gender relations of power promote and constrain the social action of men and women police officers. . . . Police work is defined culturally as an activity only "masculine men" can accomplish. As Allison Morris [1987, 111–44] shows, police work is viewed by the police and public as a masculine pursuit: the imagery is "of the armed man of action fighting crime and criminals," the Clint Eastwood model.

Accepting women as police officers who are equal to men challenges the "masculine association with police work—if women can do it, the value of the practice as a means for exhibiting masculinity is cast into question" (Messerschmidt 1993, 175). Messerschmidt also suggests that even when male and female officers work together their actions remain gendered: with team policing, the male partner will drive the squad car, decide the activities, and conduct interviews, whereas female officers tend to play supportive roles, such as recording responses and doing paperwork (Messerschmidt 1993, 175). Research by P. W. Remmington (1981, 117) indicated that "women officers not partnered with men were frequently backed up on calls by males. The latter often usurped the female officer's role and dominated the encounter." Susan Martin's (1994) work on women in policing suggests that not only sexism but also racism further divides police officers, with men of color and white men ending up more closely aligned because of shared masculinist assumptions of male power. Women of color, however, remain separated from both white men and women as well as from men of color. Sexuality is another arena in which dynamics may be altered and masculine-feminine polarities may be realigned.

Community policing, thus, challenges the traditional policing paradigm. These new approaches reject the "aloof, authoritarian, detached" model of the police officer, and they also reject the traditional policing style "structured around random patrols and response to service calls . . . respond[ing] 'by the book,' [and] carrying out policies as directed in a mechanical fashion" (Metchick and Winton 1995, 115). Community policing has instead implicitly embraced "feminine" qualities as ideal or superior traits for neighborhood officers to possess. The words that were used in the past to characterize these unwelcome, feminine qualities have faded from the present-day dialogue. But they have not completely disappeared. Once the previously disdained "feminine" qualities are elevated to a desirable status, disenchantment with the new community policing model merely becomes more muted and insidious. In fact, the negative connotations associated with femininity remain present in the references to NPOs made by other officers who oppose or misunderstand the ideological premise of the policy change.

A discussion of the shift in police practice and ideology wrought by community policing models raises some important questions: How can policing, with its paramilitary and masculinist structure, be transformed to honor the values of care, connection, empathy, and informality? What changes must occur to reconcile the contradictions between "masculine" and "feminine" police activities? What matters more, the gender of the officers, or that officers of *either* gender actively integrate "feminine traits" into their social control and policing ideology? Will male and female officers be evaluated differently because of gender-based assumptions? For example, if women are involved with children's programs, will perceptions of the success of those programs be diminished because of assumptions held about women's "natural" nurturing abilities? Whereas, if men develop great rapport with children and spend time with them, will they be praised as atypical and terrific officers because they are seen as having gone above and beyond the traditional parameters of male policing? Can these questions be empirically explored?

Such issues fit into the larger literature on the gendering of skill. Joan Acker (1992) argues that the restructuring of the global capitalist economy necessitates changes in skill demands. New technologies may upgrade skilled work, but firms or institutions may not recognize or reward increases in skill, particularly for women workers. In fact, according to job evaluations women's positions are typically viewed as requiring less skill than comparable men's jobs (Acker 1989, 1992). Similarly, Cynthia Cockburn, in her studies of gender and technology, found that "skill" is gendered, with boundaries redrawn and maintained "between male and female, skilled and unskilled" (Acker 1992, 61; Cockburn 1991; Cockburn and Ormrod 1993).[2] In community policing, a similar "adjustment" may take place in which the "feminine" traits that characterize the objectives of the new approach will be masculinized in order to fit into traditional policing frameworks (in other words, a readjustment of the rules to fit men only).

A parallel construction can be drawn from research exploring the occupational cultures of "street cops" and "office cops" (see Reuss-Ianni and Ianni 1983). For example, in her work with New York street cops, Jennifer Hunt (1984) found that their assessments of office cops were not flattering, and that these assessments were based on gender-related factors. The street cops saw the office cops as

> engaged in "feminine labor" such as public relations and secretarial work. These "pencil-pushing bureaucrats" were not involved in the "masculine" physical labor which characterized "real police work" on the street. High-ranking administrators were also viewed as "inside tit men," "ass kissers" and "whores" who gained their positions through political patronage rather than through superior performance in the rescue and crime-fighting activities associated with "real police work." (Hunt 1984, 287)

What is the relevance of these "renamed" traits to the tenets of community policing? The new approach stresses communication, familiarity, building better rapport and trust between police and residents, informal problem solving, and fostering citizen-police cooperation. Community police officers are taught to use conflict resolution and mediation skills and to go beyond immediate crisis responses to focus instead on longer-term solutions to problems that will facilitate greater connections between police and citizens. Informal styles of policing are perceived as more effective tools for enhancing the recognition, trust, and support that citizens develop for their "neighborhood cop." These are the same skills that have been associated with women's roles, not traits typical of the crimefighter image of police (men).

Contemporary research has also examined the conditions under which men have embraced, and often sought out, jobs that were once seen as "women's work." Whereas there is ample historical evidence that women "flock to male-identified occupations once opportunities are available" (Epstein 1988; Cohn

1985), this "flocking" is not true of the few men who enter female-identified occupations. "The stereotypes that differentiate masculinity and femininity, and degrade that which is defined as feminine, are deeply entrenched in culture, social structure, and personality" (Williams 1992, 264). Such a difference suggests that a "redefinition of the occupations as appropriately 'masculine' is necessary before men will consider joining them" (Ehrenreich and English 1978). This has implications for the role that supervisors play in minimizing stigma. In particular, research has revealed that if male applicants were recruited, and later supervised, by other men, stigma attached to doing traditionally female jobs significantly diminishes. For instance, in her investigation of men's entrance into the female-dominated profession of secondary-school teaching, Christine Williams found that these men did not experience a need to manage their stigmatized identity. They did not perceive their jobs as inconsistent with the male gender role because of how they were recruited and mentored by men and because of their opportunities for promotion (Williams 1992, 262). Promotion, in fact, gave men *more* authority, status, and pay. She concludes that "the social status of the token's group, not their numerical rarity" is the determining factor, and men benefit from having a higher social status simply because of their gender.

Achieving this "redefinition" of what constitutes a "man's job" may be necessary for male police officers to successfully manage the previously stigmatized identity of doing "women's work" as a neighborhood police officer. Redefining their jobs is especially crucial so that men who are NPOs will still be viewed as masculine by their (mostly male) peers on patrol and by their (mostly male) supervisors. However, Elaine Hall (1993, 463) argues that any status conflict for men is often mitigated by their gender privilege: "men's higher gender status mediates the effect of their lower occupational status." In order for men to seek what could be considered a more feminine police assignment, such as foot patrol, it is likely that they will deliberately select neighborhood police officer positions in communities where aggressive law enforcement is needed and, perhaps more important, where other officers know that aggressive police action is needed.

Another way to reestablish one's masculinity is to recast "feminine" virtues associated with "women's work" and imbue them with honor. This is a difficult task, as these denigrated traits are virtually antithetical to the masculinized construction and organization of policework.[3] Without such a recasting of the definition and the value attached to the feminized positions, however, neighborhood officers will continue to be seen by others as "pansy police." The word "pansy" is a typical slur that has been used by traditional patrol officers to demean NPOs (Miller 1996a). Intertwining the concepts of gender and sexuality, "pansy" has a dual meaning: it suggests that, for men, their heterosexuality is as much on the line as their masculinity.

Thus, some police researchers have exposed the images and realities associated with stigmatized positions within a hypermasculine profession. In the analysis of community policing presented in this book, the two police cultures of neighborhood patrol officers on foot and rapid response patrol officers in squad cars also have different goals, exercise different systems that structure, control, and guide decision making, and are afforded different opportunities for "doing gender." My research thus extends the police literature by examining the development and interactive process of gender dynamics within the community policing context. In addition, there is a need to examine the relevance of gender-based differences within policing. Both women and men can apply different skills to solving community crime problems, and in fact many already do so. Women alone cannot do the job of emotional labor, despite the numerous "feminine" traits that have been associated with them as women and reintroduced as ideal qualities for today's NPOs. In fact, skills that are most compatible with a neighborhood policing model may ideally be gender neutral. Community policing may be best practiced when it blends both masculine and feminine traits, traits that can be utilized by all men and women on the force. The "feminine" attribute of caring may need to be "de-skilled" and "neutered," however, before it can be embraced by a male-dominated police force. This "de-skilling" could move us toward a more androgynous police model. Thus, it may be that the feminine attribute of caring associated with community policing will be redefined in order to be accepted into the existing masculinist "skill" framework (see, in general, Martin and Jurik 1996).

In sum, as an institution the police combine social control and social service functions. Yet these are provided against the backdrop of a hegemonic masculinity, one that elevates "manly" pursuits and the role of the tough, aloof, detached professional while rejecting qualities or behaviors that are reminiscent of femininity or femaleness (Messerschmidt 1993). As an emerging paradigm, today's neighborhood policing policies stress a more community-oriented role, emphasizing increased interaction between police and citizens as well as greater accountability to the locale in which officers serve. Its success seems to rest upon favorable citizen evaluations of how police deliver services, as well as upon the community's acceptance, and the support from individual officers, of this new police role (Wasserman and Moore 1988). By definition, this necessitates greater accountability to community members for police behavior; in fact, citizen satisfaction is tied to establishing or reinforcing police legitimacy. But, the "hearts and minds" of police officers are not yet won (Lurigio and Skogan 1994). Successful community policing programs also require a shift in how the activities of NPOs are viewed by their entire departments—that they be seen as "serious work." Community policing's connection to the fundamental goals of crimefighting, and the role it plays in achieving them, must be understood and accepted by the rank and file and the administration alike. This requires that officers reconcile the contradictions that arise when feminine traits are appropriated by masculine experts, when women officers' behavior is dismissed as passive or natural while the same behavior is commended in men. With these questions and issues in mind, I now turn to the historical underpinnings of contemporary community policing.

The History of Policework

Work is far more than a means to get a paycheck. We are defined by the work we do, and this definition influences our own thoughts about who we are, how others see us, and how much we value ourselves (Dunn 1995; Pavalko 1988). Work "provides social and emotional rewards and affects many aspects of life and identity. . . . It defines social status and shapes income, lifestyle, and children's life chances" (Martin and Jurik 1996, 3). The workplace, however, becomes contested terrain if "outsiders," such as women, dare to cross traditional gendered boundaries of male occupations.

Women have played peripheral roles within the male-dominated criminal justice system; even today, they remain relative newcomers to the upper levels of power within administration. In the nineteenth century, women's entrance into the male world of policing was only halfheartedly embraced, even though the scope of their authority was limited to other women and to children. (For women to exercise power over men was simply not acceptable.) Historical archival writings demonstrate that feminine talents were only accepted when they did not threaten men's spheres or challenge perceived masculine talents. It was only when women demanded more job equality in the latter half of the twentieth century, when they claimed the freedom to do work outside their assumed natural female "specialties," however, that men began to fiercely oppose policewomen's inclusion in departments.

Before looking in more detail at the relevant connections between early policework and today's community policing models, though, I must explore the path that women followed to "break into" the gendered culture of the police organization.

Women in Policing

[P]olicewomen do not wish to be policemen nor do policemen's work, but . . . work which women are better fitted for, . . . with and for women and children, thus releasing men to meet the increasing demand for traffic regulation and other types of police work that are peculiarly men's work.—*IAP Bulletin*, May 1925

[P]olice work is, in a certain measure, social work, and that in it there exist problems which can be handled better by women than by men, has led to the employment of women in many police departments throughout the country. —Eleanor Hutzel, 1933

Policing as an institution was introduced into municipalities in the 1840s, with departments drawing their power, resources, and mandate from the local political machinery (see Fogelson 1977; Walker 1977; Haller 1976). In essence, the police were a political arm of local leaders. Their relationship was reciprocal: politicians recruited and employed police officers, whereas police assisted politicians in maintaining their hold on power by bringing out the vote for favored candidates and sometimes even rigging elections (Kelling and Moore 1991, 7). Police were given a range of duties beyond crime control, such as directing traffic,[4] fighting fires, assisting in health services, inspecting buildings, maintaining animal shelters, licensing pets and livestock, returning runaway animals to their owners, cleaning streets, and standing by until dead persons were removed to hospitals or morgues (Schulz 1995, 3). Despite the formally hierarchical structure of the early departments, actual police command was decentralized. Smaller precincts ran their own territories, and poor communications and limited mobility resulted in tremendous discretion for individual officers. In fact, the call box (which could connect officers with the central command station) was instituted only during the later years of this era; officers resented its intrusiveness into their previously unsupervised daily routine.

Policemen of the day were recruited from the neighborhoods in which they lived. Thus, they were intimately connected to many of the residents, and at the very least were members of their neighborhood's dominant political and ethnic group (Kelling and Moore 1991, 7). Police responded both to the calls for service from the neighborhood and to the calls of the political leadership. By default, foot patrol was the norm; even when automobiles appeared, they were at first used simply to transport officers to their beats. Although ostensibly there was some focus on fighting crime, police duties were expansive, covering riot control, maintaining order, social services, and activities that emerged from industrialization (such as running soup kitchens and providing limited shelter for the homeless, finding work for immigrants, managing elections, and returning lost children; see Haller 1976). Also, police regularly stopped by local saloons for a drink with the customers, who were their friends and neighbors. The police scholars G. L. Kelling and M. H. Moore (1991, 8–9) contend that the strengths of this initial period were the deep integration of police into neighborhoods and their acceptance there and the force's provision of helpful services. There is some evidence that parents appreciated police help in disciplining their recalcitrant or mischievous children (Haller 1976).

Women's entrance into policing was initiated by early social reformers who focused on the conditions of care provided for women and girls in jails and prisons in the 1820s.[5] Upper-middle-class Quaker and other female volunteers sought to reform inmates and train them to be domestics in their Christian homes upon release. During their visits to the jails and prisons, the volunteers became cognizant of the sexual abuse perpetrated by male guards and of the general neglect of women. This situation influenced the introduction of the prison matron position. Female matrons were viewed as better suited than men to care for and protect other women. Female social reformers, such as these new prison matrons, were tremendously concerned with issues related to sexual purity (Schulz 1995). They viewed prostitutes as evil and beyond redemption, yet these very women constituted the largest percentage of female inmates. This forced the reformers to rethink their condemnation and begin to fight for sex-segregated prisons and for women inmates to be cared for by an all-female staff (Schulz 1995). The writings of the time reflected this message of women's superior morality and their uniqueness, and hence their intrinsic ability to provide the best care for other women. Female prison historians, such as Nicole Hahn Rafter (1990) and Estelle Freedman (1981), also have noted women's belief in their ability to care for others of their sex: "women had unique, feminine virtues that should be embodied in social policy" (Freedman 1981, 39).[6]

By the end of the Civil War, women were seeking entrance into all aspects of city life, with their particular efforts revolving almost exclusively around issues concerning women and children. The reformers believed in municipal housekeeping, which "encompassed virtually all activity that placed government agencies into contact with women and children" (Schulz 1995, 2). Despite women's interest in cleaning up government and addressing social problems, most of them "were not interested in rejecting their female roles and identities . . . [;] men and women feared the demise of the female sphere and the valuable functions it performs," thus necessitating a connection to "concepts of female moral superiority and sisterhood" (Freedman 1979, 515–516). This opened opportunities for women who wished to move into the public realm while retaining women's uniqueness and roles. Prevailing ideas of womanhood included maternal activities and emotional sensitivities, so these traits could easily be brought to bear in social housekeeping ventures without compromising femaleness. Thus, the belief in a unique female ability to care for other women was used to bring women into all public arenas: "the nation had become a macro-cosm of the home, where the women cared for other women, children, and those unable to care for themselves" (Schulz 1995, 13).

Reformers after the Civil War resembled those of earlier days: upper-middle-class daughters of native-born families, well connected, and worried about exploitation of women and children by any government agency, particularly the police, since homeless women (often intoxicated) and children were given overnight shelter in stations and were vulnerable to and preyed upon by men (Schulz 1995, 2).[7] Many of the reformers had been abolitionists, and they had shifted their focus to carving a role for women in the rapidly developing cities and their governments. The women's "social crusade" reflected their zeal and their "struggle to 'save' wayward youth and helpless children from the evils of industrialism, alcohol, and other abuses" (Martin 1980, 22).

As the policewomen's movement took hold and women established distinct roles for themselves, female officers began to move beyond providing custodial care in jails toward preventing crime through an expansion of social service roles. They particularly focused on conditions that facilitated moral degeneration and posed dangers for girls and women. For example, at the world's fair in 1893, the city of Chicago hired a woman to "enforce morals regulations and protect the virtue of local women when groups of men were drawn to the area by economic conditions, large-scale events such as expositions, or the establishment of military bases" (Schulz 1995, 21–22).[8]

But policewomen's presence was still not wholly welcome; they were there because chiefs succumbed to pressure from outside reform groups, not because male administrators or officers saw any need for them. Policewomen's allies remained other male and female social workers, Progressives, clubwomen, and other reformers (Schulz 1995). This sponsorship differed by geographic region; the South, for example, was less likely to hire policewomen (Schulz 1995). Regardless, male officers and police departments hotly debated women's physical abilities, emotional stability, and capacity for functioning in a paramilitary structure (Martin 1980, 22).

Thus, policewomen's dedication to service and nurturing followed traditional gender roles, thereby not threatening male police officers or their scope of control. Early policewomen typically were paid from different sources (often by volunteer groups or women's associations), were selected differently from men and by different criteria, and were confined to performing social-work roles: guarding female prisoners in jail, searching female suspects, and dealing with female victims and children. The male policing world was primarily composed of working-class immigrant men who had met the standard requirement of being able to read and write English; until as recently as the 1950s, not even a high school diploma was required in some departments (Schulz 1995, 3). Policewomen, on the other hand, were typically required to have an undergraduate degree, plus a master's in social work or several years of social-work experience. It did not help warm their reception by male officers and administrators that the women (whether black or white) also saw themselves as superior in social class and education to their counterparts.

By the early 1900s, the police matrons' movement was seeking to expand and further professionalize women's roles (Schulz 1995, 3). In the larger arena, policing was struggling to become a legitimate occupation for men, with stable employment no longer based on political patronage and with full-time salaries, benefits, sick time, and pensions; this was a far cry from the corruption and political patronage of early departments. Policewomen of the era continued to embrace the social worker role and its emphasis on social service. They were

> eager to act as municipal mothers to those less fortunate or those whose lifestyles they believed needed correction and discipline. . . . They agreed with their supporters that many elements of the [male] police world were contrary to their mission of servicing women and juveniles in a professional, non-threatening way. They did not view themselves as female versions of policemen, a concept they derogatorily termed "little men," and they refused to wear the distinctive uniforms men wore, or carry firearms, even when permitted. (Schulz 1995, 4)

Policewomen defined and sought these roles themselves; they were not segregated into such positions by male administrators (Schulz 1995).

In 1910, Alice Stebbins Wells became the first woman appointed to a police department (Los Angeles), although both she and her new employers called the early policewomen "operators" or "workers" (Schulz 1995) so as not to draw attention to them or to imply any parallels to "real" (male) policework. The newcomers were viewed as oddities. Journalists often characterized a policewoman as "a bony, muscular, masculine person, grasping a revolver, dressed in anything but feminine apparel, hair drawn tightly into a hard little knot at the back of the head, huge unbecoming spectacles, small round disfiguring hat, the whole presenting the idea in a most repellant and unlovely guise" (Owings 1925, 103). Many groups, however, welcomed the idea of women officers as a way to solve social problems. Alice Stebbins Wells gave speeches around the country about women in policing, arguing that they could help men by taking care of women in custody (so that male officers did not open themselves to false accusations by prostitutes), thus reassuring audiences that women would not replace men (Owings 1925; Schulz 1995, 25). To further bolster public support, a typical policewoman was described by journalists (in 1913) as

> usually quiet, often slight in build, filled with a seriousness of her work, and [having] no use for the big stick. . . . [M]uch of [her] work . . . has not been done by men; it has . . . been left undone because men were not fitted to do it. (quoted in Schulz 1995, 26)

Although this picture stressed physical differences, what was left unsaid, but was certainly true, was that men did not *want* the jobs that women were seen as best qualified to do.

Preventing crime was firmly established as women's domain. This function was trivialized as one of service or maintaining order, not to be performed or valued by male officers. Policewomen's duties included enforcing laws at "dance halls, skating rinks, penny arcades, movie theatres, and other places of recreation frequented by women and children. [They] searched for missing persons and provided social service information to women," as well as tearing down any "evil" pictures outside arcades or unwholesome still shots outside the theatres (Schulz 1995, 24). Early policewomen were immersed in protective and preventive measures, and they carried out their duties with determination and enthusiasm, particularly since their efforts were legitimated by law: "they are *legally* charged with the *active* searching out of conditions which tend to produce juvenile delinquency and those minors who frequent places where these conditions obtain" (Owings 1925, 225). Upholding moral standards was a big part of their role. For example, in Newark, New Jersey, in 1918, policewomen stopped a group of young girls and forced them to remove their makeup (Schulz 1995, 33).[9]

Like their police matron predecessors, early female officers believed women possessed unique skills based on their gender. For instance, in 1915 Alice Stebbins Wells remarked:

> The need for policewomen is one angle of the very general need for women in lines of activity once wholly occupied, and without dispute, by men. . . . With today's social complexity has come a corresponding social responsibility, as playground workers, associated charities, juvenile courts, truant officers, and a score of other forms of service attest. Always, women have cared for and protected the young, yet the police department, which has charge of these strategic places where the young gather, has been composed of men dependent upon the voluntary collateral help of women, if any were given. (quoted in Schulz 1995, 44)

These words inspired the birth of the International Association of Policewomen (IAP) in 1915, whose objectives and policies "illustrate the social work, crime prevention, and educational aspirations" of female officers (Schulz 1995, 44). One of the IAP's early newsletters asserted that "although the old-time penologist and the practical police officer [would] raise their eyes and their hands in holy horror, police jobs would allow women to take an important part in the salvation of the world, a practical sort of salvation" (quoted in Schulz 1995, 43). This view established a need for women to continue their roles as "municipal housekeepers," focusing on two things: women as professionals and women professionals caring for other women. As Schulz (1995, 43–44) contends,

> Combining ambitious professionalism with feminine altruism to secure recognition was not unique to women in the social services. Even women physicians and lawyers achieved advancement primarily through separation rather than through equality. Not only the few women who became doctors, but also those who became lawyers, typically undertook tasks related to feminine roles.

Twenty-five cities had appointed female officers by 1915; three years later, 220 towns and cities recorded policewomen and matrons (Martin 1980, 21).[10]

Meanwhile, the police occupation in general was having its own legitimacy crisis. The problems grew out of the political patronage system. Corruption was rampant, particularly since politicians often used police against unpopular ethnic groups or laws. Supervision of officers was essentially nonexistent. The closeness between the police and residents made officers more susceptible to kickbacks and bribes, whether these were used to sway the conduct of elections or to encourage selective enforcement of various laws. Once Prohibition descended upon the country, police corruption became much more extensive (see Haller 1976). "Curbside justice" also reigned, particularly in cases where officers distinguished between residents and strangers, those who followed neighborhood norms and anyone who (because of race or ethnicity, for example) was found to be violating them.

The professional model that has come to characterize the occupation of policing originated in the 1920s. Although citizen-initiated reform attempts had been tried and ultimately failed in the nineteenth century, efforts at change met with greater success in the next century, since police administrators joined forces with external reformers (Fogelson 1977). As a direct legacy of the Progressive Era, professionalism was seen as a key to moving police away from the corruption and political pandering that characterized the early departments. In addition, the reformers relied on influential writings on police administration, such as those by August Volmer and O. W. Wilson. These and other authors stressed officers' power to shape and maintain morality by suggesting that policing was a legal and technical method for social control (Kelling and Moore 1991). In this era, controlling crime at any cost became departments' reason for being. Police organizations adopted a bureaucratic, hierarchical structure. Such "top-down" power meant that the chief and upper-level administrators set policy and made operational decisions, which filtered down to patrol, the backbone of the force. The autonomy and discretion of officers were restricted in order to discourage selective enforcement, corruption, and partisan politics. Isolating the police from their social environment was viewed as crucial in developing professionalism. Officers were expected to be detached, remote, stoic, conveying dispassionate objectivity. Note that the only method devised to curb corruption was to promote dehumanization; only when man is a machine can he be free of vice. (Nature, and community policing, suggest a different, more feminine path.)

A centralized command structure with a military-style chain of command was promoted to further reduce individual discretion. And, controlling demands for police service through central dispatch systems made it easy to limit or punish individual initiative. Criminal law and control functions were also emphasized in order to lower crime rates. In sum, police policies operated to restrict individual officer discretion and autonomy. Various reformers also hoped that the negative public image of police departments as disorganized, inefficient, and lacking in accountability would change once tighter controls were established. These efforts mirrored the highly publicized drive by J. Edgar Hoover to reconstitute the FBI as an efficient, rational, prestigious institution whose preeminent mission was suppressing crime. Urban police chiefs joined this trend and sought to eradicate political ties to their departments. State governments took over hiring and firing officers by implementing civil service exams. In order to sever links with neighborhoods, some cities required officers to live outside their assigned beat (Kelling and Moore 1991).

Like their male colleagues, policewomen were also involved in efforts designed to increase professionalism. By the 1920s, they were actively criticizing "untrained" police matrons and campaigning to limit the role of volunteers in order to create a more credentialized profession. On this point, Lieutenant Mina C. Van Winkle, president of the International Association of Policewomen and director of the Women's Bureau of the Metropolitan Police Department (Washington, D.C.), explained:

[V]ulgar, uneducated, untrained policewomen degrade the service in the eyes of both the public and the policemen. They are a bad influence with

clients in the community and a menace to police service in general.
(quoted in Owings 1925, xi)

As greater numbers of middle-class women replaced the earlier cohort of upper-middle-class reformers, policing began to be viewed as a viable career for women for the first time. Idealistic policewomen also believed that their presence would act as a catalyst to socialize the entire force and that they would provide models of how to treat women and children that men would follow (Owings 1925).

World War I brought more acceptance for women because of the work they did to keep women and girls away from military men, thus limiting the spread of venereal disease, preventing unwanted pregnancies, and discouraging prostitution (Schulz 1995). Schulz (1995, 35) argues that after 1925 policewomen concentrated their efforts on keeping dance halls in order and maintaining curfews especially geared to limiting juvenile activities and autonomy. This work dovetailed with the legacy of the Progressive agenda, enabling the state to be active in regulating both the private and public activities and the welfare of its citizens (Schulz 1995). Policewomen across the nation agreed that "protective and preventive work is the police function of their sex" (*Policewomen's International Bulletin* 1927, 5). This emphasis had a profound impact on the professional development of female police officers as a group: Schulz contends that they created a gender-based social service role for themselves in their departments, which "reinforced the concept of women's sphere and affected the professional lives of policewomen until the modern era" (Schulz 1995, 36). It is also apparent that these self-assigned moral guardians were usually of the middle class or higher and that their efforts to control and restrict public activities were concentrated on immigrants and citizens of the lower classes (Schulz 1995; Martin 1980).

All of these transformations of the police force trickled down from the Progressive reform agenda. In keeping with other actions that reflected the ideology of the Progressive Era was the effort to promote police as "experts." This was similar to the efforts of other professions that were developing specialized bodies of knowledge, codes of ethics, membership rules, and licensing, such as medicine and the law. Police officers saw themselves, and encouraged the public to see them, as the only group possessed with the breadth of knowledge and skills necessary to carry out law enforcement. This vision, along with the severing of political ties, was believed to put an end to patronage and corruption. In fact, "[p]olitical influence of any kind on a police department came to be seen as a failure of police leadership" (Kelling and Moore 1991, 11). As a result of this redefinition of the policing occupation, earlier tasks related to providing social and emergency services were "identified as 'social work,' becoming the object of derision" (Kelling and Moore 1991, 11), and other municipal agencies took over these duties. Only a narrow definition of policing existed: controlling crime and apprehending criminals. Hierarchical command structures were reinforced, with policies developed and implemented from the top down to an even greater extent. Police administrators sought to routinize tasks and limit individual discretion, guiding patrol officers with uniform procedures and intricate record-keeping systems, of a piece with the generic effort designed to control workers through supervision by middle-level managers (Kelling and Moore 1991, 12).

The relationship between police and citizens was redefined: "police would be impartial law enforcers who related to citizens in professionally neutral and distant terms" (Kelling and Moore 1991, 12). Citizens were expected to acquiesce in crime control actions, deferring to officers' expertise. Policing was response driven and reactive. Policemen patrolled in their cars, rarely venturing out to connect with law-abiding citizens. Patrol signified stability and "police omnipresence," deterring bad guys and reassuring good guys (Kelling and Moore 1991, 14). Citizens were discouraged from contacting their beat officer when they encountered problems; instead, they were urged to call central police dispatch (Kelling and Moore 1991, 14). In keeping with the crime control model, the effectiveness of officers was evaluated by the number of arrests made, by the timing of rapid response to calls for service, and, in some jurisdictions, by "the number of times a police car passes a given point on a city street" (Kelling and Moore 1991, 14). Kelling and Moore contend that the image sold to the public was that the police were the "thin blue line" between citizens and external threats.[11] This helped to establish the status and authority of police officers as well as to solidify stronger intradepartmental controls. In particular,

> Foot patrol when demanded by citizens was rejected as an outmoded, expensive frill. Social and emergency services were terminated or given to other agencies. When citizens persisted in their demands for those other services, police explained that citizens had to learn that police were not social workers and that police could deal with crime effectively only if they were not perceived of as such: social agencies did social work and police did law enforcement. (Kelling and Moore 1991, 13)

Since policewomen were usually housed and supervised in their own bureaus, they did not directly compete for men's duties or positions. Writing in 1933, Eleanor Hutzel, an early deputy commissioner of the Detroit Police Department, states that policewomen were "kept at arm's length from the main organization and, perhaps, a little despised by the remainder of the force" (Hutzel 1933, 3). Deputy Commissioner Hutzel's handbook reveals that women in policing were not highly esteemed, being "regarded by 'old-timers' as a fad and an unjustified excursion into social work" and as "an unwarranted invasion of the uniformed man's field of work" (Hutzel 1933, 2). The women, however, by their willingness to do clerical jobs that men did not want, and by defining their sphere of influence using gendered language (being mothers or protectors of children and controlling public morality), "took the very feminine attributes that had been used to disqualify females from policing and turned them into occupational assets" (Martin 1980, 23).

Some early female officers did not join in promoting the idea that women possessed unique skills—or that men could not learn them. For example, Hutzel (1933, 7) suggests that although women were most likely the best candidates for directors of policewomen's bureaus because of their experience in dealing with female employees and delinquent girls, "a man may be found whose experience is adequate to the task. The choice should, in any case, be made on the basis of the special qualifications possessed by candidates for the position and not on theoretical grounds." At the same time, Hutzel (1933, 8) believes a policewoman "should be the type of person who can become a real policewoman without in any sense ceasing to be a real social worker, and finally, be capable of projecting that spirit into her organization."

One consequence of the sequestered women's bureaus was that women were removed from the male power base of the police organization, with a negative impact on the scope of their responsibilities, salaries, prestige, and opportunities for promotion. Thus, the policewomen's movement began declining during the 1930s and 1940s since its members were associated, not with the police hierarchy, but with women's reform groups and private social agencies. In addition, the focus on service remained peripheral in police departments, since "professionalism became synonymous with crime fighting and managerial efficiency, rather than with crime prevention and social intervention" (Schulz 1995, 55). In her historical analysis, Schulz concludes that by accepting women's and men's roles as being different, and by accepting segregation in their own bureaus, women did not prosper. This remained the situation until 1972, when women began to demand to be hired on the same basis as their male counterparts.

By the time of the Great Depression (1929–1941), the dominant emphasis in mainstream policing had become crimefighting and bureaucratized efficiency, with social service and prevention taking a back seat. Women were viewed as not emotionally capable of leadership. Worsening economic conditions reinforced traditional gender roles by encouraging women to be content as housewives and not seek employment outside the home (Schulz 1995, 79). As unemployment continued to rise, the faces of the police began to change: better educated middle-class men joined departments, which thus further profession-alized policing by moving the force away from being an enclave of working-class immigrants. There were also efforts to get out from under political control and to change the image of the police officer in the eyes of the public. "By the 1930s they had shed many of the more obvious housekeeping roles, such as lodging the homeless and overseeing street cleaning. Agencies created specifi-cally for these purposes became part of the urban landscape" (Schulz 1995, 81). Chiefs remained under some pressure to respond to changes in standard police practices that involved the use of force and to increase the service elements of policing. By continuing to channel policewomen toward service roles that were seen as peripheral to their departments, the chiefs could address these concerns without having to make any real changes for women. Female officers continued to specialize in working with other women and children (the social control of the powerless) or in clerical tasks, although between 1930 and 1970 there were a few women who did investigative or crime lab work (Martin 1980).

In conformity with the 1930s progressive ideology espoused by New Deal Democrats was the image of the aggressive law enforcer promoted by J. Edgar Hoover, director of the Federal Bureau of Investigation:

> Professionalism had special meaning for Hoover and the FBI. Profes-sional cops were tough, fearless crime fighters . . . were well trained and utilized the latest scientific crime fighting techniques . . . were expert sharpshooters. . . . The Bureau advanced this image of police profession-alism. As a consequence, the crime fighting or law enforcement aspects of the police role overshadowed all others. . . . Order maintenance and service . . . sank to second-class status. Officers derided them as not being "real" police work. (Walker 1983, 15–16, cited in Schulz 1995, 83)

Such masculinist battle language promoted the fierce warrior-robot, devoid of emotions or personality, and this became the ideal of the new-model police officer. Police*men* relied on technology, expertise in marksmanship, and their courage to bring criminals to justice. This masculine image carries as its foil what was *not* considered to be legitimate or valuable policework, or desirable individual traits: anything not related to capturing or annihilating the enemies of law and order, or personal styles that were open, warm, and communicative.

> Police agencies became law enforcement agencies, and activities identi-fied as "social work" became the object of derision. A common line in

police circles during the 1950s and 1960s was: "If only we didn't have to do social work, we could really do something about crime." (Kelling and Moore 1991, 11)

Juvenile crime increased after World War II, stimulating male officers to encroach upon this previously women-only domain. They began to work with delinquent boys by befriending them through athletic leagues, junior cadet units, and so forth (Schulz 1995, 100). Neither male nor female police executives noticed or mentioned the parallel to women's work that signified men's new responsibilities mirrored women's traditional domains (Schulz 1995, 100). Meanwhile, female officers continued to focus on policing the sexual activities of girls and women, driven by the increased presence of servicemen and the growth in street prostitution (Schulz 1995, 101).[12] There was also a split between female officers' previous allies, social workers and women's reform groups. Without the IAP, which had disbanded in 1932 and did not reestablish itself until 1956, there were not enough policewomen to lobby successfully without the power of the other two groups behind them (Schulz 1995, 117). In addition, social workers were well established in their own profession in governments and private agencies and they no longer needed police positions (Schulz 1995). As Schulz (1995, 103) argues, "The feeling by social workers that policewomen, if not truly competitors, at least overlapped their functions, continued through the decade [of the 1940s] and persisted to some extent until policewomen relinquished social service functions to join the ranks of police crimefighters." By 1956, the new International Association of Women Police had divorced itself from the earlier bent toward social work and had taken on a new, and contradictory, mission: both to fully integrate women into police departments and to maintain gendered duties for them in separate women's bureaus (Schulz 1995).

The era of reform began to wind down in the 1960s and 1970s, when police effectiveness was challenged and crime rates, despite the increases in resources and technological advances, rose (Kelling and Moore 1991). Even though more money for equipment had poured in and more police had been hired, rapid response and preventive patrol measures remained ineffective and crime rates still increased. Well-publicized research on preventive patrol revealed that the greater police presence had no effect on neighborhood crime rates (Kelling and Moore 1987). Nor did rapid response efforts result in the promised increase in the arrest rate. Research indicated that, after about two minutes, there was no payoff for quick response, as the perpetrators were long gone (Biecke 1980). Detectives were typically stymied in solving crimes after they had received the initial officer reports and accounts from eyewitnesses and victims. Fear of crime led those city dwellers who were able to leave their communities for the sub-urbs, thus abandoning public parks, neighborhood stores, and public transpor-tation—the fabric of neighborhood life. People of color resented the unfair, neglectful, and racist treatment they received from police. The legitimacy of the government and the police was challenged in the wake of civil rights and anti-war protests. Many officers felt betrayed by the liberal decisions emanating from the Warren Court, particularly rulings that restricted the scope of their author-ity during interrogation and search and seizure incidents. And, surprisingly to some, empirical studies of police patrol work revealed that, contrary to the promises of routine uniformity, much discretion still existed (Kelling and Moore 1991, 15–16).[13]

Meanwhile, opportunities for women on the force remained stagnant until the 1970s. This decade witnessed a shift from the emphasis on specialist "police-women" to one of more-generalist officers (Schulz 1995), stemming from the concerns of the 1960s with the rising crime rate, a shortage of personnel, and riots and chronic tensions that laid bare hostile police-community relations. In addition, the due-process revolution set in motion by the Warren Court left lasting limits on police power and established crucial procedural safeguards for citizens against abuse of authority by the police.[14] The 1967 President's Com-mission on Law Enforcement and Administration of Justice, formed to examine the tense relations between police and communities, urged departments to un-dertake many reforms, among them hiring more racial minority, female, and college-educated officers (Schulz 1995, 132). With regard to women, one rec-ommendation read:

> Policewomen can be an invaluable asset to modern law enforcement and their present role should be broadened. Qualified women should be uti-lized in such important staff service units as planning and research, training, intelligence, inspection, public information, community rela-tions, and as legal advisors. Women could also serve such units as com-puter programming and laboratory analysis and communications. Their value should not be considered as limited to staff functions of police work with juveniles; women should also serve regularly in patrol, vice, and investigative divisions. Finally, as more and more well qualified women enter the service, they could assume administrative responsibili-ties. (President's Commission on Law Enforcement and Administration of Justice 1967, 125)

The women's movement, by challenging sex roles presumably correlated with "masculine" and "feminine" work, opened up the labor pool. In 1968, two female officers in Indianapolis became the first women to have the same patrol responsibilities as men, wear guns with their uniforms, and ride in a marked squad car (Schulz 1995, 131). The 1970s became a period of unprecedented growth in opportunities for policewomen. Some departments hired women to ensure long-term secretarial support for administrators; others hired them to avoid lawsuits or to comply with court orders (Martin 1980, 27). Racial and sexual integration happened more consistently in cities with large African American populations than in those with strong European ethnic leadership and populations that were more resistant to change (Martin 1980).

In 1972, the amending of Title VII of the Civil Rights Act of 1964 (which prohibits employment discrimination based on sex) paved the way for more women to be assigned to patrol, a position typically reserved for men. Court cases challenged practices that favored men in criminal justice occupations: height and weight standards, physical agility requirements, veterans' preference, and limits to pregnancy leaves (Moyer 1992). Social science research demonstrated that women on patrol performed just as effectively as men.[15] Government-funded pilot programs in Washington, New York City, Philadelphia, Denver, Miami, and Dallas showed that although male officers still questioned the effectiveness of women and whether they could physically handle the job, these concerns were not substantiated by performance evaluations (Townsey 1982). Although some barriers to hiring women had been lifted, many others still existed that excluded them or led to only partial use of their talents (Milton 1972). Given public concern with the escalating number of reported rapes (and with female delinquency and criminality), one trend was to assign women to special rape investigation units. There is some irony here: even as women were seen, somewhat patronizingly, as better suited to handle these domains, this specialization offered more prestige by creating investigative positions for them (Martin 1980). It was also suggested that women could elevate departmental standards and improve the bad public image that plagued police during and after the tumultuous 1960s: "women could 'gentle-ize' the department, improve the tarnished public image of the police, and provide a pool of heretofore untapped personnel who were both well educated and sensitive to individuals, as well as dedicated to community service" (Martin 1980, 39). All of these factors coalesced to challenge restrictions on and opposition to women as officers; by the late 1970s, most large cities sent women to patrol and other assignments by using criteria that were not based on sex.

By the early 1980s, criminal justice research revealed that citizens' fears seemed to be more closely associated with general disorder than high crime rates (Police Foundation 1981; Wilson and Kelling 1982; Skogan and Maxfield 1981). Yet, in the push to make crime control a priority, order maintenance was one of those functions that police had been downplaying over the years. They collected no data on it, provided no training to officers in order maintenance activities, and did not reward officers for successfully conducting order maintenance tasks. (Kelling and Moore 1991, 16)

Relations between police and the communities they served were still tense. Officers were remote and detached, estranged from the citizens, whom some of them saw as "assholes" (Van Maanen 1978) and "symbolic assailants" (Skolnick 1994). Overreliance on answering 911 rapid response calls brought overexposure to bad people, bad places, and bad things. The suspicion and distrust were reciprocal: the police did not see citizens as a source of support; citizens saw officers as sunglassed automatons (Trojanowicz and Bucqueroux 1990). Civil suits against departments and individual officers increased, and the explosion of urban problems, many of them related to poverty and race, magnified the public's antagonism toward and disconnection from the police.

Thus, it became clear that policing as an institution was under siege and was viewed largely as ineffective and unresponsive to the demands of an increasingly diverse society. Scholars and practitioners began to seek new ideas about how police *could* contribute to neighborhood social control. The "broken windows" theory of James Q. Wilson and George Kelling (1982) instigated yet another change in policing's role, this one toward more focus on the community. Although not without its detractors, the broken-windows theory emerged as a potential cure for the ills that had arisen from the bureaucratic policing style of the reform era.

Simply put, Wilson and Kelling suggested in their article that what people feared most was disorder, not crime, since ongoing, unchecked disorder has a profound effect on the quality of life. To counter disorder, rather than put a premium on their minimally effective crimefighting ability, police could shift their focus. This could be accomplished by strengthening their mandate to maintain order and by addressing nuisances that lead to more serious crime if unattended, such as those involving drunks, solicitors, loiterers, panhandlers, vagrants, and graffiti artists. In what is also called the "incivilities model," Wilson and Kelling hypothesized that signs of physical disorder (abandoned buildings, broken windows, litter) and social disorder (public intoxication, public drug use) that remain unaddressed convey the message that citizens do not care and police will not resolve the problems. This inattention leads to the community's inability to control itself through confronting residents' shared concerns: communal obligations break down, and crime flourishes.

As social incivilities become more widespread and/or intense, residents
make fewer efforts to exert formal social control over one another. . . .
This lessening of regulatory efforts results in further expansions of incivilities. . . . Faced with the spread of incivilities, residents use the streets
less, resulting in less eyes on the street . . . and the alienation of residents
from co-residents will also ensue. The fabric of community is progres-
sively abraded. . . . At this point in the process of community decay . . .
criminals may move into an area. . . . These developments further inten-
sify residents' fears. (Greene and Taylor 1991, 198–199)

The implications of the broken-windows theory are pivotal for community
policing. This "new" model of policing works to reduce fear by addressing the
physical and social incivilities, or disorders, that have weakened social control.
Community policing emphasizes reestablishing and strengthening community
attachments and invigorates residents to help in this mission. If these efforts
succeed, then fear will diminish, public places will no longer be avoided, and
police will regain citizens' respect and trust.

Not all scholars of policing believe that this approach is the answer to reducing the fear of crime. David Bayley, for example, contends that community
policing is the reconfiguration of an idea that did not work in the past:

It is probably fair to say that community policing in 1988 is more rhetoric than reality. It is a trendy phrase spread thinly over customary reality.
Unless this state of affairs changes, the most likely future for community
policing is that it will be remembered as another attempt to put old wine
into new bottles. (Bayley 1991, 225–226)

The challenge facing advocates of community policing was how to "sell"
their new product. The rhetoric used to "market" the new approach shows a
remarkable similarity to that used to explain the mission of early policewomen.
It is to this connection that I now turn.

Contrasting Models: Early Policewomen
and Contemporary Community Policing

The policewomen of Indianapolis do not wear uniforms. Instead they go
clad as they would go to market or to the shops—just the real women with
"human-bein'ism" stamped on their souls. —*Literary Digest,* 1921

By insisting upon the social protection of women, children and the community, rather than upon the vindication of "rights" . . . policewomen

are introducing into the administration of criminal justice a social view-point which should influence a change of attitude on the part of the courts and the public. —Chloe Owings, 1925

Community policing models of the late 1980s and the 1990s follow ideologies and implementation strategies that are very reminiscent of the turn-of-the-century social welfare roles of police, an approach that was discarded in favor of the "aloof professional" model. Writings from the time that describe the duties of policewomen illustrate this reclaiming of previously denigrated duties; these descriptions presage today's more gender-neutral model of the neighborhood police officer. Contrasting the historical writings with contemporary expectations and duties of NPOs offers some "new" insights about "old" issues. Descriptions of the roles and responsibilities of neighborhood officers today are strikingly consistent with those of police*women* in the late nineteenth and early twentieth centuries. Ironically, the stereotypically "feminine" traits once used to exclude women from patrol, or to separate "real" crimefighters from "office or social worker cops," are now used to describe valuable community policing skills, albeit no longer in "feminine" terms.

As mentioned at the beginning of this book, many expectations are associated with today's neighborhood policing. It has been suggested, in fact, that community policing is "a conveniently elastic term which is often loosely used to accommodate virtually any policing activity of which its proponents approve" (Weatheritt 1987, 7). Neighborhood police officers are expected to be intimately familiar with their particular community, relaying and exchanging information about residents, trouble spots, and leaders with other neighborhood and patrol officers. They are encouraged to become familiar with their neighborhood by gathering and integrating information from multiple sources: detectives, probation and parole officers, and liaisons with schools, government agencies, social workers, and other groups. Information received from such professional contacts is added to that gathered from residents and other persons in the community who can, if they choose, easily provide background details about relationships, families, criminal offenders or incidents, and victims. However, the officer must instill trust and cultivate relationships for such disclosure to happen. Creating personal connections, gathering family history data, and forging connections with other government and social service agencies are not activities typical of patrol officers. Rather, they are rapid responders, call driven, who do not have the luxury of time to follow up on their calls or collect family histories.

The process of creating ties with the community is strikingly similar to what Detroit's Eleanor Hutzel, in the 1930s, described as the patrol duties expected of policewomen. Indeed, this captures the first similarity between the pioneer female officers and today's NPOs. Hutzel, in her instruction book, *The Policewoman's Handbook,* called on female officers to learn all about their assigned districts by speaking with other policewomen who may have preceded them, studying police department and juvenile court records, and conferring with "individuals who have worked in the district, and who are likely to be familiar with delinquency problems, namely: patrolmen, probation officers, teachers, recreation leaders, public health nurses, and other social workers" (Hutzel 1933, 13). She also urged policewomen to

> make friendly contacts with certain residents and persons in the district who can most often supply needed information. These include store-keepers, restaurant managers, janitors and managers of apartment buildings, night watchmen, landladies, taxicab drivers, theater managers, and newsboys. (Hutzel 1933, 13)

The goal, she wrote, was to ferret out information regarding rooms or houses used for illicit purposes, collect the names of young women seen loitering, and so forth. Hutzel warned that not everybody would welcome this kind of intelligence gathering, but added that "antagonistic persons sometimes prove helpful, for in their anger they often unconsciously give out valuable information" (Hutzel 1933, 14). The activities that community police officers emphasize today are virtually the same as those emphasized by the early patrolwomen.

A second similarity between the context of early policework by women and modern community policing involves the decentralization of power. It is typically accomplished today by creating a separate, informal, "drop-in" environment through the use of police ministations. These settings put neighborhood officers into closer, more casual contact with the residents they serve. This "modern" idea is also easy to find in descriptions of police stations run by women in the early twentieth century:

> In removing from the Women's Precinct all the earmarks of a regular police station it at once became a center where a woman could seek information, advice or aid from . . . her own sex without fear of . . . the grim atmosphere of the average police desk. The red geraniums in the window boxes would attract . . . a woman. . . . The worried mother or weary, runaway girl could find the help, understanding and protection that only a motherly policewoman can give. (Hamilton 1924, 18, 20)

This description connotes a womblike environment, where residents would be safe from harm and comforted by a listening (female) ear and a pleasant, woman-filled environment, in contrast to a male-run administrative desk at an ordinary police station.

A third similarity between the two ideologies is the emphasis on prevention, particularly activities directed at juveniles. Today's NPOs are encouraged to work with the community to create ways to keep children and juveniles constructively busy as an alternative to joining gangs and as a way to foster more and better interactions between young people and the police. Many community policing programs use sports leagues, computer workshops, and other such efforts to attract juveniles and provide a crime-free and safe environment. Similar goals and activities were embraced by female officers decades ago. For example, in Philadelphia in 1936, delinquency prevention combined the resources of civic associations with those of policewomen, who

> worked from an abandoned school building, apart from male colleagues, handling boys and girls under 16 years of age, supervising recreation, organizing a bootblacks' club, arranging for underprivileged children to attend summer camp, and taking youngsters to the circus. (Schulz 1995, 92)

The interest in forging connections between police and social service agencies to prevent juvenile delinquency was a large part of women's contribution to early-twentieth-century policing: as a segment of New York City's Crime Prevention Bureau, "policewomen perform their duties in plain clothes and have been able to foster social activities and athletics among groups of boys who were drifting into anti-social pastimes. The Bureau is developing close interrelationships between social agencies and the police" (*Encyclopedia* 1933, 361). The emphasis on social work for early policewomen meant that their patrol duties targeted areas that attracted delinquent boys or wayward girls and young women, such as dance halls, motion picture houses, railroad stations, and parks. Other activities of early policewomen related to social work stressed the need to develop alternative gathering places for juveniles, such as "facilities for more wholesome recreation" (*Encyclopedia* 1933, 361). Today's community police officers are often expected to design similar programs.

Thus, a fourth comparison can be made between the social-work activities of early policewomen and what is done by contemporary NPOs. This is perhaps the most contested contrast, and the one that most clearly reveals how formerly rejected female roles have been resurrected and transformed into gender-neutral skills in community policing. In the early part of the twentieth century, the domain of women police officers was social work:

The cases with which policewomen deal cover the whole field of social maladjustment—missing persons, shoplifters, disrupted domestic relations, rape, neglect, delinquency, and waywardness. In well-conducted bureaus these cases are investigated according to case work methods, and where adjustments require facilities beyond the capacity of the policewomen the cases are referred to other social agencies. (*Encyclopedia* 1933, 360)

Proponents of the social, rather than the police, approach to solving problems believed that opposition to their ideas indicated "technical ignorance on the part of those promoting appointments or political nepotism of unusual strength" (*Encyclopedia* 1933, 361). Much of the social-work emphasis for early policewomen was influenced by the belief that they were not as physically competent as men to perform certain tasks, such as patrol. It was also influenced by the desire to elevate women to a specialized role. Stressing social work capitalized on women's differences, giving them control over peripheral policing duties (and thus not threatening men's power).

Accordingly, values related to social work and maternal thinking were emphasized:

There is a tendency to stress the social side of police work, rather than its punitive side, with positive efforts on the part of officers to train children to look to them for guidance and assistance in their troubles. An example of this spirit is the chintz-hung room in Berkeley, California, equipped with toys and games, and used expressly for children who are sometimes offenders under the law, but more often voluntary seekers of advice and aid. (*Encyclopedia* 1933, 361)

Again, the description of a cheerful, well-decorated room symbolizes feminine touches and maternal protection and guidance. In addition, early police used a case file approach to record family histories and other information. Today's community police officers frequently rely on similar case studies to keep track of neighborhood residents.

As noted earlier in this chapter, in the early twentieth century conflict surrounded the perceived value of social work as compared with law enforcement. For their part, female social workers believed that "police departments are sadly lacking in the social service point of view" (*Police Journal* 1929, 20). On the other hand, policemen believed that social workers were "swayed by sentiment and have too little knowledge of legal matters" (*Police Journal* 1929, 20). Social workers vehemently argued that police officers were indifferent to identifying and correcting societal conditions that facilitated juvenile delinquency, as well as more serious adult crime. From the vantage point of the present day, this argument closely parallels the broken-windows theory, with its calls for paying greater attention to underlying and contextual causes of disorder and crime. Policewomen familiar with social work believed that nothing in men's "previous experience, in the curriculum of the training school, or in their experience as police officers gives them the needed social background or the social interest necessary for intelligent investigation of the cause and prevention of bad social conditions" (*Police Journal* 1929, 22). Women experienced in social work, however, were seen as crucial to doing this kind of social investigation, and they were more eager to undertake such tasks than were their male colleagues. Moreover, it was believed that even when men with proper social service training led successful investigations of social conditions, "the fact remains that in most cases women also have participated, and frequently have done all or most of the planning and work" (*Police Journal* 1929, 22).

At least one area, though, was not contested by early female and male officers. They agreed that women were best suited to handle the physical care and safety of women and children taken into custody: "Even the most 'hard-boiled' police officer of the old type will not seriously maintain that a woman arrested by the police and held pending trial should be placed in charge of a man. The same is true as to lost children who are found by the police or who are obtained for any reason" (*Police Journal* 1929, 22). This widely read article proclaiming women to be the best guardians of children's welfare concludes with this sentiment: "The practically universal decision of the human race in matters pertaining to the custody and care of the young is that men are goodhearted bunglers at best and that women should be given this responsibility" (*Police Journal* 1929, 22). Today's community policeman, however, challenges women's exclusive control of this domain and is actively involved with the children in his neighborhood.

For decades, the belief in the appropriateness of social work for women remained a dominant ideological underpinning of their limited role in policing. The Indianapolis Department of Police Women (organized with eleven members in 1918, and growing to twenty-three women and a supervisor by 1921) took a different approach, actively circumventing formal law enforcement. The department made

> it a special point to avoid arrests. Jail sentences and a large record of convictions, the standard upon which the efficiency of most police organizations is based, [were] not considered important. They handle[d] most offenders "in a little court of their own." (*Literary Digest* 1921, 41)

Women were seen as having ample energy to do the job of social work, but not having enough energy to perform the policework done by men. The following description of a female officer in Indianapolis provides an idea of a typical policewoman's workday:

> One thinks of a police officer as having to possess a sturdy physique. Miss Burnside [supervisor of policewomen] defies that tradition, because she easily could walk under the outstretched arm of the average policeman. But what she lacks in physique she easily overbalances in energy. Hours on duty are not her problem. She constantly is on the job, striving to right some domestic ship that threatens to go on the rocks, or seeking, with the aid of her loyal force of policemen, to make some erring girl take the better path. (*Literary Digest* 1921, 41)

This description is not so different from that of the typical day of a community police officer in the 1990s. Indeed, the sheer physical demands on any NPO who takes seriously her or his role as liaison or ambassador to families, children, social service agencies, landlords, and the criminal justice system require the energy of at least one Miss Burnside.

Thus, contrasting the roles of early policewomen with those of contemporary community police officers suggests several conclusions. First, women were reluctantly accepted as police so long as they confined their activities to narrow spheres. Second, these accepted spheres never involved areas in which men desired to work. Third, once women wanted to become patrol officers, men's jobs and masculinity were threatened. Finally, to retain their masculine status, men steered away from any police job or style that evoked femininity. This boundary separated the macho crimefighter from the female social worker. Men's exclusionary practices are now challenged by community policing. This new approach implicitly demands the assertion of the feminine side of policing. It also demands respect for "feminine" jobs, long eschewed by male officers and even by female officers who wanted to fit in with the established police subculture and prove their competency to their male peers. In fact, in Jackson City the community policing activities mirror the similarities revealed in this contrast: gaining intimate knowledge of the neighborhood and the details of the residents' lives; decentralizing power through ministations; undertaking prevention-oriented activities, particularly for young people; and using the case study method of social workers.

An article published in 1929 in the *Police Journal,* "Police Functions Best Performed by Men and by Women Police Officers," delineates the issue:

There is now almost universal agreement that policewomen should not attempt to do general patrol work. Police work of this type is rather exacting in its physical demands, and men as a sex, have greater physical strength and endurance than women as a sex. The police officer doing patrol work, moreover, is engaged in the main protection of property and the prevention of crime—types of work for which women have no peculiar or unique qualifications. In view of the general and specific nature of patrol work, the requirements as to strength alone are sufficient to be a determining factor. (*Police Journal* 1929, 20)

These words from the 1920s clearly show that only men were believed to possess the necessary skills and talents needed to be crimefighters. Seventy years later, not only do women in the law enforcement arena possess these "masculine" abilities, but *both* men and women are being called upon to deploy the very same skills and talents in the ostensibly gender-neutral realm of community policing. However, a careful examination of what the officers say and do in the interview and fieldwork data that follow suggests the persistence of a subterranean effect of gendered expectations and task divisions in the neighborhoods of Jackson City. The next several chapters explore these dilemmas and contradictions, and their implications.

Notes

Parts of this chapter previously appeared in Miller 1998.

1. Elsewhere, I (and others) have examined how the concepts of "different voices," described by Carol Gilligan (1982), lend themselves to critiquing the male voice of law and legal practice, although the law is ostensibly gender neutral (see Miller 1998; Daly 1989, 1; Menkel-Meadow 1985; West 1988). Gilligan casts female and male "voices" as opposing ethical styles used in resolving conflicts or dilemmas: men prize individual rights, autonomy, and impartiality, whereas women reject the male values of objectivity and detachment (ethic of justice) and instead honor and emphasize care, responsibility, and affective connections (ethic of care). Although she has been criticized for her sample and methodology, and on conceptual issues such as essentialism (see MacKinnon 1989, 1984; Lloyd 1983; Code 1983), Gilligan's notion of different voices has permeated the discourse across a wide range of academic disciplines, among them education, psychology, and the law.

Other theorists, such as Kathleen Daly (1989), have used different-voice constructs to suggest that justice concepts, such as proportional punishment applied in a depersonalized context that stresses deterrence or retribution, reflect a "male" justice model. She sees the "female" care model operating when treatment and rehabilitation concerns are raised, based on the potential to reform individuals and reintegrate them into communities. Thus, Daly does not believe that only the "male voice" operates within the criminal justice system. This is particularly so because prior and ongoing victim-offender relationships *are* routinely taken into account in culpability assessments, sentencing practices, and other policies that provide evidence of a strong "ethic of care" approach to processing cases.

2. Researchers in the growing area of gender and technology have found that although the introduction of computers and other new technologies upgraded women's skills across a variety of occupations, such as engineering, banking, and insurance, men remained in charge (see studies conducted by Cockburn [1988, 1991]; Cockburn and Ormrod [1993]; Acker [1990]; Acker and Ask [1989]; Hacker [1990]; and Baran [1990]). Men were perceived as having more skills than women, and the latter's skills were undervalued; female workers remained at the lower levels of the organization's social and professional hierarchy. Given the gendered skills inherent in community policing, future performance evaluations will reveal whether "feminine" skills have been upgraded to be perceived as more highly valued masculine ones, and how skill assessment will be interpreted for male and female officers who exhibit such skills.

3. Investigators who look at social-psychological factors that influence policing often write about competing, or oppositional, police subcultures. For example, Jennifer Hunt (1990) characterizes a gender-linked occupational dualism in her schema of gender-stereotyped opposites (masculine/feminine), occupational work themes and activities (crimefighting/service and maintaining order), and situations (public/domestic, dirty/clean). Of course, the concepts associated with the feminine are undervalued and disparaged, whereas their opposites are revered.

4. Handling traffic was seen as potentially very dangerous work, and therefore it was part of men's domain in early policing. Typically, two reasons were offered in explanation: "The physical demands made upon traffic officers, who must stand on their feet for lengthy periods, are considerable; while these demands are not beyond the strength of some women, they impose a considerable strain. A traffic officer, moreover, does not need the social service background which is usually given as one of the compelling reasons for employing policewomen" (*Police Journal* 1929, 20).

5. The career path of modern women police officers is less well documented than the trajectories of other women's careers; in-depth analyses can be found in books by Dorothy Moses Schulz (1995) and Janis Appier (1998), as well as in a groundbreaking book by Susan Ehrlich Martin (1980). Although archival records exist, the works by Schulz and Martin provide rich syntheses and analyses of these early movements; I recognize the influence their work has had on my own efforts and the debt I owe to their scholarship.

6. Women actively promoted moral and maternal reforms through such groups as the Women's Christian Temperance Union (WCTU), the General Federation of Women's Clubs, the National League of Women Voters, the National Young Women's Christian Association, the American Social Hygiene Association, and Jewish and Catholic social

agencies; there were also at least two men's city clubs, in Chicago and Philadelphia (Owings 1925). Along with its support for the women's suffrage and kindergarten movements, the WCTU was particularly important in promoting the use of prison matrons. By 1890, thirty-six cities had hired matrons and forty-five more were seeking to increase the number of positions; most of them were sponsored by private groups or paid through donated funds (Schulz 1995).

7. This help, of course, was provided for whites only; blacks were sent to the poorhouses, and they were often refused help even there (Monkkonen 1981).

8. These functions were similar to the activities of the Travelers' Aid Society; in the 1880s and 1890s, groups of women began to "greet female arrivals at seaports and railroad stations to advise and shelter them" in order to prevent these "innocents" from being lured into immoral activities or prostitution (Schulz 1995, 22).

9. This is not to suggest that the early policewomen did not contribute to other operations in their departments; for example, in 1887 in New York City, policewomen took care of forty-two thousand female lodgers and fourteen thousand female prisoners (Schulz 1995, 15).

10. The ideology promoted by policewomen was similar to that of other reform groups, such as the child savers (see Platt 1977). Middle-class women extended their role of homemaker and mother to public service: "By moving from volunteerism to government supported reforms, the women created career opportunities which neither threatened men nor challenged society's view of the female sphere" (Schulz 1995, 46). Other occupations that had begun as volunteer efforts, such as nursing, social work, and home economics, moved toward professionalization and paid positions. Within police departments, women created separate bureaus, which reinforced the idea that they would not have the opportunity to threaten men. For their part, men would not be inclined to enter women's specialty fields of service and thus would not block women's success in this endeavor. There was a downside, however: "Because the women had separated themselves from all facets of the police function not concerned with social service, there was now a need to assure that men did not enter this specialty and eliminate the need for policewomen." Writers who were policewomen, though, were very quick to point out that the focus on women and children, the low pay and poor conditions of work, and the long wait for promotion would be less than likely to attract men (Owings 1925, 217). However, by delineating a distinct role for themselves, women's separate sphere, even as it allowed access *into* the occupation, also blocked opportunities to move beyond the restrictions of being municipal housekeepers. Of course, attaining patrol positions equivalent to male police officers took several generations to achieve (Schulz 1995).

11. Following Hoover's lead in his reinvention of the FBI, municipal police executives sought to shape opinion by appearing on radio shows, using media consultants, and staging public relations campaigns, all designed to promote the image of police as aggressive crimefighters (Kelling and Moore 1991).

12. Earlier, during World War I, policewomen established Committees on Protective Work for Girls that attempted to redirect the morals of young women and the ener-

gies they expended in connection with military camps: "Girls were following the wave of emotionalism which was sweeping the country and making a hero of every man in a uniform" (Owings 1925, 110).

13. Kelling and Moore (1991, 17) suggest other issues bedeviling law enforcement in the 1960s and 1970s: patrol officers (unlike administrators) did not "buy into" reform ideals, particularly the removal of officer discretion; fiscal crises in cities led to the dismissal of officers, with no change in crime rates; and private security and community anticrime movements competed in attempts to protect citizens and their property.

14. A number of landmark Supreme Court decisions established or enhanced citizens' rights in the areas of self-incrimination, illegal searches and seizures, exclusion of evidence, confessions gathered illegally, right to counsel for indigents, and so on (see, e.g., *Mapp v. Ohio* [1961], *Miranda v. Arizona* [1966], and *Gideon v. Wainwright* [1963]).

15. For a review of these studies, see Sulton and Townsey 1981; for a critique of these studies, see Morash and Greene 1986.

Competing Police Roles

Social Workers or
Dirty Harry/Harriet?

If you've got a good NPO, you've got five
patrol officers rolled into one.
—Lisa, white lesbian, former NPO

We don't need any more cowboys. . . . [W]hat good is
it to be a cowboy or cowgirl? It just gets you into a
fight.
—Francine, white woman, former NPO

There's a lot of anonymity in a squad car,
there's the uniform and it's almost like you're a
centaur, you know, with a head of a human and the
body of a squad.
—Pam, white lesbian, former NPO

When you become an NPO, some patrol officers act
like you give up your gunbelt and put on a sweater
and you are now going to be in Mister Rogers'
neighborhood.
—Stewart, black man, current NPO

Some officers feel that the only person with any
testosterone and any manhood is somebody who
works patrol; nobody else is of any use whatsoever.
—Evan, white man, current NPO

Scott, a white man who once served as a neighborhood police officer, recalls a
turning point in his career:

When you are in patrol, a felony arrest is considered good work, something that should be done, and everyone understands its significance. One of the amazing things to me when I took the NPO position was how priorities changed shape. The neighborhood business association wanted more trash cans put on Davis Street. At first, the city said no, we don't allow that, and then the second time, the city said okay as long as you follow these conditions: you have to get a specific type of can, it's gotta be painted this way, using a certain size lettering, and be this size, etc. So by the time you figure the costs for all those requirements, it was about fifteen hundred dollars per garbage can. Well, the business association didn't have that kind of money, but prior to our city going to a full recycling program, a grassroots organization from that neighborhood started recycling on their own and they had raised quite a bit of money. And they came to the business association and said, we'll donate this and buy trash cans because it's consistent with our work. Then the business association purchased the cans and put them out there, but the ones that were currently out there now looked terrible—they were all rusted and bent. So, their argument to the city was, we're purchasing all these new ones, can you replace or upgrade these old ones. And the city was real staunch about it, no, there are other things we need to do and they are not due to be replaced. So the association asked me if there's anything I can do. So, I took my Polaroid out, and took a couple of shots of the worst trash cans. And then I went and saw the [former] chief. And I explained to him that people from the community are trying to make their area look better, they did all this work and bought all these trash cans, and this is what the city has done. Well, the chief immediately went to the mayor's office and within the week there were new trash cans out there. And the people in the community acted like I was this big hero and I had all this pull with city hall. And it was amazing to me because in patrol, I could have made a dozen felony arrests, but most citizens wouldn't have known. But because I took those photographs, I was a big hero.

This story typifies the cognitive dissonance involved when a patrol officer, accustomed primarily to answering calls from a squad car, becomes a neighborhood officer and is expected to handle noncriminal incidents. No longer do officers put a priority on arrests; instead, they look at the underlying problems that generate community discontent, and they size up situations in order to address minor disorder before they explode into more serious crime. As Scott's account indicates, it is unheard of for a patrol officer in a squad car to be concerned over, let alone have the time to do anything about, a garbage can; yet, the neighborhood clearly wanted this kind of police help. Drawing on the data from research in Jackson City, this chapter explores the uniqueness of the neighborhood and patrol officer positions and why their interactions might be supportive or antagonistic. I also investigate how men and women "do" community policing differently. The chapter examines several other subjects in greater detail. First, the officers discuss the changes in their identities brought about by neighborhood work, as such changes relate to both police image and police practice. I go on to examine how patrol officers negotiate the images and practices of neighborhood officers. The chapter then explores how and why conflict or coordination arises between the dual images of crimefighter and social worker. Further, I look at strategies used to address these dynamics and how the approaches varied by race and gender of the officers. This section also investigates how officers negotiate their emotions. Finally, I examine how sexual orientation may introduce differences in how policewomen and policemen do their jobs.

Making the Transition

The move from patrol to neighborhood policing was dramatic in Jackson City. It entailed a negotiation of images for the officers as well as a change in their style of operation. The transition was further complicated by the symbolism of the patrol officer as crimefighter and the neighborhood officer as social worker. Although some NPOs welcomed this change and saw advantages to the new position, others were frustrated in their move away from the predictable routine of patrol. Without exception, though, the thirteen current and twenty-seven former neighborhood officers involved in the study talked about the difficulty of the transition. Although most NPOs agreed that the regular routine and expectations of patrol officers were sometimes more advantageous because the guidelines were clearer, many of them also believed that the routine got boring and there were few opportunities to be creative in traditional reactive patrol. All of the current and former neighborhood officers felt unprepared to generate their own agendas in the neighborhoods, since the new positions lacked the familiar structure of patrol shifts. Most of them mentioned liking the freedom of no longer being "slaves to the radio," but they felt a little intimidated when the "props of policing" were stripped away, props such as having permanent patrol hours and shifts, set days off, a protocol of quick-in and quick-out when responding to calls, and a squad car of their own.

The neighborhood officers repeatedly spoke of their unease during the first few months of their new jobs. They were accustomed to being dispatched to calls, with the expectation that they should secure a quick disposition and then move on, as is the nature of call-driven policing. However, officers who were burned out by the routinized nature of patrol echoed the sentiments of one current NPO, an African American man: "Welcome to the patrol officers' world, where the decisions are made without your input, without knowledge of the job, and the expectation [is] that you'll carry it through above and beyond the call of duty." He welcomed becoming a neighborhood officer and the chance to be more creative and flexible with his time. The NPO position carries the pressure of making a long-term commitment to a relatively small area. Some women and men, however, relished the idea of getting more intimately connected to an identifiable neighborhood. The first wave of neighborhood officers in particular spoke of the "tug" of community as being important. Familiarity between police and community, however, also brought its share of concerns. For instance, by the time neighborhood policing was in its third wave the officers felt more pressure to make a difference in the troubled districts. This concern, expressed by both former and serving NPOs, is captured in the comment by a current NPO, a white man: "You feel like you have the whole weight of the neighborhood on your back."

Furthermore, residents did not always welcome the newcomers; often, they did not know what to make of a permanent foot patrol officer "living" in their neighborhood. And the new officers frequently were just as confused about their roles as the residents. Bill, a white former NPO, described a situation he encountered early on: "[A] big-time young male drug dealer said to me, 'Officer, I tells you what, I'm just gonna hate you. You're one of them smart cops. We just never know what you're thinking.' " The kind of ongoing, daily, noncriminal encounters with residents expected of NPOs ran contrary to the "quick-in, quick-out" style of traditional patrolling by squad car.

All of the officers agreed with a colleague that neighborhood positions were "hard to get used to initially, you just wake up and you're still pretty much in that reactive law enforcement kind of mode, and all of a sudden when you get out of the car and start walking, that car's getting farther and farther away!" This same officer, although initially trepidatious, grew to love being an NPO and said at the end of his assignment, "I went through a period of withdrawal when I was promoted out of the neighborhood because [you don't] have that positive contact with citizens anymore when you are back on regular patrol."

The perceived second-class status of foot patrol and neighborhood policing in general was linked to a major shift in thinking about policework. William, an African American and a former NPO, explained:

> The neighborhood position was seen as undesirable initially because it
> was seen as the chief's latest experiment. And also, it was not embraced

because police officers, like in most organizations, are creatures of habit, we're even more so, for very practical reasons, and this was breaking the norm. It was viewed as a real touchy-feely way of policing, that NPOs were not really doing policing, they're kind of like Officer Friendly.

The stigma attached to the social worker image of neighborhood policing meant that most members of the department were not interested in trying the new approach. In fact, patrol officers were typically loath to pursue the neighborhood positions. Foot patrol seemed antithetical to the nature of policework as they knew it, call driven and aggressive. Current and former NPOs were very cognizant of patrol officers' disdain. One advantage of such a lack of interest, however, was to make it much easier for officers who had very little time on the force to become NPOs, since no one with more seniority was competing against them. As one of the early community officers, Scott, pointed out: "It was an easy position to get, even with only two years on [the] force, because that was before NPO was popular. So, a lot of people thought of it as social work, and you're not doing real policing." Thus, the transition to a neighborhood police program in Jackson City has been characterized by confusion over the new role and conflict between patrol and community police officers. It has also been marked, however, by some enthusiasm, expressed by some officers, about the opportunity to do something different that might have a lasting impact on communities and crime.

Social Worker or Crimefighter? NPOs' Perceptions

Time and again in the interviews, questionnaires, and fieldwork encounters, the current and former NPOs talked or wrote about the pejorative labels and mockery that seemed to appear whenever patrol officers mentioned community policing. More than half of the neighborhood officers admitted that they, too, laughed about the new approach or dismissed the idea until they had experienced it themselves. Patrol officers harbored the perception that NPOs were not "real" police. I explored whether this perception made sense among the NPOs and if they thought of themselves as social workers or crimefighters. Most *current* officers were very quick to assert that they were police first and foremost and that they would always enforce the laws. Without exception, however, the serving NPOs said that although law enforcement undergirded their work they drew upon many different resources to do their jobs, and some of these included the skills and activities associated with social workers.

The *former* NPOs, in contrast, were much more likely to expand on the social-work aspects of the job. The women of this group in particular viewed social work as a defining feature of the position. It is probable that the former officers felt "safer" in admitting the existence and importance of the social-work aspect, since they were no longer in the NPO position.

> I think you do far more than enforcing the laws as an NPO. You're parenting, and you're social-working. You're thinking more about first aid possibilities. You're a community organizer. You're looking at physical environmental things. You *never* do that in patrol. It is very unlikely that you would look for ways to make neighborhoods safer. (Terry, white woman, former NPO)

It seemed as though the newest officers tried the hardest to address and fight the negative stereotype that NPOs were merely doing social work. Both men and women who were currently community officers stressed law enforcement. The female former NPOs, however, were the most up-front about the components of the job related to social work. For example, in thinking about her early days as a neighborhood officer, Andrea, a former NPO (white woman), described how aggressive she had planned to be in order to decrease the stigma associated with "doing social work" in the neighborhoods:

> I initially went out there, even announced this to the board members of the community center, that I wasn't gonna be any kind of social worker. I said I am out here to do *policework* and *not* social work.

Andrea went on to explain that this stance softened as she learned her job and the neighborhood's needs:

> [M]y denial of the social-work aspect came back to haunt me . . . I was doing more social work than I ever expected. . . . [S]ome days this was rewarding and some days, like policework, it was really frustrating. . . . [A]t least with patrol you're there and then you can leave and not worry.

In the everyday world, there is often an assumption that women are drawn to people-oriented jobs and thus excel in positions that create and maintain emotional connections. Men, on the other hand, are often seen as more naturally suited to aggressive and competitive activities. This was the pattern with neighborhood policing in Jackson City. Women were drawn to, or at least acknowledged, the job's social-work aspects, whereas men unreservedly steered clear of this informal style of policework. However, not all of the female former NPOs displayed a social worker style. In the second wave of neighborhood officers, for example, one woman followed another female NPO who had used a softer style. Residents criticized the newcomer for her tougher approach. One of her initiatives was to publish a neighborhood newsletter that included a column on criminal happenings and arrests. Some residents approved because it informed them about local events; others saw the column as an intrusion into their privacy. However, feelings about toughness could run both ways. A woman who had been a neighborhood officer heard from patrol, "You are too nice; you should have kicked more ass down there."

The male NPOs (both current and former) addressed the social-work image in different ways. They did *not* want to be seen as doing "women's work." Thus, the men tended to justify their involvement in service or social-work activities by emphasizing the connection to law enforcement. One former NPO, a black man, explained:

> I did not want to be utilized as a social worker because I wasn't out there to solve people's problems. I wanted them to solve their own problems. I took it upon myself to try to guide them, use techniques or types of strategies that would get these people to work things out on their own; I'd give them resources. But if they had to do it themselves, they felt it was their project without relying on me or calling me on the phone, "I got this problem . . ." I didn't want that. You'd still, however, get people who called because of their plumbing, their pipes broke. (Keith)

Another NPO, a white man, responded in a similar vein:

> I was always more of a pro-police type presence. I would be in a squad car in uniform and it was known that I was a police officer first and [if] I could help or assist in a situation in another way, I was there to do that also as long as it didn't interfere with my job. I set guidelines; in the neighborhood position you have so much latitude in what you can do. And you can stretch yourself so thin where you become ineffective, I feel. When you try to do so much and try to solve so many problems . . . you're not getting anywhere and you're just touching base here and there. So that's why I tried to keep a more police perspective rather than getting into social work or counseling. But you still wear those hats. I mean, there's no way around that. I'd spend the time, I'd try to do as much as I felt I could, but there was a gray line I didn't want to get near. So I try to talk to them as much as I could. Then I'd refer them or try to hook them up with qualified persons, social workers, counselors, or

someone like that, people who were far more experienced and knowl-
edgeable. (Garth)

The interview data raised a question: If the neighborhood officer position
was a "feminized" aspect of macho policing, how would men manage their masculinity? In the interviews and fieldwork, both women and men addressed the
issue by giving information that demonstrated their competency. Data that I
gathered on career histories demonstrated that the men who requested an NPO
position had a background in traditional, "macho" policework. Most of the men
who were former or serving neighborhood officers had previous (or ongoing)
experience with elite law enforcement units, such as the SWAT team, drug and
gang squads, undercover detail, and hostage negotiation team. These specialty
positions were very well known, and the male officers were eager to tell me and
members of the research team about this part of their background, often before
we asked for the information.

What the male officers revealed is in accord with similar research that followed men who entered other traditionally female professions such as nursing.[1]
Male nurses recognized that others could see their choice of career as effeminate. They expressed some reservations about their work, such as the fear of
being perceived as unmanly. During interviews, the male nurses explicitly pro-
claimed their heterosexuality to the researchers by mentioning their wives or
children or displaying their wedding rings. The men were attracted to the more
dangerous and risky positions within nursing, favoring emergency room work,
assisting with surgical procedures, and learning new technologies. Female
nurses, on the other hand, were more likely to favor patient care and pediatrics.
In my research with the NPOs in Jackson City, the male officers were similarly
motivated. They mentioned choosing policing for its excitement twice as often
as the female officers did. Like the male nurses, they also engaged in impression
management about their masculinity, stressing their macho experience and de-
tailing their credentials. The male NPOs deliberately wove some mention of
their heterosexual status into the interviews and fieldwork, usually offering information about their female dating partners, wives, and children.

My data also revealed that the female NPOs had two very different responses to competency- and gender-based assumptions about skill. Those who
were single or no longer had to care for children followed "macho" career paths,
similar to those of "career-motivated" men in the department. Although the
women were reluctant to initiate conversations about their experiences and earlier participation in elite law enforcement squads, once asked they spoke openly.
The interviews revealed that many of them had macho experience before becoming NPOs. However, this was not always the case. Several women spoke of

being drawn to neighborhood policing for reasons other than promotion or career advancement. For example, an African American from the first wave of NPOs was committed to racial justice and cultural diversity, which sparked her interest in community policing.

The issues were different for lesbian officers. In interviews and in conversations in the field, they tended to exaggerate either their femininity or masculinity. This dichotomy is well documented in the work on women and policing conducted by Susan Martin (1980): police*women* emphasize the feminine aspects of being an officer, by emphasizing female identity, passivity, weaker leadership ability and less autonomy, and flirtatiousness; *police*women, on the other hand, downplay femininity and strive for more-masculine characteristics, such as leadership skills, aggressiveness, and occupational competence and achievement. In Jackson City, the emphasis depended on the intended "audience" more than on any favored or stereotyped skill. For example, if lesbian officers were assigned to a tough, criminally active neighborhood, their actions depended on how comfortable or expert they were in using aggressive law enforcement techniques. This, in turn, reflected what kind of police style they had while in patrol positions. At the same time, though, they were aware of the need to use gender-based skills that drew on their female status because of the receptivity, or lack thereof, of the residents. Some local people sought a more nurturing and empathic response from them because the officers were women. This more flexible, androgynous style is reminiscent of the "inventive role" in Lynn Zimmer's (1986) study of female prison workers. Women in this role do not evaluate themselves as being equal to or less capable than the male officers; rather, they view themselves as being an asset to the criminal justice system because of their more finely developed communication skills and respect for suspects or prisoners. But it was not always clear what behavior was linked to gender and what was linked to sexual orientation. The lesbian NPOs' behavior might also be inextricably connected to others' perceptions and their own levels of experience and skill, thus having little to do with gender and sexuality.

Part of the reason the neighborhood officers emphasized their competency in previous aggressive policework was that they anticipated a mocking reception from their patrol colleagues. In the interview and fieldwork data, current and former NPOs discussed at length their struggle to remain connected to patrol while trying to carry out their new responsibilities. By 1996, community policing in Jackson City had existed for a decade, and the program had expanded from the original six to twelve neighborhoods. Even after ten years, however, uncertainty remained on both sides as to how NPOs did or did not complement patrol officers. There was tension between patrol and neighborhood officers for at least two reasons: first, there was a simple misunderstanding of the work demands of the new jobs; second, there was a tendency to see the new positions as stepping-stones to promotion. Patrol officers struggled with the issue of promotion because they often did not believe that the NPOs were conducting "real policework." Instead, patrol officers often believed that their colleagues attended community meetings all day long and had the luxury of working whenever they wanted to, since they could structure their own hours. There were no formal evaluations for either patrol or neighborhood officers. Accordingly, the NPOs were not subject to any greater standard of accountability for their time or for how they set their priorities in the neighborhood than were patrol officers. This situation is being reexamined under the leadership of the new chief of police. Not only did the current and former NPOs believe that their counterparts harbored these perceptions, but the majority of patrol officers interviewed raised these matters as well. (This issue will be discussed more fully in Chapter 5.) The conflict was heightened by observations from the second and third waves of NPOs, including the current neighborhood officers, that a disproportionate number of NPOs had been promoted in the last several years. Even though there was some legitimacy to these assertions, it is in the very nature of neighborhood policing to facilitate standing out, and being noticed by promotion panels.

The NPOs were very aware of the patrol officers' feelings:

> I don't know how things have changed now, but when we started, it was like, oh, another new program from the chief, and patrol believed NPOs weren't gonna do anything. So that was something that was really hard for me because I felt like we had no credibility. People would make snide comments and stuff. And even if it wasn't directed towards me, it was still hurtful. It was really hard to not only feel like you were out there exposed, but then feel like the rest of the department was not supporting you. Although I didn't feel any personal lack of support from the patrol officers in my beat because they saw me do stuff, . . . the general attitude was that NPOs don't do anything. . . . [I]t also depends on the neighborhood officer, there are some NPOs that were more popular or more well-liked than others . . . people just like to second-guess new programs. But it was really hard for me to be in that position away from officers who I'd worked with, my classmates and stuff, and feel like there was very little support from the rest of the department in general. (Pam, white lesbian, former NPO)

> There was a lot of anger when the NPO positions were first created because we were chronically understaffed to begin with, and when they took this chunk of officers out of the patrol bureau, it created a lot of

hard feelings. That's pretty much gone away. Most of the officers, as much as they bitch about it, they'll tell you that they like having the NPO in the neighborhood. And you'll hear right away, generally, if the NPO is a problem. (Hank, white man, former NPO)

By the time my research project began the NPO program was well established, and the new chief carried on the existing policies. He envisioned that community policing would spread to become a department-wide priority. In fact, everyone on the force had become much more familiar with neighborhood policing, and an increasing number of former NPOs were now upper-level managers and supervisors. This helped legitimize community policing positions among the top administrators of the department. It was also clear that the current NPOs benefited from patrol's now lengthy exposure to neighborhood policing. They experienced greater understanding and cooperation from their colleagues, particularly so among the NPOs who proactively sought liaisons or connections with patrol officers assigned to their beat. There were still some problems, however. One female current NPO remarked:

I think it depends on the officer. Officers like Daniel see the benefits. And there's other officers that are by nature more reluctant to change, they see us more as like social workers, and that we're doing a job that we shouldn't be doing. [I asked if that bothered her.] No, those officers' attitudes don't bother me one way or another. But I think those officers are in the minority. At the beginning of the program, there were more who were very hesitant about the whole idea. Patrol officers did not like that NPOs were not responsible for answering the radio all the time, being able to change your hours, being able to play basketball. It sounded like we're not doing the job. But now a lot of them see the benefits. . . . [T]here are a lot of good officers in this department and some get more visibility. But there are some that do their job very, very well, but do it quietly, so they don't get a lot of recognition, and there's other ones that do a very good job but do it in a manner that's different than what some managers like. And I can see that they might be overlooked and not given the chance, just because of somebody's perception (and wouldn't get [an] NPO position except for seniority). I think that a person should be able to get to grow into the position of NPO. If they don't do the job, then they should be moved out, which takes work because management has to be able to back up why they're taking a person out.

These words raise an important issue: some NPOs performed as well as or better than others, but often their modesty prevented them from making supervisors and administrators aware of the facts. This meant that the braggarts, more prominent and thus more closely associated with neighborhood policing, were rewarded. Men tended to emphasize their external accomplishments, whereas women talked more about their internal satisfaction with how the neighborhood was doing, which for them translated into more-personal "rewards."

One strategy NPOs used to gain more respect and understanding from patrol officers was to increase their law enforcement visibility. More than half of the current and former male neighborhood officers, although none of the female NPOs, suggested that acceptance and respect were more likely to be accorded to individuals who built a reputation for answering dispatchers' calls for service in their neighborhoods. This made patrol more aware that community officers were doing something besides attending meetings and playing games with children—they could hear over the radio that an NPO was taking a call.

> I think an NPO is much more apt to be accepted because you are doing a lot of patrol functions in terms of answering calls for service. What really doesn't help is, there are some NPOs who, and I'll be very frank with you, nobody sees or hears from. And they're not answering calls for service in their neighborhoods. . . . Some NPOs view the position as a place to hide, and they can kind of make their own hours, because there is flexibility. Or the other thing is that sometimes you can get "meetinged out," meaning you're never available for calls for service or to service your neighborhood because you're so busy tied up in meetings. . . . [I]t's up to each NPO to develop a working relationship with the officers you work with . . . I mean, you've gotta take your share of calls, and then patrol will be glad to take their share. (Evan, white man, current NPO)

Despite the interest in forging stronger connections, relations between NPOs and patrol officers remained uneasy. Many former and current neighborhood officers described the pejorative ways in which their colleagues continued to characterize them:

> Patrol never lets up. From day one, till the time you leave, the jabs are never-ending; they never stop. Patrol officers believe that if you've left patrol, you don't do policework anymore, and you're never there, and you never take calls . . . just a whole array of suspicions that you're out there doing something but nobody knows what or where or when. Mean-

while, patrol thinks they are the only Dirty Harrys of the department. (Garth, white man, former NPO)

Again, this mean-spiritedness may stem in part from professional envy, based on the patrol officers' perception that community policing positions were tied to promotion within the department. The NPOs had a greater chance to shine because they were better known and more visible to management and city residents. But worthy candidates for promotion among patrol officers often got overshadowed by NPOs, causing even more bad feelings:

> Although NPOs do a lot of good out there, it makes them much more likely to be recognized for what they're doing . . . than the patrol officers, . . . many of the patrol officers are doing the same things but don't get any credit for it. I think the spotlight tends to be on the NPO. It can't hurt your chances for promotion unless you burn a few bridges along the way. (Pam, white lesbian, former NPO)

At the same time, however, promoting neighborhood officers served an educative function, giving greater visibility to the position's varied activities and roles.

> [I]n the last couple of announcements of vacancies, there's been an abundance of people who put in, so now I think everybody wants that challenge and that change. And it could be for two reasons, one, the direction the department is going, and then also, a lot of the last promotions were former NPO. And so I think people are understanding that it's broadening your horizons because you're doing something, not just policing, but you're also being a liaison to different organizations, you're a spokesperson, you're fine-tuning your investigative skills because most of the time they will send cases back to you and let you do the investigations. So obviously, it helps you develop, it helps you supervise things because you do your own projects and so you have to work and coordinate, and I think that's good for whatever position you want or [for] promotion. (Wendy, white lesbian, former NPO)

> It seems to fit right into going to detective because you're doing follow-up cases, you learn a lot about resources and how to utilize those resources, how to find certain resources, and you could make those work to your benefit. . . . [T]hat's also part of being a detective because it takes more than just going out and doing follow-up investigation, you gotta also utilize the resources out there because there might be one organiza-

tion that has information or one agency that can help your case, and you just gotta know how to use those resources. (Keith, black man, former NPO)

Neighborhood officers used other strategies to educate patrol on their expansive duties. For instance, a third of the NPOs changed their hours to increase their visibility. Several explained that if they worked nights in uniform, patrol officers *had* to see them. However, most NPOs agreed that, with the typical patrol officers who worked the day shift and the graveyard shift (midnight to 6 A.M.), the jokes and derision never ended.

Despite jabs from their colleagues, all of the current and former community police officers firmly believed that they could strengthen patrol's law enforcement efforts. As they saw it, NPOs had a deeper understanding and a more intimate knowledge of the residents than patrol could gain during call-driven shifts. As Helen, a white current NPO, asserted: "We are the eyes and ears of the neighborhood, along with probation. This can help patrol."

There were times, though, when patrol resented answering calls in the neighborhood, asserting that it was the NPO's domain. When on dispatched calls, patrol officers would wonder where the NPOs were. Their absence fueled the suspicion that NPOs did nothing but go to meetings. The patrol officers' attitude frustrated their colleagues even more; the NPOs believed that they *were* hard at work, even if "work" entailed talking with children at a bike rodeo or having a cup of coffee with the members of the business association. Neighborhood officers stated repeatedly that these social activities were important for addressing the long-term health of communities. Yet, they were continually discounted by patrol, since they did not fall within traditional policing responsibilities and duties.

With patrol, they had the attitude, there's an NPO here, let him handle it. But it might also be that it's hard to step into something where somebody might already be doing something and you get in the middle of a mess that you don't know anything about, so it works both ways. (Linc, white man, former NPO)

It depends how "educated" the beat officer is. . . . [I]f the NPO is there every day and answers calls and goes to calls when there's a fight, then things will be okay. But many think it's basically a bunch of window dressing, and that you picked the NPO because it accommodates your schedule, you can take off any time you want to, and they will have this attitude until they see you taking calls and being on the front line every day. If they never see you they will think you are in meetings all day and have the social worker–window dresser attitude. (Matt, white man, current NPO)

By showing up on the "front lines," particularly at night, community police officers demonstrated that they were law enforcers, not window dressing. Perhaps understandably, patrol officers grew frustrated if they never saw their colleagues. Often, they measured an NPO's quality by how many calls they had to answer in her or his neighborhood. There was a false assumption that patrol calls should decrease in districts that had an NPO, since there was now one officer assigned exclusively to handle the area. When patrol officers found themselves still answering the bulk of the district's calls for service, they became further disillusioned about the role of the neighborhood officers, and NPOs in turn felt their lack of support. As one former NPO said in a typical comment:

You can't be everywhere in twenty-four hours. Problems were gonna happen. Basically, if you weren't there when they had that problem at that time, then the beat officers feel like they're taking calls in your neighborhood. I think they forget sometimes, that we are all in the same department, and it is just as much their duty to go out there and take calls as it is my duty. (Keith)

Moreover, if patrol officers never left their cars to get to know their beats on foot, they never experienced the advantage of knowing a neighborhood and its residents more intimately. Carol, a current NPO, believed that patrol's dismissal and denunciation of community officers was most typical of the graveyard shift, since it was then that NPOs were least likely to be working and thus least likely to come into contact with their colleagues. She explained:

[T]o be quite honest, [graveyard-shift] officers have very little respect for most of the NPOs. They never see them, they're not there during the night, and that is the time when the stuff happens. There's not a lot of information sharing between the NPO and the people that are out there at night that really could utilize that information. And they just feel like it's this black hole that NPOs go into, and take time off whenever they want and slough off and really aren't held accountable. And, after all, night shift is like this whole other breed of cop.

After the first few years of the community policing program in Jackson City, the NPOs began to stagger and adjust their work hours to respond to the needs of the neighborhood, as well as to their personal needs. Although this meant that some NPOs worked some nights, usually they did not work the graveyard shift. That which patrol officers did not see, they believed did not exist. This perception, or lack of it, reinforced their belief that the neighborhood officers were getting a free ride. NPOs found this assessment untenable, since the majority felt that they did vastly more work than did patrol officers. On this point, a former NPO, an African American woman, added:

> There was a lot of resentment from patrol, they believed because we had to set our own hours and because they never saw us, we didn't do our jobs. They made this complaint that everything was so cushy, cushy, lovely, lovely, and it really wasn't, because we were doing everything. (Katie)

Not all patrol officers were unsupportive of or ignorant about their colleagues' goals. Some expressed a desire to do more meaningful policing, similar to the NPOs' duties. Although a number of patrol officers tried to get out of their cars more often or be proactive, the structure of call-driven, rapid response policing interfered with these efforts and led to frustration. The NPOs were well aware of the patrol officers who "bought into" the proactive and personal style of community policing, and they appreciated their dissatisfaction.

> A lot of patrol officers can't get out of their car. Some tried. I myself did prior to becoming an NPO, but every time I was in the middle of trying to do something proactive, dispatch would send me out on a lousy barking-dog call. . . . [I]t gets real frustrating and dispatch hasn't got any idea of what's going on and neither does the citizen who wants the dog to shut up. There are some cops that just sit in their cars and wait for the calls to come and others that try to do things, but it was a real frustrating combination to me when I was a patrol officer. (Linc, white man, former NPO)

Those neighborhood officers who had already tried to act like NPOs while they were still in patrol believed that this experience made their transition to community policing much easier.

> As a beat officer, I had a reputation for being the type of officer who would carry things through all the way to the end and not leave any portion of it undone, and sometimes that would annoy the people that I dragged with me, saying is that really necessary, isn't that someone else's

responsibility. This prepared me for the NPO position. (Carol, white woman, current NPO)

Overall, the officers' thoughts reveal an ambivalence about each other's roles that has more to do with the structure of policing than with any direct antagonism toward individuals. Although their activities were often invisible to patrol officers, the NPOs felt as though they were working harder and longer than they ever had in patrol. Yet, their absence mystified and exasperated the patrol officers, particularly those who were already hostile to the social-work aspect of neighborhood policing.

Negotiating Conflict and Coordination

Given the potential for antipathy between neighborhood and patrol officers, all of the current and former NPOs recognized the need for building greater cooperation and understanding. Hank, a current NPO (white man), explained that patrol officers could "be your friends or your enemies; they're part of your neighborhood, just like the mailman, and the fireman." Some community officers actively pursued stronger relationships with patrol by encouraging them to join in walking the neighborhood. These efforts met with more success and greater interest from patrol officers when there appeared to be a law enforcement need. Increased interaction with NPOs also reflected the personal style and interest of patrol officers. During our fieldwork, many of them expressed a desire to break away from the monotony of the call-driven routine. (Note that these patrol officers had the most contact with neighborhood officers.) Since most of the serving and former NPOs talked about the isolation and alienation of working solo, their loneliness motivated them to come up with appealing reasons for their colleagues to work with them.

The circumstances in which patrol officers left their cars and walked with NPOs reflected a mutual interest in carrying out more traditional crimefighting actions, however, rather than serving an educative function, such as learning more about neighborhood officers. Regardless of the catalyst for conducting joint activities, a positive side effect was that the process *did* teach patrol officers more about the realities of neighborhood policing. In their descriptions of walking the beat with NPOs, what was most revealing was that the patrol officers promoted the need for a greater law enforcement presence in the neighborhood. This may, however, have been no more than a rationalization for walking around. An emphasis on law enforcement would reinforce the crimefighting image that was more likely to be associated with patrol and less likely to be associated with neighborhood policing.

Patrol officers got out of their cars for a variety of reasons. For example, one often walked with Barbara, a former NPO, when she spoke of the drug deals occurring in back hallways or in basements and emphasized that she wanted other officers with her for safety when checking buildings. Christine, another former NPO (white lesbian), worked with patrol officers when she needed help with plainclothes surveillance in a park in her neighborhood. Tony, a white current NPO, described his joint activities with patrol this way:

> I feel I have to maintain some type of friendly posture and attitude with people in the 'hood, not throwing officer safety out the window or any-thing, in order to get things done. In most cases, I'll use the task force people and the beat officers as my muscle when I need it . . . then the residents will continue to treat me well because I am not the bad guy. And there's other ways that I can play little head games with people so it comes to my benefit. . . . [A]nything is a useful tool.

In this case, the neighborhood officer cast his colleagues in the role of law enforcement "heavy" so as not to lose the residents' support. This strategy was more likely to be undertaken by lazy NPOs, who cared little about their neigh-borhood, or by newer NPOs; it was also most common among men. The newer NPOs' reliance on patrol officers indicates that it took a while on the job to find a balance between social work and crimefighting.

One former NPO, Pam, a white lesbian, talked about the strong support she received from day patrol officers. She attributed it to the aggressive law enforcement stance she took in her neighborhood. She also greatly respected the patrol officers for what they could teach her, and said she actively sought their guidance rather than setting herself apart from them. This situation was atypical; it could indicate that she was young, one of the first six community officers, and struggling to be embraced by the police subculture early in her career. Pam explained:

> I never had a problem with day patrol and I think it started out because they were happy that I was willing to take calls. But we really worked well together, and I think they were much more of the feeling that, you know, that there were big separations between the newer officers and the older officers. And the new officers, most of the time, had college degrees, and so that was intimidating to the older officers. And my feel-ing was always, they've been doing the job, and they know more about it than I do, so let me learn from them. And once they realized that I was interested in learning from them and stuff, that barrier sort of disap-

peared. And I think the day officers, much more sometimes than the newer officers, see us as "all blue," sort of the phrase, all cops, and we back each other up.

However, most neighborhood officers did not experience the same strong bond with daytime patrol. Pam's situation may have been different because of her concerted efforts to be accepted by the older, male day shift while in a stigmatized new position.

Thus, the NPOs' lingering perception that their jobs were misunderstood and discounted propelled them to pursue various strategies in their attempts to remain connected to others on the force. Links between neighborhood and patrol officers were more solid when the need for law enforcement action was emphasized.

Negotiating Stigmatizing Images

Another way to impression-manage the perception that the neighborhood position was weak, or feminine, was to focus on universally recognized "male" activities. As stated earlier, the fieldwork and interview data revealed that NPOs' choice of activities was driven by patrol officers' perceptions that they were not "real" (masculine) crimefighters, but had turned in their badges to become social workers. This was difficult for male NPOs, in particular, to negotiate, since the nature of community policing reflected a less aggressive, pro-social emphasis. One current NPO, a white man, explained the resultant contradiction between impression and reality.

> I think patrol is expecting law enforcement out of me, but the reality is
> that since I've been out here, it's been easily 60 percent social work and
> follow-up investigations and meetings with Joining Forces for Families
> activities, neighborhood association, etc. Hey, I've been in law enforce-
> ment eighteen years now, and to me this is a break. . . . Granted, the
> reason I selected to be a cop to begin with was that the military taught
> me that no one day is the same . . . you might deal with the same players,
> but there's always a little different twist or something else that's gonna
> be different about that scenario, and that's what I like, constant change
> and excitement. . . . If I want to do the real cop stuff and get into guns
> and all that other stuff, I'm on the SWAT team. I've been on that team
> now for four years. I shot a guy last year on a SWAT call; I've done a lot.
> And I still continue to do that, I'm available for the high-risk warrants,

and whatever types of stuff, and training the other department members. So, the social-work aspects of this job [are] a welcome change. (Tony)

What was revealing in these words, and consistent with the comments of other men in interviews and fieldwork, was that no sooner had they acknowledged the social-work aspect of being a community officer than they pointed to their previous "manly" work and other masculine background experiences (such as the military, the SWAT team, or time spent with other police departments). Tony, for instance, was quick to say he shot a man while on a SWAT call. The jokes and examples that male NPOs used when talking about their work in the neighborhoods had a distinctly masculine flavor. On the other hand, the fieldwork and interview data revealed that women's descriptions and language focused more on building interpersonal connections. Apart from reflecting unique officer styles and personalities, these different emphases may also have simply reflected variations in neighborhoods' needs. The fieldwork observations did suggest, however, that patrol officers often joined female NPOs to socialize and gossip in program development neighborhoods and to play a supportive law enforcement role in criminally active neighborhoods.

The language used by the men in their interviews carried a metaphoric emphasis on action and aggressive enforcement, with attention paid to differentiating between good guys and bad guys. In one example of "male talk" by NPOs, a serving officer remarked:

We need to bring the hammer down, now, and start writing twenty-dollar citations for No Parking. . . . In some cases, for the people who aren't with the program and want to dabble with selling drugs or something, they need a knock on the head every now and then to get them focused on that this isn't the place for you to be doing this, we need you to go elsewhere to do it. (Tony, white, current NPO)

And a white former NPO pointed out:

It doesn't matter how bright you are, how smart you are, patrol's gonna hurt you more than they're gonna help you, in terms of swimming with some of the sharks in our place. But I found a way to do it, yet really challenging the thinking of some of the more traditional-thinking officers. Because within the context of community policing, you gotta believe there is an awful lot of crimefighting that does take place, and the bottom line is it's a lot of hard work, and hey, you old traditional

crimefighter cops, if you want to do it, here's your chance to . . . there are
a lot of warrants to service and people to arrest in neighborhoods. (Bill)

On the other hand, the women we interviewed spent more time describing programs and family problems in the neighborhoods. They highlighted the different interactions they had with various agencies working with local residents.
One black former NPO, Barbara, who typed a neighborhood newsletter herself,
discussed the limitations of clerical support in the neighborhood (there were
no computers in her office or the community center). But at the same time,
Barbara did not want the patrol officers to think her neighborhood position
consisted of glorified secretarial or stereotypically feminine work. Accordingly,
she made sure that patrol officers and any passing members of the drug and
gang task forces saw her out doing "real" policework. Nonetheless, Barbara still
proudly described her indoor working environment as being very homey; she
was quite attached to her office, especially since she and her husband had
painted it and decorated it with furniture from their own home. Men never
referred to their offices with such affection.

The interview and fieldwork data from the former and current NPOs revealed striking gender differences in what, specifically, the women and men
planned to do. For instance, when asked about their priorities and activities in
the neighborhood, the male NPOs (current and former) again framed their issues using crimefighting imagery and examples. Rarely did they offer names or
provide personal examples of individual or family struggles. Rather, the men's
words revolved around enforcement issues. For instance, Hank, who took over
his NPO position from Lisa, stressed (with apparent disapproval) how their
priorities were different: whereas he emphasized street-level enforcement, she
emphasized building rapport and relationships with the owners of retail stores;
whereas he emphasized street crime, such as that involving drugs, she emphasized retail theft and sought to establish more personal connections with the
potential victims. Hank said at one point in the interview, "On occasion, Lisa
was *forced* into that kind of policing," meaning street-level enforcement (emphasis mine).

Some officers believed their personal interests influenced which neighborhood they chose. Matt, a former NPO, observed that "a woman might want to
work with kids and a man may want to get the drug dealers out of the neighborhood, but then it probably doesn't matter as long as the officer picks the right
neighborhood where he or she can do the things they wanna do." Steve, another
former NPO, left his position before the three-year term was up. He recalled,

I was ready to go. It had actually gotten to the point out there where the
drug dealing had declined a lot, and there really wasn't much of anything

going on . . ., and it just got boring for me driving around in circles out there, and I guess I was bored with it because there wasn't anything going on. I wanted to get back in patrol work where I could be more active.

Tony, a serving neighborhood officer, bragged, "I am up to my ass in arresting people, it's needed and I keep very busy." A black current NPO, Hugh, thought he had an enforcement mentality; he saw this as good for his neighborhood, which he believed to be very disorganized and plagued by drug dealers. He routinely patrolled on foot with employees of a local private security company, TREC. I asked what the acronym stood for. Hugh replied that although it was derived from the initials of the four men who started the company, the NPOs now said it stood for either Tactical Response Emergency Crew or To Rid Enemy Crap.

One of the serving neighborhood officers, an African American named Wallace, took over his position from a well-liked, respected, hard-working female NPO. His interest in the job reflected a desire to work outdoors; Wallace also liked the male camaraderie involved in working with the department's special drug or gang task forces and with the private security officers. He freely admitted, as well, to a liking for "being wooed" by the single moms in the neighborhood and for getting coffee, food, and flirtatious attention from the women. He compared himself to his female predecessor in this way:

> I love to be outside, seeing people. Terry knew everybody's name, where they lived, how many kids they had, the mother's maiden name, and you know, I just haven't been that skilled, and she kept the office much cleaner. For me, filing reports, that's secondary. I love to be out, seeing people. And I get along with the women a lot better, too; the guys who live here are a little more doubting. The women are a lot more friendly.

Wallace also boasted that he "lets" the team of female probation-parole officers assigned to the neighborhood use his office so that they could "keep [it] nice and clean for me and neat." I will examine the neighborhood officers' activities and how they vary by gender more fully in Chapter 5.

The Disproportionate Representation of Women and People of Color

More and more men became interested in the neighborhood officer position, especially during the cusp of the second and third waves. Consequently, discerning the reasons behind this rise in popularity becomes important. Recall that when community policing was just beginning, only women or people of color were actively interested in becoming NPOs. Although Jackson City boasted of having the highest percentage of women in the country on its police force, their representation in upper-level management remained low. Yet many of the female officers were ambitious and sought opportunities for advancement. It is possible that the first wave of NPOs, already at the bottom of the organizational hierarchy in rank, gender, and race, had less to lose if community policing did not work out, and something to gain, at least potentially, if it did. Although some nontraditional officers did everything they could to fit in with the established, white male power base (see Martin 1994 for how this works in some police departments elsewhere), other non-traditional officers used creative means that deviated from the organizational norm. Taking on the position of neighborhood officer offered one such avenue.

It could also be that since the first wave achieved such success in their evaluations by the chief, the city, and the residents, the chief became even more enthusiastic about and committed to community policing. Consequently, the pioneer NPOs, by creating a new path to advancement, became role models for other ambitious, nontraditional officers. Perhaps this was one career trajectory where gender and race were not barriers to advancement. This could also help explain some of the backlash against "excessive promotions" of NPOs driven by officers who were not currently in neighborhood positions, since the NPOs were disproportionately women or people of color.

More men entered community policing, reflecting their presumption that serving as an NPO gave one a "glass escalator" ride to the next rank on the force. In her work on gender and occupations, Christine Williams (1992, 260) discovered that even though "women are eager to see men enter 'their' profession," they *do not* like how easily men advance once through the door. Within the Jackson City Police Department, as the number of male NPOs increased, and as some were promoted to supervise newer NPOs, the community policing program began to be viewed as more legitimate. A relatively young cohort of men now occupy high-ranking positions within the department, reflecting earlier promotions made by a supportive chief who valued community policing. These younger administrators were second-wave NPOs, and they became supervisors of second- and third-wave neighborhood officers. The chief rewarded the career risks they took before community policing positions were seen as desirable by more members of the rank and file. Other men followed suit, becoming neighborhood officers under the tutelage of male former NPOs, who are now upper-level managers.

This lessening of stigma may reflect patterns similar to those that Williams (1992) found in her research exploring men's entrance into female professions:

contrary to the experience of women seeking employment in male-dominated occupations, there was a *preference* for hiring men, and their token status was considered advantageous. In fact, in some cases, the more female-dominated the job, the greater the apparent preference granted to men. For instance, those in pediatrics might be told by managers and supervisors, "It's nice to have a man because it's such a female-dominated profession" (Williams 1992, 256). Likewise, male NPOs heard this kind of praise if they were being supervised by other men. Since community policing had the stigma of being thought of as "women's work" on the force, men sought out peer support in order to risk doing it. In fact, only one woman has been a supervisor of neighborhood police officers in Jackson City. Although the absence of female managers could reflect the larger reality that women have not attained many upper-level positions within most police departments, it could also be the case that men, especially those doing "unmanly" tasks, were more comfortable being supervised by other men. With same-sex supervision, the existing perception of the femininity of community policing would not be strengthened by female supervision of men doing so-called women's work.

Many of the men, but *not* the women, mentioned that they liked dealing with disenfranchised populations, such as the homeless, drunks, and the mentally ill. Steve, a white former NPO, remarked:

> I enjoy dealing with them; there's a lot of interesting personalities and characters and it's a lot of fun. . . . It really is a lot of fun, especially the chronically mentally ill, to deal with them repeatedly and learn more about them and what their habits are and what their problems are. . . .
> I get a lot of satisfaction from helping them from time to time.

What was interesting in the male NPOs' discussion of the special populations was that because such persons were less attached to conventional relationships and families, police officers exercised a stronger function of social control when dealing with them.

Under the new chief's leadership, new strategies were implemented to make it easier for patrol officers to take part in activities that were similar to neighborhood policing. Approaching "women's work" within a community policing context of problem solving, rather than aggressive crimefighting, could help destigmatize the duties for male NPOs. In 1996, one serving community officer explained that the chief's new plan was to instill the idea that neighborhood activities were beneficial to policework. "In the last couple of newsletters from the chief," the officer recalled, "he made it a point to highlight things that patrol officers are doing that are very similar to what NPOs are expected to do, and give them some well-earned credit, too." This strategy was wise; it rewarded patrol officers for doing things they may have believed were part only of community policing. By encouraging the whole department to "buy in" to the idea, the chief hoped to gain the cooperation of the rank and file. The strategy would also encourage patrol officers to think about community policing in a gender-neutral way, and it would build stronger connections between officers on foot in the neighborhoods and officers in squad cars.

"Doing Gender" Differently

No matter why men and women sought to become neighborhood officers, in conversation they stressed different aspects of the job and presented different goals and styles. Competing images of skills competence and gender concerns occurred simultaneously. Gender-role expectations and socialization experiences shaped most of the activities of the NPOs. Officers who wanted to be evaluated by occupational measures, not gender, stressed the neutral or masculine parts of the job, even if their daily focus in the neighborhood revolved around concerns more commonly seen as "women's work." The *residents* also projected certain competencies onto the officers or held expectations about the NPOs. These were based on how they perceived gender roles and gender-linked expertise, which might have nothing to do with the officers' own skills or priorities. From the interview and fieldwork data, it appeared that male NPOs had learned to delegate more. The men also avoided taking the job's emotional problems or stresses home with them. As Scott, a white former NPO, stated: "Initially, I was very intimidated and didn't know how I was going to do all this stuff, but after a while, I got pretty confident thinking, well, I don't have to do it, it's not my job to take care of everything, I need them to do it. And I learned to delegate things and not take them home with me and internalize them." Another white former NPO, Greg, echoed these sentiments: "I had to separate emotionally from the neighborhood. I lived near my neighborhood, I shopped there occasionally, so I thought it could be a problem; I could get too attached. But I never did bow to that. I never bowed to neighborhood expectations at the expense of my private life." African American men who had been NPOs reached the same conclusions. One of them, Keith, contended, "You gotta watch out and be firm and not compromise your beliefs. . . . [S]ometimes people can suck you in, and you start feeling sorry for people, and then you're gonna get burned."

At the same time, however, the male NPOs acknowledged that their work opened up an opportunity for them to learn or perfect new skills, such as better interpersonal communication. As Keith, a former NPO, sees it,

We deal with people, whether they're victims, witnesses, or suspects, and you have to treat them with some respect, and you have to let them know that I'm on your side [as a detective], I understand what's going on, and let them know you have feelings. I think that's the big thing. I think that [being an NPO] helped a lot because it developed my communication skills. It really helped me deal with interpersonal relationships, and it helped me understand people from what's going on in their lives as opposed to what I think should be going on in their lives.

A current NPO, Patrick, said:

Female officers, I have found, are more patient, and they communicate a lot more than male officers. Male officers will communicate to a point, but after a while, it's like, okay, we're gonna go with this program or we're not. We can learn from the women.

For their part, female NPOs acknowledged that they often had to resort to more aggressive means of establishing social control when verbal skills were not powerful enough for the situation.

A lot of times there's no choice but to fight. If we're going to the cement, we're all going together. True. But there's a lot of times where a good verbal skill helps ease the situation. . . . If you can think of a way to avoid a problem by talking—I've been in enough fights, I didn't need to be so brusque that I had to end up insulting people, I mean, that wasn't why I was put here. I'm just not into it. I just never was, and maybe I am not the perfect police officer because of that. Well, fine, I go to sleep at night and I can get up in the morning feeling okay about my job, even though I have to take people in and arrest them. I don't batter people unless it comes to the point that they're hurting me or someone else. When I can't get anywhere by talking, I know how to handle the situation a different way. (Lisa)

Because they got to know families and extended families so well, the female community officers, former and current, were frequently invited to share a meal with the residents or be a guest at one of their family get-togethers. They believed that accepting such invitations ultimately paid off, imbuing them with a sense of power, particularly the power to achieve good outcomes. One of the women said:

I went to a few things, so they're familiar with you, and they see you, and they say hi to you, and I like that. It makes me feel safe. It's my nature, I like to talk to people and deal with people, and I like to be helpful, too. And because being a police officer gives you a little more, you know. I mean if I want to call someone, I'm Police Officer So-and-So, they're probably going to listen to you a little more, so you have a little bit more . . . power, I mean you can do some things for people, if you wanted to. So, I like to feel that. It's not that I feel like I'm so power-ful, but at least I have something to offer. (Carlena)

Although most of the female NPOs raised this as an advantage, the preceding words were from a Latina officer. She may have received a bigger welcome from residents because of shared ethnicity and culture. Her experience brings to mind residents' receptivity toward male African American officers, discussed earlier in this chapter.

In contrast, men who had been NPOs had dissuaded residents from getting too close. Charlie, a white man, talked about his frustration with becoming too tied to the neighborhood's needs and expectations. He also sought to avoid becoming too responsive to the patrol officers:

I tried to vary my hours to what the patrol officers on the different shifts were telling me were hot times or problematic times, that's how I did it. And that was a downside, that was something that posed a problem for me. I felt compelled . . . to always be out there. I felt a sense of guilt, if something major happened in my neighborhood. Either I should have been out there on foot patrol, or I should have had some contact, or made my presence known, or had some inside information that this was going to happen. And that for me was a big problem. I spent probably twenty to thirty hours of my own time on work, be it paperwork, doing follow up, whatever.

Men talked more specifically about their good deeds and the corresponding payoffs. Most of the male current and former neighborhood officers said that their morale rose when they heard about or witnessed direct improvements in residents' attitudes toward police officers; the men liked feeling that they were on the "good team" for once. One NPO described how he solved a problem of frequent bicycle thefts by juveniles. The officer designed and coordinated a bike rodeo, in which boys and girls could "earn" bicycles and helmets donated by local merchants by performing odd jobs and doing well in school, thus building up "bike points" over a specified period. Parents and teachers also became in-

volved, because they had to document the children's activities. The officer recalled the satisfaction he received from the project:

> What happened is my bicycle theft problem disappeared pretty much,
> but the greater benefit was that a lot of the parents and relatives of kids
> who got bikes were from larger cities, and they would come up and talk
> to me on the street and say, all my contacts with the police have been
> negative, and you got my nephew a bike, and that's great. And everybody
> in the community checked in and got involved. (Scott)

Men and women had different ways of prioritizing their achievements as
NPOs, particularly in how they kept supervisors apprised of their work. Male
officers volunteered this information, whereas their female counterparts had to
be prompted. The men expressed more concern that their supervisors would
not know what they were doing, or how well things were going, unless they
made a special effort to keep them informed. Except for one woman, this concern was virtually absent in the interviews and fieldwork data with the female
NPOs. In observed encounters between NPOs and supervisors, the male officers
provided information about their activities, especially those concerning law enforcement; the female NPOs, however, typically asked the supervisors questions. The one exception was Suzanne, a white woman. She was the only former
neighborhood officer to leave the position after only one year of a three-year
term, and she was very frustrated and disillusioned. Having encountered racial
and gender barriers in connecting with residents, she spoke to her supervisors
so that they would be aware of the situation and could assist in developing
possible solutions. Suzanne felt her supervisors did not help her. The only former NPO to express any bitterness about her time in community policing, she
attributed a neighborhood officer's success to popularity, with African American
men particularly at an advantage. Suzanne believed that nonwhite persons in
her neighborhood preferred nonwhite NPOs. She watched black officers receive
warm support from adult residents for just walking around saying hello. Yet
Suzanne felt that although she worked extremely hard no one, except for some
of the children, seemed to appreciate her efforts. She also hated planning so
many activities (although children loved the outings she organized). In fact,
Suzanne concluded our interview by exclaiming, "I found out that I was not a
party planner!"

The issue raised here is not unique to community policing: men often seek
external acknowledgment and praise for their behavior; women just do whatever is necessary without fanfare. Research in the field of work and occupations
suggests that, when no formal evaluation criteria exist, men "toot their own

horn," being quite vocal about their accomplishments so that their supervisors are aware of their effort and successes. Many of the male NPOs talked about their performance in this manner. The words of Keith, an African American former NPO, indicate their thinking:

> The lieutenant is your supervisor, so I made it a point to let the lieutenant and the captain know what I was doing, what projects I was getting involved with, what information I had gotten about drugs, because it's good to keep them abreast of what's going on because a lot of times they're more focused on what's happening in the district on [the] patrol aspect, they don't have the time all the time to come down and see what you're up to, so I like to let them know what's going on so that, say, the chief or the deputy chief asks them, So what's going on in such and such a neighborhood? they would know, and you know, in that way you're kind of working with each other and they don't think you're just hanging out.

The men's efforts to keep supervisors informed could also reflect their awareness that other police officers trivialized the NPO position and believed that it involved little or no "real" policework. The male community officers wanted to claim their occupational status and publicize their efforts. Greg, another former NPO (white), talked about his strategy of letting others know he had not just disappeared in the neighborhood:

> I would put stuff in the department's daily bulletins so that patrol would know what was going on, especially those with permanent beats. And I would call patrol over if there was a certain situation they needed to be aware of, so depending on what the situation was, I'd try to involve them as much as possible.

Many officers, neighborhood and patrol alike, believed that promotions were tied to taking on the community policing position. This perception helps explain why NPOs, men in particular, were eager to keep their supervisors informed of their work in the neighborhoods. Greg explained:

> Initially, probably the thing that attracted me the most is that, you know, I will be up-front, part of the reason I went into neighborhood policing was I wanted to find avenues to better myself in this department. I'm a firm believer that the more things that you get involved in, the better that you see the entire picture and how the whole thing works. And

that's pretty indicative of me going into the detective bureau, and now into a supervisory position. . . . So initially it was for personal growth, within this organization. I also have a strong desire to get involved with younger people, with kids, and I saw Water Lane as a really good opportunity for me to because there were two hundred kids in just that neighborhood alone.

Gender differences also emerged in the striking pattern involving the *kinds* of activities that the male and female NPOs organized. (More detailed discussions of these activities will be found in Chapter 5.) The men talked primarily about the sports programs they began, directed, and played in themselves, as well as other recreational events they organized, such as camping, boating, and fishing trips. Several male NPOs had been featured in articles in the city's newspaper for the Little League team and other such programs that they developed; almost all of them were geared toward sports or recreation. One former community officer talked about how he would walk up to young teenagers and say, "Hey guys, how you doing? My name's Greg and I'm the new NPO. You mind if I quarterback for both sides?" Youngsters, particularly boys, were fascinated with sports and the officers' guns. A number of the men mentioned showing their firearms to the boys. Several male NPOs also wrote letters to companies and newspapers asking them to sponsor sports equipment for the youth programs.

Whenever the men were asked if these activities were open for girls' participation, they said that few showed an interest. The only story told about a girl in sports concerned one child who wanted to join the Little League team during the second wave of neighborhood policing. She was not good enough to make the club. When pressed, the officers provided more details about what activities were available for girls. The list included getting school supplies, jumping rope, and, several times, having them make get-well cards for nursing homes and help clean up the neighborhood. The available pursuits thus followed very traditional gender patterns: active, competitive programs for boys, and passive or less strenuous activities for girls; team sports for boys, and caring for the elderly and cleaning activities for girls.

With several exceptions, the female NPOs seemed less concerned about sports programs, although they were still not necessarily promoting gender-neutral activities for girls. One former neighborhood officer, Carlena, flatly stated that it was not their job to get involved with recreational pursuits. But some of the female NPOs did try to stimulate interest among the girls, since they felt that going through the children was an ideal way to reach out to the parents. However, except for some soccer teams, the programs that existed for girls were minimal and often stereotypically feminine: sewing, Girl Scouts, and gardening. In one of the neighborhoods with a female officer, though, there was some talk of beginning a new computer club that targeted girls as members.

This picture of the male NPOs' daily routines in the neighborhoods contrasts sharply with how female officers described their activities. Terry's account is quite representative:

> You have to make your day happen. It is a very loose position. You have to be creative. You have to be a goal setter. All management said to us was, "You will just figure it out, and it'll just happen." You have to have some markers, be able to measure it for yourself, so you can answer people who want to know "How's it going out there?" They might not see you for a month. You may be out there every day and not even come downtown to the department. Or you come down here and everybody's working on their own thing and they just don't really know anything about your neighborhood because it hasn't been in the paper, nothing bad has happened. It's hard to measure what's going on. . . . [S]ome of the things are seemingly small to the big city, the whole big picture, or the department as a whole. Somebody had a good day that day because we found somebody's child or whatever it was. . . . [I]t doesn't rank real high with the rest of everyone else's work so it's hard to describe it to other people when they ask.

Again and again, the female NPOs (current and former), unprompted, talked about the children and families in their neighborhoods. For some, a number of years had passed since they had been community officers, yet they still could vividly recount stories and names and family dynamics and relationships. Andrea, a white officer who had been out of her former neighborhood position for about six years, recalled:

> Leigh-Anne was four at the time, she was another one of Rebecca Johnson's kids, and Leigh-Anne was actually my most favorite kid. She was always dirty, snot running out of her nose, nonstop. She had summer clothes on for a cold day. She had her shirt on inside out, and pants that didn't really fit her, and they were—she was—filthy dirty, and she had dressed herself. . . . I learned that Mom wasn't even in the house. . . . I don't want to be too critical . . . Rebecca did what a lot of women did, she got involved in seasonal work at the cannery. So, Rebecca left the house at something like 6 A.M. and she was going to put in about a twelve-hour day, but nobody was watching Leigh-Anne, except that she

was supposed to have been left with Gramma or a neighbor, but Leigh-Anne isn't with anyone and can't really tell me, but I could usually find a relative out there to help Rebecca.

Many female NPOs believed that their gender helped to break down some of the distrust that local people usually felt toward police officers and that residents confided in them with greater ease. The view of Terry, a former NPO, is again representative:

> It was both a positive and negative that I was a woman. I think because there were so many single women and single women with children out there that that was easy for them to do, it was more approachable. A lot of people have a fear because there's a uniform in the way and all this equipment, and that throws people right away. But as people got acquainted with me through the [community] center, I think they became less and less aware of that part of the body . . . that a barrier wasn't there as much and they would talk to their friends or they'd say, "Well, maybe Officer Terry can get that answer for you," and word just spread. I would get out more and more and get to the other streets and the people that didn't come to the center, some of them already knew who I was. I'd already met the landlords or I already went to the school and went to Head Start and met kids there, so their parents heard about this Officer Terry, so word spread a lot in neighborhoods, good and bad things.

Many of the women also explained that for certain populations of particular ethnicity, such as Southeast Asians,

> Being female was a negative also because some of the Asian population have a very strong patriarchal type of hierarchy in their society, and the uniform is a negative to them, and being a female is a very low status compared to being older or being a male, so if you're older and you're a male, you're almost like the leader just because of your gender. If you're a female and you're young, and I appear young to them until they find out that I have children, and if you have children, well, that puts you up a little bit higher.

The women also believed that since there were so many female officers throughout the department citizens were no longer surprised when one responded to a call. Usually, the women saw this as advantageous, especially when dealing with male residents. They were very aware of men's need to "save face" and of their macho posturing; the women said that their female presence changed the volatile atmosphere. Based on chivalric notions, and on women's ability to defuse situations by talking to combatants to calm them down, female officers said they relieved the tension using verbal skills.

> [W]ith us, men don't have their guard up or their ego up or need to have that competitive edge, and that's what is typical on patrol as a rule. I think a woman could go into a crisis situation and maybe start talking with either party and [things] either would stabilize or maybe even get better, sometimes it got worse no matter who you were, but oftentimes, some men—well, many men just unfortunately because they're male would walk into a crisis and the male might like it, and the female may not like it. They feel a power or they feel a flight-[or]-fear kind of response right away. . . . I don't know if there's some kind of mothering image or something out there, but I think it was a positive in a lot of ways that you could go into some households or some people that even though they had negative experiences with people in uniform, sometimes it was better that you were a woman and they could maybe set back a little bit and then start talking to you, and maybe even get acquainted with you [which they might] not have if you were a man, but it's still a gut feeling and it's probably a generalization. It depends on the person. (Terry)

The female NPOs with children credited their understanding of the residents' family and relationship struggles to their own parenting experiences. They felt that they could identify with the local people, since they knew what difficulties the families were going through; this was helpful in an environment "saturated with children, and parents who don't have the best parenting skills." The female officers believed they could be supportive rather than judgmental. This issue was not always clear-cut, as one former NPO, Karen, suggested:

> It helped more being female, than it hurt me . . . although maybe it was because of who I am. I was a lifelong resident of Jackson City, from the east side, I had kids, I went to school here, and I'm from a large, very middle-class family. I certainly could relate to some hardships these families were relating to, I mean, I know what it is like to share a bedroom with three other sisters. . . . It also wasn't my style as a police officer to get in people's faces and do a lot of finger pointing at people's noses and chests. I'm fairly tolerant to a point, probably more than some people, but people also knew what I would tolerate and what I wouldn't. And a

lot of it just had to do with common courtesy, just common respect for other people and their property. . . . I don't like to be lied to, I am very up-front with people and truthful.

These words suggest that Karen's empathy resulted from similar family circumstances and her individual style of gaining authority, which may not be correlated with gender. The fieldwork data confirm that both men and women were emphatic about not wanting residents to lie to them. Community officers and residents alike wanted to be treated honestly. However, the familiarity established between the NPOs and the residents had its share of potential shortcomings. The women volunteered that, once they had become well known and integrated into the community, they felt more vulnerable because they were no longer faceless, anonymous officers responding quickly to a crisis call and then leaving. In fact, half of the heterosexual current and former NPOs talked about the concern expressed by some of their husbands and lovers about the NPO position:

My husband had always been supportive because he knew I wanted to do neighborhood policing. But when this detective assignment became available, he said, "Please take it, I want you out of there." He had never ever expressed to me in any way that he was ever concerned about my welfare out in that neighborhood. . . . I expressed how difficult it would be to rearrange childcare, etc., but he said he didn't care, he wanted me out. He was too worried all the time about me in the neighborhood. It was because I was more vulnerable there than on patrol. You are no longer a cop in a uniform in the neighborhood. People knew me almost too well. They knew my comings and goings, I had threats made on me, to harm me, and once to specifically shoot me. It could happen. I had that brought to my attention a couple of times from people who I considered trustworthy confidants, people who I could trust in that community who had shown over a period of time that they were credible and trustworthy and had been helpful to me in the past. They would come to me and say, "You need to know that there's some people out there who are really not happy with you and angry, and somebody might take a shot at you." (Andrea)

They also focused on the emotional tugs—"There were just some things in there that would just rip your heart apart." Many of the women spoke of having learned that they were not as tough as they thought or liked to think.

I can't tell you how many times you'd walk through there in the winter and the kids would be inappropriately dressed . . . they're out there and they don't have adequate winter wear. Or if I got out there kind of early for one evening, I'd see little kids who were not school age just out and about, and the adult in that household was just nowhere to be seen. . . . [O]ne young lady, she had her shoes on the wrong feet. (Tina)

Without exception, the former and current female NPOs joyfully told us stories, complete with names and detailed descriptions, about many of their "favorite" residents, as well as some of the more problematic ones.

Not everything the male and female community officers said was different. Women and men spoke of the importance of treating all citizens with dignity and respect, and we observed this approach during the fieldwork. Although some NPOs highlighted gender differences in an individual officer's style, women and men were equally likely to state that, although there were some officers they sought as backup and some they would avoid, this was not necessarily related to gender but to individual personality and competence. For instance, one current NPO, a white man, was concise about gender and policing:

I have not personally seen gender having an effect as to whether or not a person was a "good" officer. Frankly, there's men in this department that I don't want backing me up on a high-risk call, and there's women in this department I *definitely* would want. It doesn't matter that they're men or women, it's just what I know about their ability. (Patrick)

A former neighborhood officer, Carlena, held a similar view:

I definitely think that men and women have something unique to bring to this job, and we complement each other. I have seen male officers who are as sensitive or more sensitive than some females. The main thing is that you have a real interest in helping a community. Men seem to be a little more aggressive or something. See, . . . it's not the gender thing, because I assume some officers, male officers, are very sensitive, they are very good with people.

Clearly, men and women bring different things to the job, and these reflect traditional expectations of masculinity and femininity. At the same time, however, a more androgynous style often emerges, with some male officers appearing comfortable with nurturing tasks and some female officers displaying aggressive crimefighting skills. Experimentation with oppositional gender-role behavior is facilitated by the department's open-ended mandate to NPOs to respond to the needs of the neighborhood. Perhaps the lack of everyday visibility among their fellow officers creates an environment in which NPOs of both sexes can "try on" new roles that they may have been reticent about playing before. Hypermasculine displays among the patrol officers and the crimefighting image are disrupted by the need to connect with the residents and to get to know them in a more intimate way. Exaggerated masculinity among women may be tempered by gender-neutral skills best suited to the situational context of neighborhood policework.

Sexual Orientation

Despite the masculinist organizational culture of policing, the data revealed practices used by officers to integrate more feminine and gender-neutral styles into their work. A further complication of gender dynamics was sexual orientation. The Jackson City Police Department was atypical in some ways for its acceptance of gays and lesbians on the force. Throughout the two and a half years of data collection, many officers offered unsolicited comments regarding the range of diversity in the department, notably mentioning the high numbers of lesbians and at least one openly gay man (as discussed in Chapter 1). Five policewomen revealed their lesbianism during the interviews or fieldwork, not as a confidence-sharing kind of interaction, but matter-of-factly. Some officers have marched openly in the city's annual gay and lesbian pride parade. Just as a number of heterosexuals had dated and married while serving together on the force, so had lesbian officers formed long-term relationships with other policewomen.

To what extent did sexual orientation influence neighborhood policing practices? It is often difficult to separate this aspect of life from other social statuses, such as gender and race. In fact, Patricia Hill Collins (1990) has criticized dichotomous "either/or" thinking and favors a "both/and" approach. Within the image-laden occupation of policing, adding issues of sexuality to the already complicated masculine-feminine dynamic creates even more confusion.

What makes the question of sexual orientation even more intriguing in the context of neighborhood policing was that heterosexual men initially steered clear of the program because it represented denigrated feminine traits. It was not until the positions grew better known to the majority of the force, and came to be seen as linked to promotion, that men began to want them. Policewomen, on the other hand, have always faced the stereotypical assumption that they might be gay, regardless of their true sexual orientation. The pervasiveness of this stereotype might free female officers to pursue nontraditional careers. As suggested in Susan Martin's (1980) research, mentioned earlier, women adapt to policing either by emphasizing their femininity and by portraying themselves as relatively weak and passive in relation to male officers, or else by emphasizing masculinity and by embracing a dominant and equal position. This phenomenon got turned on its head in the ambiguous, gendered context of neighborhood work, since today's community policing models have transformed an undesirable, feminine position into a potentially male-driven, popular one. Men have adapted to taking on socially less dominant jobs by exaggerating their masculinity, using verbal aggressiveness and displays of authority to "prove" their ability. (This is similar to what was found by the gender researcher Beth Schneider [1989].) Men overemphasize masculinity because of a culture in which any suggestion of such traditionally "feminine" traits as gentleness or sensitivity encourages colleagues to brand them as sissies, girls, or faggots (Blumfield 1992). Yet community policing promotes a more personal approach to law enforcement, and men (by the time of the second and third waves) were clamoring for a part, at least in Jackson City.

Whereas heterosexual women in "male" occupations may also feel pressured to demonstrate masculine traits to prove their abilities (Zimmer 1987), lesbians may try to assert their feminine side. In other research (see Miller, Forrest, and Jurik 1997), it has been suggested that lesbians may feel a need to be especially feminine in order to avoid hostile confrontations with (mostly male) homophobic coworkers (Schneider 1989), reflecting Susan Martin's police*women* style of adaptation. Most female officers, straight or gay, realized that although policing calls for such masculine characteristics as assertiveness, strength, and competitiveness, to act in this way would confirm the assumptions of other officers that they were lesbian (Burke 1994; Pharr 1988). Since lesbians are not just tokens in the Jackson City Police Department, however, they may be under less pressure as women to "prove their masculinity," and thus may be more free to develop their natural styles.

Lesbian officers gravitated toward the neighborhood position. One possible reason could be word-of-mouth reports. Since community policing yielded greater job satisfaction, current members of the force encouraged their friends (both straight and gay) to apply to the Jackson City department. Another possible explanation, one that a few of the lesbian officers raised themselves, is that the appearance is deceiving: the numbers merely reflect the overall representation of lesbians on the police force. Thus, in reality it may be that no increased or disproportionate number of lesbians requested the NPO position.

Another possible approach to the officers' sexual orientation is to acknowledge that, just as community policing afforded men an opportunity to play a more nurturing role in a socially acceptable fashion, the neighborhood positions provided the same role flexibility for lesbian officers. In our society, "out" lesbians, in particular, do not always have the same access to or support for nurturing roles, especially ones such as becoming mothers or retaining custody of children. Thus, if lesbians are not seen as "real" women in society, they may seek other ways to confirm their female status. This again calls to mind how Susan Martin's police*women* emphasized their femininity to find a place in the masculinist subculture and working environment of policing.

With its opportunities for androgynous practice, neighborhood work may constitute a unique alternative to the macho police culture. Officers can draw upon *both* masculine-linked and feminine-linked sex roles. For example, sometimes an aggressive crimefighting stance is necessary; on other occasions, female or male NPOs can "mother" the neighborhood, its children, and the broader community as well. For lesbian officers, this opens up ways in which their status as women is not as negated, because of homophobia, as it might be in the larger society. To extend this argument a little further, lesbians who are already mothers may appreciate the public confirmation of a nurturing role even as they capably do what is still ultimately thought of as "men's work."

I asked the openly lesbian officers to speculate on the reasons for their high numbers in the neighborhood positions. Some believed that single women, lesbian or heterosexual, were probably more career oriented. Others suggested, as mentioned earlier, that the apparently strong lesbian presence among NPOs could simply reflect the demographics of the department. A number of officers also suggested that lesbian NPOs who did not have children, and hence did not have to juggle daycare and other parenting responsibilities, found it easier to maintain a flexible schedule and work late hours. It was possible, too, that the higher number of lesbians in neighborhood policing simply paralleled the number of women who were childless. In addition, any officer with children who was married or had a permanent domestic partner could depend on shared childcare. As one NPO said, "I think there's more understanding and working it out when your partner has worked the same job or in the same place to understand the goofy schedules and demands that are put on us." Married male officers also acknowledged receiving this help from their wives.

In general, sexual orientation could be inherently unrelated to competent job performance. Jackson City and its police department may be particularly enlightened in this respect; since job candidates were explicitly asked about diversity issues and comfort levels as part of the hiring process, there may be a higher comfort level among successful applicants. All of the current and former officers, gay and straight, when asked whether sexual orientation played a part in performance in community policing, said that since NPOs were selected based on seniority the gay and lesbian officers had already been on the force long enough to demonstrate their abilities and to establish a reputation for themselves. It may be that the greater openness and visibility of homosexual officers increased pressures to prove that social minorities could do the job as well as social dominants. In other research, lesbian and gay police officers have described themselves as becoming overachievers or perfectionists so that their performance would be above reproach and their effectiveness would not be challenged on grounds of sexual orientation (Miller, Forrest, and Jurik 1997). The lesbian officers' solid reputations may have been established before they became NPOs. It is also likely that gay and lesbian persons have a unique "outsider" status that enables them to see the world slightly differently. In particular, they may be more cognizant of how individuals interact socially and of how such factors as racism, economic struggles, and social injustice may affect their lives.

The qualities admired in police officers have moved away from those typified by the efficient, stoic loner; today, expressive qualities that display a more humane dimension have come into favor (Jurik and Martin 1999; Manning 1984). The need for aggressive law enforcement action endures, however. As community policing grows in popularity, what may become most salient are the quality and effectiveness of one's work and one's ability to excel as a humane law enforcer. Just as heterosexual men can adopt a more caring approach without fear of being labeled homosexual, women can expand upon their preferred style of policing without concern about appearing too masculine (or too feminine). In fact, the social psychologist Sandra Bem (1974; 1993) contends that rigid sex-role differentiation is out-of-date and no longer useful in a society where flexibility and androgyny are strongly associated with higher standards of psychological health and professional performance. Even though the lesbian neighborhood officers in this study were more similar to male NPOs in their activity planning than they were to the heterosexual women, they still eagerly shared detailed stories about the relationships they formed with residents. They, too, talked about the emotional tugs of community policing, just like all of the heterosexual female NPOs, current and former. Perhaps lesbian officers in Jackson City had enough peer support and respect to be able to display both masculine-linked and feminine-linked traits in their policework. The data suggested that adopting this duality of style was easier for lesbians than for male neighborhood officers. The obstacles for men involved the stigma of doing "feminine" work; they were greater than those the women encountered for doing "masculine" work.

This chapter has addressed the identity changes and pressures experienced by women and men as they moved from being patrol to neighborhood officers. I have explored how the NPOs created strategies for their work duties and community activities in order to maximize acceptable public images, as well as how their ambiguous new roles were shaped by race, ethnicity, gender, and sexual orientation. This tale is a complicated one, with many nuances that are not to be neatly resolved or categorized. To shed more light on these issues, in Chapter 6 I will look more closely at the working relationships between neighborhood officers and patrol officers.

First, however, I will turn in Chapter 5 to an examination of the relations between neighborhood officers and their communities, and some of the possible ramifications of these for both groups.

Note

1. For studies examining men who enter female-dominated professions, see Williams and Heikes 1993; Kelly, Shoemaker, and Steele 1996; and Perry 1996.

Police and Community

Interactions

You can't talk to a drunk dog.
—Linc, white man, former NPO

People get very uneasy when they see blue polyester.
—Theresa, white woman, current NPO

Cops on patrol get to be sort of twitchy and paranoid . . . we
may not start out that way, but it gets worse over time.
—Pam, white lesbian, former NPO

Being an NPO developed my communication skills. It
really helped me deal with interpersonal relationships. It
helped me understand what's going on in people's lives, as
opposed to what I think should be going on in their lives.
—Keith, black man, former NPO

People during the day would be out washing their cars,
and they would be the same people at night, drunk and
taking a swing at a beat officer. There were people who
would refer to me as Officer William during the day and
Officer Asshole at night, and they were the same people.
—William, black man, former NPO

This chapter investigates contacts between police officers and citizens and the
situational ambiguities related to such encounters. First, I explore how an offi-

cer's style and interests influence the choice of a criminally active, program development, or maintenance neighborhood as a place to work. Next, I examine what officers do, and how neighborhood policing shapes connections, both formal and informal, between NPOs and residents. The officers reveal the advantages and disadvantages introduced by the "personal touch" of neighborhood policing. Finally, I look at how an officer's social status characteristics, such as gender, race, and ethnicity, influence her or his perceptions, behavior, and actual policework.

Neighborhoods develop a character of their own and, with that, a reputation, albeit one that is not always accurate. It is the residents who make the neighborhoods. Often, these persons share and express the joys and the struggles of their lives behind the doors of their homes, in the yards and streets, with neighbors and friends, and in interactions with visitors. No matter whether they arrive by foot, bicycle, horse, or squad car, police officers are such visitors. The quality of their connection with residents rests on how well the officers' activities, interests, and policing styles match the needs of the neighborhood.

In Jackson City, within each residential area that was assigned an NPO, there were identifiable reasons to justify a more intensive police presence. Self-selection, and the seniority process used by the Jackson City department to fill neighborhood positions, however, meant that officers whose styles might best complement a certain district's needs could not always be matched with that area. The result was that officers adapted, often developing new styles to add to their policing repertoire. Those who were less enthusiastic about or less effective with neighborhood policing ultimately retreated from high levels of involvement. In fact, low morale resulting from frustration or disillusionment with being an NPO led officers, even before the three-year commitment had been fulfilled, to withdraw from the program completely and ask for reassignment. Alternatively, women and men who were more interested in aggressive law enforcement and crimefighting purposefully selected neighborhoods that needed to be "cleaned up." In this way, they focused on obvious, immediate concerns directly related to crime, such as writing tickets for trespassing, serving outstanding warrants, and displaying a strong police presence. This strategy was often used to rid neighborhoods of nonresidents who were seen as undesirables by some local people and the police because, for example, they were involved in the drug trade. The city enacted a statute that allowed for huge fines for violating particular ordinances. Thus, it became common for police to "paper" communities with tickets until the message got across. This aggressive action often displaced offenders to other neighborhoods that lacked such surveillance and enforcement. Other visible strategies that emphasized traditional, aggressive law enforcement included increased foot patrol by day and car patrol by night, frequent drive-throughs by patrol officers, and teaming up and walking the streets with uniformed employees of private security companies.

Initially, it was not always clear if the law enforcement emphasis was necessary because of the collapse (or potential for collapse) of neighborhood norms and informal controls, in line with the broken-windows theory, or if such an emphasis simply reflected an individual officer's style. In other words, although a man or woman who wanted to do more crimefighting might select a neighborhood where this approach was needed and welcomed, only afterward would one know the NPO's personal style. For example, it would be revealed when, although aggressive action was no longer needed, the officer retained an aggressive posture. In addressing high-crime neighborhoods, strong police presence and authority needed to be established and used *prior* to any introduction of longer-term strategies based on the broken-windows theory. This level of enforcement activity was reminiscent of more traditional (masculine) policing, and in consequence these neighborhoods might attract men and women who were more comfortable with an aggressive, macho, crimefighting style. It was also the case that officers who ordinarily shied away from the more personal, "feminine" style and stereotype embodied in community policing might be more strongly drawn to these "hard core" neighborhoods, since the need for crime control was so well known.

All police officers were aware of problem spots, and the department was very cognizant of the need for crimefighters in particular neighborhoods, especially since patrol received a disproportionately high number of calls for service from these areas. Accordingly, selecting a high-crime neighborhood could be very attractive for officers who sought an NPO position as a way to advance in their careers, yet felt conflicted or ambivalent about becoming one of the "pansy police." Since the "tough" neighborhoods were well known across the force, these reluctant officers could retain their masculine identity. At the same time, they could be publicly associated with upholding the "party line" of doing something different for the community, such as providing round-the-clock surveillance or enforcement, not just waiting to be dispatched on crisis calls.

If, however, an officer selected an NPO position in a high-crime neighborhood, but had a personal style that was oriented more toward social service, the need to be an aggressive crimefighter could sour the officer's enthusiasm for her or his assignment. This would be particularly true if the NPO favored a more emotive, nurturing, and conciliatory approach to community policing. Thus, the officer would need to draw upon or develop other strengths and skills in order to put the neighborhood back into shape and make it a community that ultimately valued these kinds of police-citizen interactions and interpersonal communication styles.

Greenwood constitutes a good example of how an officer worked to transform a neighborhood. Linc, the former NPO, spent the initial half year or so cleaning up, focusing on "bad guys and drug sales." Only then did he feel able to concentrate on other "broken-windows" and longer-term problems. Linc had to be patient through the community's transformation:

> I wandered around and talked to people and listened to people to just see what's going on and what people had in mind that were problems, and then acted on that accordingly. There were people from the schools that I dealt with on a daily basis, people from neighborhood associations that were very important, public health nurse, social workers, probation and parole that I talked to all the time . . . the building inspectors, property managers and owners, jobs and job development, Dane County, sheriff's department people . . . there were usually a hundred things going through my head at the same time and it was all an ongoing process that seems as if it was a process of sorting out the problems, identifying how to attack them, and then hooking up with the other people that actually had responsibility or expertise. Then staying in contact with them and moving ahead a piece at a time. . . . I enjoyed the kids . . . most of them got along with me, too. There were one or two families—this one mother, she was a real horror. The father of the kids, he was wanted on the run out in Indiana, and she left the kids alone to go off and do her dope and drink in town on a regular basis. These kids weren't old and were often hungry. . . . I started putting pressure on her and she would see me coming down the street from the second window and would scream and swear at me . . . so she trained her kids not to like me. . . . I felt like I had accomplished something when these kids found some rocks in a baggie and gave them to me.

In another high-crime, unstable neighborhood, Taylor, the NPO never became involved in nonpolice activities, such as those for children, unless another officer set it up. He recalled,

> I thought that my time, as far as for everyone who was going to have to be living there on a continuous basis, would be better spent dealing with trying to improve things and get certain elements out of there, rather than taking kids on walks at the state park or something. My first year, I didn't want to get too latched onto people, I thought my time would be best spent dealing with that other stuff. (Matt)

Using the words "certain elements" to describe unwelcome residents suggested a racist assumption that all offenders were black. Matt later expressed this as a belief.

The NPOs' policing needs and perceptions differed in the neighborhoods that had developed a reputation for stability. Two particular officers and their districts were consistently raised in the interviews and fieldwork data as examples of the maintenance neighborhood model. One of the areas had a very economically diverse population, with some residents owning lakefront homes; the main local problem seemed to be excessive noise at the nightly pickup basketball games in the public park. Both neighborhoods had veteran officers as NPOs, and each man was very close to retirement. One officer, Curtis, was an African American. He seemed very personable and extroverted to all who encountered him and appeared to know everyone. In fact, his home was in the neighborhood and his children went to school there. Other officers confided that they believed Curtis was biding his time until he retired, since no one who might be interested in the NPO position would outrank him in seniority and thus bump him out.

Frank, the other NPO, a white man, did not live in his district but did own rental property there; thus, he too was personally invested in quality of life issues surrounding residents and community services. All of the officers who mentioned Frank did so with grudging respect for how he had surprised them with his leadership and energy level in the neighborhood. They assumed he wanted a cushy job in which to relax until his retirement. His colleagues discovered instead that the neighborhood position revitalized Frank, and his enthusiasm and spirit reflected a much stronger commitment than they had anticipated. As one officer (Steve) said, "Frank's one of those guys most people expected [to become] an NPO as a retirement job as some people would, but he's very busy and keeps himself that way." This remark stood in contrast to how officers discussed Curtis's "retirement NPO job." Tony, a white serving NPO, claimed:

> The Fairlawn neighborhood is dead. Fairlawn, that's the gravy train right now. Curtis is the kind of guy that he's got himself adjusted into a work schedule that is nothing but Monday through Friday day shifts, and he's not doing a damned thing else. The NPO of the adjoining neighborhood, Greenwood, is really frustrated because he's getting the workload dumped on him, and Roger is saying, this is supposed to be Curtis's problem, not mine. If you've got a problem with it, you have Curtis get out here and with it, not me. So there's a little bit of tension out there.

Since NPOs were located in places designated as "troubled areas," many government agencies, social service workers, and researchers have taken an active interest. Some officers believed that residents tired of being guinea pigs for local progressive groups; yet most of them believed that citizens were pleased to get an officer solely for their district. According to members of the force, many residents were initially antagonistic to the philosophy of community policing, since they had witnessed the popularity and financial support of other persons and programs come and go.

> Occasionally, people get pissed off and they'll let you know that you're not part of the neighborhood. That you make your paycheck and you work here and go home at the end of the day . . . and you can't really be hurt by that because it's the truth. But the thing is that after some point, they know that you're still coming back every day, and you're still committed and you haven't gone away, and you get something back. What's really missing in some of these neighborhoods is that nobody's ever been around consistently, whether it's from the school or the police or from housing, or social workers, you never feel like you were anything more than a fly by night . . . people tinker around for a while and at the end of the project, they're gone. And the next person comes tinkering and poking and prying and asking questions probably after the same damn information. And people resent being used. (Helen)

In criminally active neighborhoods, residents may not appear to appreciate NPOs' efforts until they feel the benefits, such as decreased fear, increased autonomy, a decline in visible drug dealing, and more stability and program development. Of course, the "bad guys" felt the NPOs were getting in the way of their (illegal) business, and they resented the intrusion; often the arrival of a community officer displaced the crime to a new area not under such supervision.

Moving away from examples involving individual officers, I turn now to examining some of the issues encountered by both male and female NPOs. These similarities involved relationships (both advantageous and disadvantageous) with residents and strategies NPOs used in their interactions with the community. All but one of the officers discussed the time they spent developing relationships between themselves and the residents. Much of this involved helping local people deal more easily with the criminal justice system. For instance, family members turned to NPOs if they encountered a situation that they did not know how to handle.

> When you're in the 'hood, if you walk somebody through a restraining order or something else, you can see it's not that easy. . . . [A] lot of

people have a hard time filling the forms out, and a lot of these people are disadvantaged and don't have the education, so I think that it gave me a different perspective. (Scott)

But not all community police officers were as sympathetic to such needs.

When you are an NPO, you are so accessible, and you have your phone number out there, people don't really realize that government is this huge bureaucracy, that more people are afraid to deal with. They have a problem, they don't call because they don't know who to call. So when they have an NPO, it's, gee, I'm having a problem, my neighbor's putting his garbage out twenty-four hours before he's supposed to. Do you think you could do something about it? And those are not really an NPO's jurisdiction. (Hank)

In other cases, the officer acted almost as an ambassador to the family by being a personal liaison between an offender and the criminal justice system: "Let's say somebody was seriously injured or even dead—the NPO could actually be the one to go with the coroner to deliver that message to the family members." Other times, "Criminals turn themselves over to you: All right, Lisa, I've messed up, if I've gotta go in, . . . I'd rather you took me in."

This attentive and sometimes benevolent focus did not mean that NPOs ignored their law enforcement obligations or relegated them to the back burner. But officers mentioned over and over that they undertook these routine law enforcement duties in a more caring way, which could ultimately pay off by decreasing hostility, suspicion, and distrust between citizens and police. Both male and female NPOs believed that their more informal personal styles meant better law enforcement results.

The bottom line is that I am a police officer, and my job is to arrest. . . . I think I would give more explanations than a beat officer could because I had time to do that, and I could do some crisis management. . . . I might try to give them a little leeway—if a group of young adults was drinking open intoxicants in the little playground area on Crestview, I didn't see that my first thing was to say, "Okay, I am writing everybody open-intoxicant tickets." I would say, "Hey guys, why don't you take it up to your balcony or to your own apartments, it's bad to let the kids see this, a bad example," and you know, that worked . . . so the numbers dwindled. . . . [W]ith patrol officers, writing citations or cutting slack is often based on mood, the type of day they are having. . . . [I]f they had a heavy day of calls, or they have just been running to all kinds of situations and they come to you and at first they are respectful, but you're flipping off at them, they're gonna say, "You know, I really don't have to take this, I'll just take enforcement action." (Keith)

Treating residents, whether victims, offenders, or ordinary law abiders, with dignity and respect, no matter what they might have suffered or been alleged to have done, was a consistent theme raised during the interviews, questionnaires, and fieldwork. The officers felt that emphasizing dignity was the right way to treat another human being, and they also suggested it paid off in other ways.

Even most of the creeps know when they do something wrong and most of them if you treat them fairly, and you treat them like human beings, are going to go along with the program anyway. . . . [I]f you treat somebody with decency and respect you usually are going to be given that back. . . . [O]ver time, they know I am not going to throw anyone down a well and leave them there and they knew I *had* to arrest. Sometimes I would call them up and they would come down to the office and off we would go. (Linc)

Another benefit to the police of developing and maintaining relations with the good side of communities was that it renewed officers' beliefs in the good side of people and countered any cynicism with at least some hope. "As an NPO, I actually cared about the people I arrested, and how their families were affected, and it helped me realize that most people are not evil" (Pam). The neighborhood officers expressed a renewed optimism about humanity, since they routinely saw residents during the daytime hours going about their lives, not just in response to some emergency call. Establishing rapport before and after a crisis was refreshing and helped in doing the job. As one former NPO, a white man, remarked, "You can't talk to a drunk dog; you have to talk to people when they are not in crisis."

There was also a reciprocal effect. Residents aligned themselves with officers, either preserving the NPO's reputation for fairness and caring, or else "sharing the glory" if they played a role in giving police information that led to an arrest. According to the officers, local people who respected them often rendered support during public or unpopular law enforcement actions. The result was that a suspect might back down from a potentially violent confrontation, in front of residents, but still be allowed to save face. Since much of the policework in the neighborhoods took place in the presence of community members, this sort of help made the NPOs' jobs easier.

I could walk in there, and whoever was giving me the hard time, the other people would say, "Shut up and listen to Officer Scott. He's fair and square, he'll deal with it." So it was like they almost became support for you, whereas patrol officers don't have that luxury. (Scott)

People I arrested rescued me. I had ended up in a fight with two four-teen-year-old kids, one armed with a pipe and one, when I got the kid with the pipe subdued, ran back and got a knife, and a different guy I arrested a month before, who fought with every cop in town except me, came over, grabbed this kid, held him for me, and when the other cops got there, they wanted to get backup to go get the other suspect, but I went and got him. And Willy was holding him since he appreciated the fact that last month when I arrested him, I had gone in, he had a little boy seven at the time, and I said, let's take care of little Winston. Let's get him a baby-sitter, you know, you've got to go, and I treated him decently. And he had never forgotten that. (Francine)

A lot of good community interactions stem from just time, just being there every day and helping out with life's little problems. And if you can bet that bond developed around these little things, then when a big crisis develops, they're more and more willing to help—it's a weird phe-nomenon, you're off for three days, and you come back and you're walk-ing down the street, and people take you aside and say, this happened on Friday, so I just thought I'd wait until you got back to work. You know, they could have called on Friday, but they knew they would have gotten somebody they didn't know, a faceless bureaucrat. . . . [I]t's so much easier for people who are afraid of bureaucracy—or the criminal justice system—to deal with someone that they know, taking away the anonymity factor. . . . [K]ids recognize Mickey Mouse more than they recognize the vice president of the U.S., it's the same thing. (Hank)

Serving arrest warrants was one specific area in which NPOs routinely re-sponded by using strategies very different from those of patrol officers. Familiar with a resident's personal and family position, employment, and financial situa-tion, many NPOs were able to use this information when determining the best time to serve outstanding warrants. Officers were in the neighborhood most of the time, which gave them an advantage in following up citizens' situations. Two of them described how they handled warrants:

You have that advantage because you know where they live and where they work and where they hang out. And . . . a patrol officer doesn't have

that advantage because when patrol encounters somebody, and you don't
know if they're handing you a story or if you're gonna see them again,
. . . you pretty much have to bring them in, regardless of their personal
situation. (Scott)

When I worked in the early eighties on foot patrols, we had a lot of
Mariel Boat Lift Cuban immigrants here, and we had some that were,
unfortunately, of jail quality, with serious problems. And there were just
a few of those people, but they were enough to cause problems. But one
of the things my friend, who's a past alderperson, had warned me—
watch out for macho. He told me, Lisa, never insult them, and you'll be
fine. Especially in front of their friends and their women. So, I would
just say, hey Juan, can I talk to you? (he'd say, *No!*) Juan, I gotta talk to
you, and I really don't wanna in front of your friends. Could you just
move two feet away? Okay. Total respect. Even if I'm gonna arrest him.
Now, I've gotta tell you, I've got a warrant, we could go around the corner
here. Okay, I don't want it in front of my friends. Fine. You know what
I mean? But a lot of people are not gonna take the time to do that.
They're gonna walk over and say you're under arrest, asshole, let's go.
(Lisa)

This incident was made even more delicate because the police officer was a
woman acting in a nonfeminine way with a Latino resident surrounded by his
peers. Related research has found that, in the Latino community, losing face in
front of one's peers and letting the police officer get the upper hand is seen as
stigmatizing and emasculating (see Shusta et al. 1995). Other NPOs describe
the ways in which they allowed citizens to save face:

We walked our prisoners, the people who were under arrest, without
handcuffs, without backup. . . . I had arrests by appointments. You know,
I called people up, they were on a warrant. I mean it was misdemeanors,
it wasn't anything like a felony, that's a different issue. But for misdemeanor things, you'd call somebody up, you'd say, hey, I've got a warrant
for your arrest, how about next Monday we go in, you take care of your
kids, get a baby-sitter, if you can, get the money and pay the bail, or we
can maybe make a court appearance right away in the morning, we'll set
it up. . . . I thought the chief would die when he found out we were
making arrest appointments! (Francine)

There were some basic things I had to do. I was first and foremost a
police officer, so I had to make arrests. But I have to admit that, you'd

come to know some of these people and it was harder not to give people breaks along the way because I knew them as people. I knew that if I took some people in on a warrant on a particular day or whatever, they weren't gonna be able to pay and get out, and come back and take care of their kids. So, there were times when I would say, "OK, you've got this outstanding warrant" and it's not like it was a big deal, but it still needed to be taken care of, and I'd ask, "Realistically, when do you think you can take care of it?" And then some would say, "Well, I have to wait until I get paid and then I can." I could work with this. There were still some people that left me no choice, even while I was an NPO. I would try to work with them but they would just blow me off and not take advantage of it or reciprocate in any way. (Andrea)

All of the current and former neighborhood officers had experienced this personal touch and they discussed it at length. As one black former NPO, William, remarked, arrests were no less professional, but the procedures used were more personal and the arrests went more smoothly:

[I]t is easier because they have seen me at times where we've talked and they have seen me because you are always watched; they have seen me go out of my way to help people in the 'hood whereas I didn't have to do it so they know I have their best interests at heart. So although they may fight with me the night of the arrest, 90 to 99 percent will come back around.

Another former NPO, Greg, a white man, recalled that citizens sometimes got embarrassed the day after an arrest and tried to "clean up" the situation so that the NPO would not think badly of them: "Oh, Officer Greg, I am really sorry about what happened last night, but you know, you gotta understand." Several of the male officers stressed that the "personal touch" had the potential to get out of hand when residents sought special favors or tried to take advantage of a relationship. One white former NPO captured the essence of this concern:

A big part of this job is to moderate or control the contact because you can get to the point where you get so accessible that you never get anything else done. You have to remember the law and order, maintenance and control aspects of things. . . . So you gotta balance what you do and do some of the traditional things. I don't believe in burning out on it, and I am not into our officers out there cranking out a lot of high numbers [of arrests], but you do have to do some of it. (Bill)

Some officers believed that arrests became less volatile when they knew the residents personally.

> I think it makes it easier to arrest. I try to make them responsible for their own stuff and not lessen that. Because I have a relationship, but if they aren't 'hooding up, or if they do something, they have to take responsibility for it. And that is my role, basically. I mean, if you are not going to provide an adequate place for your children, and they're not going to be in a safe environment, I'm gonna arrest you because you are neglecting your children. (Carol, current NPO)

Steve, a former NPO, responded differently when asked if it was difficult to arrest persons he knew, since he would see both the victims and the offenders again.

> Absolutely. It's this whole neighbor issue. It's like you have become, like their neighbors, and when you arrest somebody today, you know you're gonna see them out there tomorrow. Generally it wasn't a real big deal. I don't think there were any grudges, at least nobody expressed any real grudges towards me. They were more likely to apologize for the way they behaved and to say they understood me. But nevertheless, it's still an awkward situation you might not confront—at least not in such a short time frame—on patrol.

Another factor that affected both women and men was the never-ending nature of neighborhood policing; community problems would "hit you in the face again" as soon as the next day began. Some NPOs looked back wistfully at their former patrol positions; once an eight-hour shift was complete, they could go home and forget about work until their next shift started. Such was not the case for many community officers, particularly the women. Women took work, problems, and concerns home with them because they knew the residents better. They thus felt a greater emotional investment in the neighborhood, and in people's lives and their specific circumstances.

> You could have lived and breathed that job if you wanted to, and for my own sanity, I couldn't do that for more than the years I was there. I had my family, and I had enough stress at home with two toddlers, without coming home even more stressed out. (Andrea)

Only one female NPO, Carol, indicated that she never intended to bring the job home, but she had been in the neighborhood position for less than a month.

Carol was also particularly concerned about career advancement and success. She insisted,

> I am not going to take the work home. I feel that women set goals that are too high and then feel disappointed. I have no problem leaving stuff at work. I am used to doing my work, finishing it, being done, going home, and not having any ongoing cases. That's why I like patrol. That's one of the reasons that being a detective never really interested me, because even if they finish one case, they have twenty others going on. Maybe I might have to adjust as an NPO. But I'm hoping that I don't have this weighing on me, you know, the weight of the neighborhood, once I get settled in the new position.

Here, the newest female NPO said implicitly that she wanted to follow the career advancement model, the path more likely to be associated with male officers. Carol saw this model as more cut and dried; women's goals were set "too high" and caused disappointment. This raises the issue of whether women and men do things differently in the neighborhoods, which I will explore in the next section.

Gender-Related Approaches to Community Activities

Gender is another factor that shaped neighborhood policing styles. On the one hand, women and men shared some similar experiences with and feelings about community policing. These centered on the ambiguity of their new roles. (Balancing residents' desires with individual officers' agendas stimulated some differences as well.) Officers' actions and beliefs were complicated by factors that were interrelated with gender, such as race, ethnicity, and perceptions of masculinity and femininity. Given the nexus of gender, race, and sexual orientation in the lives of men and women, untangling their effects on neighborhood policing is a complex task.

Male and female NPOs gave priority to different programs in the neighborhoods, which was reflected by gender-based differences in their approaches. Although this question was not directly asked of the officers, based on descriptions of the kinds of programs they helped to develop and implement and which residents took advantage of them was obvious that differences existed. As mentioned in Chapter 4, men tended to stress physical activity, such as team sports, fishing, and camping. For example, Tony, a white current NPO, presented a huge wish list, which included bringing African American role models from the state's professional football team to talk to the boys in the neighborhood, building a gymnasium at the community center for midnight basketball, and convincing the city's human resources department to mail notices of job openings for him to post on the community bulletin board. Another idea from a male NPO was to have children construct airplane and car models, since his hobby was building and collecting military miniatures. He then set up a contest, with a local business giving away pizzas as prizes. Although the men became involved with a lot of activities after their first few months in the neighborhood, they all admitted that, before becoming NPOs, when they had heard of how community officers arranged youth recreational programs they took it as an effort to impress the administration. However, the men admitted that after a while they were having fun arranging the activities and getting local businesses to sponsor teams.

Another white male NPO worked to establish a technical center in his neighborhood. A colleague in an adjacent community had received a grant to do this, and the NPO was visibly and admittedly envious.

> [T]he owners of the homes out in Fairlawn got a HUD grant to build a high-technology center for their community center. . . . [T]he first time I visited it, it damned near brought me to tears . . . going in there and looking at what he managed to do, and I can't get a goddamned 486 [higher-powered computer] for this building without having to go out and really scramble and jump through so many different hoops to get it for the neighborhood association or the community center. But they've got brand-new Pentium 133s and their brand-new Macintosh equipment, scanners, color printers, it's unbelievable. . . . [I]f the kids don't have that access, they're gonna get smoked, they'll be so far behind. (Tony)

Male community officers, unlike their female counterparts, were much more likely to "list" their accomplishments and agendas. They emphasized how much work they were doing, indicating that they were not just "socializing." Women had lists of accomplishments and plans that were as long or longer, but they did not mention them unless directly asked. Also, the men tended to gravitate to "manly" activities, which attracted more children and adults, to a much greater extent than did the female community police officers.

Women, on the other hand, typically raised larger issues in the interviews, such as family concerns. They were also interested in enduring problems like domestic violence, teenaged motherhood, and dropping out of school; they wanted to develop programs with these issues in mind. Women also had to negotiate their occupational role as "the law" and their gender role. Their empathy and focus on people and their problems were regarded as "natural," yet when men focused on the same concerns it was viewed as extraordinary that they cared so much about "women's issues." I will discuss this contradiction in greater detail below.

These gendered patterns raise the question of why men and women followed traditional gender lines in their activities. For example, *all* of the male NPOs highlighted their sports and computer programs for children and their drug busts and law enforcement activities when dealing with adults. Only one example of a nontraditional activity was offered, and it was offered repeatedly by officers on the west side of the city as if it were the only one that existed. A former community policeman arranged for the police union to rent an Easter Bunny costume; he wore it to the children's Easter party in his neighborhood, which he had planned with a female NPO.

It appeared that men sometimes found it easier to dominate in the traditionally feminine sphere of taking care of children. In fact, research about men in professions that are largely female, such as teaching in primary and secondary schools, found that, unlike women who have moved into male-dominated professions, men do not report a poisoned working environment or being sexually harassed. Men in the schools, however, tended to be cast in stereotypical roles, such as that of disciplinarian. For example, principals and other teachers have been reported as saying that children really need male guidance and male role models (Williams 1992, 260). But some men regarded this as stereotyping, and it bothered them to be assigned all the disciplinary problems within the school system.

The issue of plugging men into traditional roles also arose in the neighborhoods. Male community officers were more easily viewed as "the law," not having to "earn" that respect as female officers have had to do. The interview and fieldwork data indicated that male NPOs, particularly African Americans, were thrust into stereotypical roles, such as that of parent or disciplinarian, by residents who were hungry to have a law-abiding male role model for their children. In this way, the male NPOs in the neighborhoods were often treated with more respect, even though the women were assumed to have more empathy with female residents' family problems simply because the officers were women themselves.

Finding the right stylistic balance between crimefighter and social worker was complicated. Often, the ideal varied by what each community seemed to need. One current NPO, Carol, described the situation (as she saw it) in one of the most unstable, criminally active neighborhoods:

> Residents liked a particular style of neighborhood officer in Taylor. Children were all playing outside with no supervision, running all over the

place. And they liked the style of an NPO who, when a big gang of black males were posturing and doing some stuff, he'd walk right in the middle and tell them none of this is going to happen around here, you're out of here. And he held people up to that standard, that this is everybody's neighborhood, and if you're gonna be dealing dope and beating people up and intimidating people, you're going to jail. This surprised me because I thought that someone who was more active and more out there and visible and firm would be kind of less thought of by the residents, but it was the opposite. The difference was these women wanted their kids to be able to go outside and play and not get jumped on or shot at, and that was what made [the women's lives] better, as opposed to when people are running loose through the neighborhood and not kept under control.

Carol believed that the residents in this disorganized residential area wanted an aggressive crimefighter to exert authority over the "bad guys." Men were seen as ideal for this function. It was a perfect match for those male NPOs who were drawn to criminally active neighborhoods, because they wanted to assert their control. This is in line with empirical research findings: some men in female-dominated professions reported that they liked "being appreciated for the special traits and abilities (such as strength) they could contribute" (Williams 1992, 261). In research on the educational system, some men reported preferring working with women to working with men: "Maybe it's that women will let me take control more than men will" (Williams 1992, 261), and women cast men in leadership roles. As an NPO, each officer was in charge of her or his own neighborhood, although (beyond taking individual interests and styles into account) women and men shaped their work agendas to reflect the needs of the residents. This allowed persons of both sexes to distinguish themselves as leaders, whereas fewer opportunities for such recognition would have been available had they remained patrol officers.

The issue of setting activity agendas, however, involved far more than gender socialization or preferences. Some of the female NPOs *did,* in fact, set up and run sports programs for the children in their neighborhoods. But they talked about them very differently than the men did. Most of the women put these efforts within a larger context, asserting that they were using the sports programs to bring together boys and girls from different racial and ethnic backgrounds in order to dispel prejudices and fears and to break down segregation and cultural misunderstandings. In particular, female NPOs used soccer as a sport (rather than baseball, basketball, or football) because they believed it emphasizes teamwork and cooperation over individual competitiveness. The female officers also favored mixed-gender teams. The men said that although they made some (limited) attempts to get girls to join baseball clubs or go to ballparks to watch games, the girls only expressed an interest when a roller-skating trip was organized over the December holiday break. Of the women, the lesbian officers were more likely to develop sports programs, especially in conjunction with male NPOs' efforts. Only one former community officer, a lesbian, coached a Little League team, which she took over from a male NPO.

For both women and men, sports seemed to be a strategy to reach out to children and teenagers. The women who were involved with sports programs tended to be the ones assigned to the toughest neighborhoods. There were female NPOs in only two of these criminally active districts. For them, the emphasis on sports could also have reflected the difficulty of being white in nonwhite neighborhoods and the need to keep crime-prone boys (and girls) active. These two female officers were concerned that girls' physical and emotional development was not being adequately addressed. Moreover, female NPOs who followed a career advancement model no doubt noticed that their male colleagues received a lot of media attention, admiration from patrol officers, and recognition by the department and city for their sports efforts, as well as loyal corporate sponsorship for uniforms and equipment. Thus, it is not surprising that some community policewomen also wanted a piece of the action and based their efforts on what had proven successful for the men. The patterns and emphases of the programs reflect gender variation among the NPOs, often contingent upon their motivations, such as career advancement or the reduction of racial tensions.

Race and Ethnicity of Residents and NPOs

Further complicating questions arising from whether an NPO was a man or a woman and how gender affected behavior were the racial and ethnic backgrounds of officers and residents. Again, following Patricia Hill Collins's thinking (1990), this was not an either/or situation, but an issue of how a melding of multiple factors and social status positions affected policework. The designated neighborhoods were typically home to several racial and ethnic groups. Community officers responded to these varied populations in multiple ways. The NPOs seemed to have a grasp, and in some cases a more complex understanding, of racial miscommunications that occurred across different groups. For instance, Francine, a white former NPO, recalled:

One of the biggest problems I encountered was blacks and Hispanics and their animated, get in your face, body language . . . which, there's nothing wrong with that, but people from the other groups may misread it or even be afraid of such expressive language; the Asians have more distance, they do not have animated body language, but believe keeping one's distance shows respect. But Asians were afraid that black people were aggressive and out to attack them. And on the part of the black or Hispanic community, they believed that the Asians were sneaky, dangerous, and that they'd knife you in the back. A lot of it was not only verbal, it was body language that was misunderstood.

In the neighborhood that housed the largest Southeast Asian population, the first officer, a white woman, tried to learn to speak Hmong and understand Hmong culture. Her successor, another white woman, was less aware of Southeast Asian cultural traditions. Several current NPOs told the story of Andrea and the pig. Apparently, she answered a call and went into a dark basement. A big pig moved toward her, as if to attack. Andrea almost shot the pig. But pigs are traditionally part of Hmong households. "They knew they weren't supposed to have it, and poor Andrea had this pig charging at her . . ." Having gained some knowledge of the community she served allowed Andrea to work out a solution with the residents, without the formal invocation of law and without disrespect to Hmong traditions. By spreading this story, NPOs at once acknowledged cultural differences and educated new officers on the customs and cultural nuances they would encounter.

Only *female* officers from the first and second waves of neighborhood policing raised cultural diversity issues. The women made an explicit link between differences in culture, including race and ethnicity, and residents' behavior and receptivity to the NPOs and to police in general.

Several community officers (two black male former NPOs, one black male serving NPO, and one white female former NPO) believed it was better to have a black or Hispanic officer assigned to neighborhoods with predominantly minority populations. One white former NPO, Suzanne, remembered:

I never felt welcomed. Especially by the black women in the neighborhood—regardless if the black women were residents or professional social workers in the community center. They were never warm and fuzzy with me, as they had been with the former NPO [a black woman] and what I have seen of my replacement [a black man]. This was really disheartening, I wanted to tell them, "Look what I do with your kids, I'm doing good, your kids like me, why can't you?" It got so that I would feel intimidated at meetings and would stop speaking up. It seemed like everything that I said was met with criticism, and I thought this is a shame because they could teach me since I was a white woman in their neighborhood, you know, a great way to break down barriers.

Most community officers, however, did *not* agree that the NPO in a minority district should be a person of color. One former officer, a black man, contended:

Everybody can't be something to everyone. I mean, just because the whole neighborhood is Hispanic, doesn't mean an Hispanic officer is gonna have a lot of success . . . but at the same time, if a person from a different culture comes in there, they need to have an understanding of that particular neighborhood's culture, and if they can't deal with it, they shouldn't be in that position. . . . The department says they try to hire people with different life experiences, but when you really look at it, there are probably a lot of officers who never had a lot of contact with blacks or Hispanics . . . and now with our growing Asian population, that's even becoming a challenge. (Keith)

Half of the former and current NPOs saw a need for Asian officers and bilingual officers, since there was only one Hmong policeman in the entire department. Many of the white neighborhood officers believed that, even though they saw themselves as very good NPOs, African American single mothers and children were desperately seeking strong male role models, and thus had more appreciation for black NPOs. One officer remarked,

The only time race was an issue was when the kids would bring it up. A lot of kids out there were really looking for a role model and they would tell me that they would like to see a black officer out there, not that I was doing anything wrong, but I think it's just because they wanted a black role model and somebody that they felt had some common experiences. Whether or not that is realistic, the kids really brought that up. The adults really didn't say too much about it, and it was just the problem people there that made race an issue, otherwise it was pretty much a non-issue. (Steve)

On the other hand, some NPOs believed "a cop is a cop is a cop."

It's not really something that I was aware of, it's more that I was there by myself and there was a lot of people out. Sometimes I was aware that I was the only one in a blue suit around, but not that I was the only white person. (Matt)

Along the same lines, several white male neighborhood officers believed that any resident who was invested in conventional activities, and who had a job, would not care about the NPO's race. The words of one current NPO illustrate the point:

> I've had black NPOs tell me that they can do more than I can. But that was one thing I walked in here thinking, yeah, they might feel that way, but I'm no different from anybody else other than culturally or racially, you know. And I can get in here and do the same thing. They know I do care, especially people in organized groups, like the neighborhood association or our JFF [Joining Forces for Families] team. (Tony)

One of the former neighborhood officers, Bill, saw himself as a community organizer and leader, "almost like I was a white Martin Luther King. I mean, there were just people who were dying to be led, and they would just follow me anywhere." Apparently, he saw no racial barrier. Since at least five other officers mentioned Bill's reputation for being conceited, it would be interesting to know if the residents shared his interpretations of his activities and charisma. Nonetheless, the officer was devoted to the community policing model; ever since his days as an NPO, he has remained involved in the neighborhood, joining many civic organizations and boards, lining up corporate sponsorships for youth sports teams, and attending national conferences to discuss his department's community policing program.

Nonetheless, it was difficult to untangle race from gender effects, since the two were often conflated:

> I truly, truly believe that most white male officers have never been in that role or position where they can say "I can take my shoes off and wear someone else's shoes" and truly understand what it feels like to be oppressed or down or ignored because of who you are. Being a black female from the 'hood meant people accepted me, even though at first they didn't look beyond the uniform, even called me "he" a lot. I mean, they never even saw what's under my hat or if I had a chest! (Katie, black woman, former NPO)

Not surprisingly, personality and personal style further complicated the attempt to reduce an officer's effectiveness to a single explanatory factor. The two comments that follow were made by black women, both of them former NPOs:

> Good interactions have a lot to do with personalities, I think, not just race. . . . [U]sually black guys, they have lied to me but at least they gave

me a respectful lie . . . some of them would try to hit on me but also I felt like they respected me, and for the most part I felt that if I ever had to get into a fight with anybody there it would have probably been with just one because of policies and the need to fight with men and their egos, and in some cases women would have those problems, particularly young women . . . they always have the tough-crew complex, so I think that personality, sex, and gender all play into how people are going to relate to you as an NPO because one thing I knew, and it was confirmed time and time again, you couldn't go out and be disrespectful and have to go back the next day. (Barbara)

People always put their best foot forward if it was a nonconfrontational situation. Later on I would find out . . . ohhh, they're a crack head. I didn't have any trouble arresting them, but I would get angry or hurt, feeling like they had done something personally to me if I found out that they were using drugs or something. . . . [O]ne of the first search warrants we had to do with the task force. I was really concerned if they had valid information because I was going to be involved in that . . . and it could put me in a bad position because you know their attitude and focus is to go in and get the people, but then any mess that comes up afterwards it rests on me. So when they went into this one apartment, I was like, god I hope you're right because I felt like my reputation was on the line and people would see me as not necessarily being an advocate for them. (Katie)

These words suggest that male residents may relate to police differently because of their desire to save face in front of their peers. The same men, however, acted with chivalry toward neighborhood officers who were women.

African American men who were NPOs felt particularly torn about the issues of race and gender they confronted in the neighborhood position. They recognized that their status signified achievement for other black persons. One of the former officers, William, said:

It's a fine line . . . it's very easy to remain separate and keep that professional distance when you're in a squad [car], but it's one of the challenges when walking the 'hood. Being an African American male, a lot of kids looked up to me. A lot of times I would be the only African American male walking around during the day when mothers and kids are out so there's also that connection. "Officer William, why don't you come on over to my apartment? I can make you lunch or coffee or something." You know, those types of things.

In fact, all of the black men who were former or serving community police officers mentioned this behavior, often with a smile. The women wanted their company because they were successful African American men, and therefore perceived as valuable. During a day of fieldwork, one of the female residents, after hearing that I was conducting a research project about NPOs, said of one officer: "He's doing good. If he just standing still, he still do real good." The men recalled getting free food, often homemade cookies, and many barbecue sandwiches. And, indeed, we observed many invitations issued and much food handed out when we were in the neighborhoods doing fieldwork with men who were African American NPOs.

Race aside, we also observed heightened enthusiasm on the part of local women whenever *any* male officer stopped to chat with them. In particular, male NPOs impressed residents to the point of awe when they expressed a personal interest in their children or family activities. At the times female officers showed such interest, the residents still embraced their informality, and seemed to look on it as above the call of duty for ordinary patrol officers. But they did not seem to regard the female NPOs' interest as something out of the ordinary for *women*, particularly ones with children of their own. Thus, when men performed "women's work" in the new neighborhood policing role, they were hailed as "supermen"; women performing the same work, however, were simply involved in traditional female tasks and responsibilities and were doing nothing out of the ordinary.

This phenomenon of men being lavishly praised when doing traditionally female work is well documented in the larger studies that have investigated gender and occupation. Feminist researchers assert that jobs are not gender neutral (Acker 1990). In analyzing gender and work issues within the criminal justice system, Martin and Jurik (1996, 4) observe:

The gender division of labor in the justice system is part of larger on-going processes of differentiation in society. Social differentiation, or the practice of distinguishing categories based on some attribute or set of attributes, is a fundamental social process and the basis for differential evaluations and unequal rewards. Differentiation assumes, magnifies, and even creates behavioral and psychological differences to ensure that the subordinate group differs from the dominant one. It presumes that differences are "natural" and desirable.

In this way, gender is extended beyond what someone *is* to include what someone *does* on an ongoing basis (West and Zimmerman 1987). As illustrated earlier in this chapter and in Chapter 4, the male NPOs tended to engage in
"masculine" activities with the neighborhood children and geared these to boys'
interests, among them sports, camping, and computers. Some women were involved with such programs, particularly in the high-crime, less-stable districts,
and officers of both genders were aware that they brought a different style to
policing.

> I think that women have a better sense of just being more aware of the
> emotional side, and more of the "just the facts" [approach] disappears. I
> think women pick up nonverbal stuff more easily . . . I could go on and
> make myself look like I am male-bashing. There are a lot of women who
> aren't good at that and who aren't sensitive and aren't aware of things,
> and there are men that are good at it and not good at it. But I think that
> women have really brought out communication skills and awareness in
> the men. Men see what a positive and helpful tool it is, and how much
> of a better job can be done by talking, instead of knocking someone
> around and giving no explanations, just hauling them off to jail. I think
> women take on more of a role of seeing the big picture or trying to solve
> other problems beyond the initial problems. (Carol)

The men recognized the positive and negative issues related to officer and gender socialization. As one former NPO, Keith, a black man, said:

> Some of the men are sensitive and aware of problems and they care. But
> there are some men, even in the NPO positions, who hate being at do-
> mestic calls because it's not the big one, and they're not going to be able
> to get into a confrontation or a shoot-out or something. They're still
> always hoping for the big one.

For Stewart, a current NPO,

> Women brought the ability to expand roles within policing, and that's
> what is needed in community policing.

Thus, the neighborhood officers recognized that women and men "do gender" differently, which was reflected in the activities related to law enforcement
that they chose to emphasize. Differences can be attributed to multiple sources,
such as the extent to which residents desired the NPOs' presence in their per-

sonal and community space. What kind of officer was most desirable? The answer would vary by residents' interests or fears or hopes, by the natures of the different neighborhoods, and by the characteristics of individual officers.

This chapter has examined issues related to interactions between neighborhood police officers and their communities. Differences in behavior cannot be reduced to any single factor, such as gender. Although some of the officers' actions resulted from gender-role socialization, others resulted more from purely gender-neutral circumstances. An example of the latter involved the reasons officers gave for seeking the neighborhood position. Although all of them stated that their initial goal as NPOs was to improve troubled communities, they also were attracted to the job for various other reasons: some sought to advance within the force and saw neighborhood policing as a good career move; some were looking for less action and a slower pace; and still others, burned out from crisis-driven, anonymous patrol, needed a change. These varied motivations caused tensions among the NPOs, which were exacerbated by unclear expectations in the different neighborhoods about what NPOs should do.

Role ambivalence characterized the neighborhood policing model in at least two important ways: first, there was tension between communities' desires and officers' agendas; second, problems arose from the dynamics related to officers' expressions of masculinity or femininity and to their race and ethnicity. Within each community, NPOs' styles and interests affected the kinds of activities they pursued. The emphasis on public visibility for law enforcement efforts indicated that community policing fiercely clung to its masculine police focus, despite being laden, supposedly, with social workers. Men and women asserted their masculinity and femininity in different ways within the various neighborhoods. The department's seniority policy also had an impact on policework, sometimes resulting in the assignment of NPOs who were not best fitted to the needs of particular communities.

Regardless of their gender, race, or sexual orientation, neighborhood officers had several experiences in common. For instance, residents grew to rely on them for help in negotiating their way through the intricacies of the criminal justice or social service systems. All of the current and former NPOs believed that their law enforcement efforts improved once they had established more personal connections with the residents: hostility and distrust between police and local citizens decreased; officers' morale improved, since they saw more of the good side of people; making arrests and serving warrants became easier; and, often, residents publicly supported officers during disagreements over neighborhood problems. This did not mean that there were no difficulties, particularly for the male NPOs. Men saw the informal style of community policing as getting in the way of effective law enforcement, and they struggled to keep job expectations separate from their personal lives.

Residents played an important role, often working in tandem with officers to mutual advantage. For instance, as noted above, greater familiarity between police and local people made such formal law enforcement actions as serving warrants and making arrests easier. For their part, residents got help and support from their NPOs, who acted as liaisons or negotiators in dealings with the criminal justice system and, sometimes, social service agencies and landlords. Such reciprocity helped to bolster officers' morale and to forge even more positive connections between local citizens and police.

Race and images of masculinity and femininity were inextricably linked to neighborhood officers' gender, and these dynamics influenced NPOs' interpretations and actions. Only white male officers (both former and current) believed that the race of an NPO made no difference in the neighborhoods. Men of all races concentrated on masculine activity, such as sports programs for children (primarily boys), and law enforcement work overall. Men of all races were also more likely to select the more criminally active, socially disorganized neighborhoods, which gave them the opportunity to display their masculinity to their police peers on patrol. Although women did not shy away from law enforcement action when necessary, their responses reflected a much stronger focus on broader social issues that might be antecedent to crime, involving them in such work as creating domestic violence programs for victims or building stronger links between parents and schools.

Kelly, the only woman to be supervisor of NPOs, contended:

> Personality is always a factor, regardless of gender or race. Just who they
> are as people and how they interact with other people. . . . [G]ender and
> race are certainly factors that may make it easier or more difficult at
> times to walk into certain situations, but personality often determines
> how an officer handles incidents.

Even though both men and women might follow an androgynous style of policing, their decisions and actions were nonetheless conditioned by years of early socialization patterns and influences that instilled particular social constructions of masculinity and femininity. Women who chose law enforcement careers were already atypical in that they selected the quintessential masculinity-confirming field. Within this masculine context, men and women drew on both perceived and socially prescribed gender roles, with men favoring higher-risk situations that promised more action and greater potential for aggression and confrontation. For their part, women gravitated toward developing more nur-

turing bonds and maintaining them, mending relationships, supporting cooperative sports (such as soccer), establishing links with community nurses, and
developing ways to improve coordination between parents and schools.

Perhaps due to social perceptions and understandings, residents granted
female neighborhood officers "expert status" in negotiating the social and com-
munity-related aspects of daily life. In this way, women could capitalize on their
strengths as law enforcement officers who had authority and as individuals who
might better understand interpersonal dynamics and relationships. (At the same
time, however, not all women strove toward both of these objectives.) They
were quick to commend some of the men who also were able to wear both hats,
those of law enforcer and social worker. Some female NPOs also acknowledged
their inclination to favor and pursue a stronger emphasis on law enforcement
in the neighborhood. Despite their disclaimers, however, these women's law
enforcement styles still reflected some gender differences. The words of both
women and men suggested that they themselves differentiated between their
fellow officers, male and female, on merit; this indicated that they felt some
officers, regardless of gender, deserved respect for their abilities and others did
not. Clearly, the men and women are not monolithic groups, but sets of individuals who were influenced by their unique backgrounds and life experiences,
and by gender, race, and sexual orientation as well.

Chapter 6 addresses how these differences and similarities are experienced
and understood by patrol officers assigned to squad cars in the neighborhoods.
It also examines how they and community officers handle the enduring social
problem of domestic violence.

Walking the Talk

Contrasting Neighborhood Officers and Patrol Officers

Each day is a fresh, new slate.
—Patrol Officer

How can you help a neighborhood if you
don't get to know it intimately?
—Neighborhood Officer

This chapter focuses on two issues. First, I turn to a group of officers who have not yet been examined, the rapid response patrol officers in squad cars, in order to uncover their perceptions of community policing. There were nineteen patrol officers in the sample, reflecting that their shifts overlapped those of the thirteen neighborhood officers (who had flexible schedules) in different ways. The fieldwork data revealed six major themes that captured the perceptions and experiences of the patrol officers. Second, I explore the special topic of domestic violence, which remains one of the most frustrating issues that police officers confront. This part of the chapter looks at how neighborhood officers handle such incidents and at how their approach differs from traditional policing models.

Earlier chapters have explored the NPOs' perceptions of being accepted or rejected by patrol officers. The community officers have also discussed how they handled policework in ways that were similar to or different from those used by patrol officers. In this chapter, patrol officers reveal their feelings about neighborhood policing. The chapter begins with descriptive material from the police department's briefing room, where officers gather to exchange information before every shift. This introduces the patrol officers' milieu, and points to ways in which how they talked about NPOs revealed their thoughts about them.

The Police Briefing Room

Most officers, community and patrol, typically began their shift by attending briefings, and our research team often went along. These meetings, at the downtown (main) police station, were jovial, somewhat disorganized events. Present in the room was a shared language, a shared way of understanding, and a sense of peer bonding and positive reinforcement. It was striking how many of the officers were young and how many were women. Although what follows is a description of just one 3 P.M. gathering, consistently similar patterns or themes emerged across multiple observations, at different briefings with different shifts, and with several trained observers.

The briefing room was a picture of camaraderie, with much joking, soda drinking, gum chewing, and mutual teasing. The total number of persons in the room fluctuated, as some officers (including the inspector, who was not in uniform) drifted in and out. On this afternoon there were around twenty-six, perhaps half of them women; of the men, two were Latino, and all the rest were white. Approximately twenty of those present appeared to be under forty years of age. This youthfulness reflected a couple of factors. Seniority provides officers with a better selection of shifts, so newcomers on the force are less likely to get the coveted daytime shifts. Some of the younger officers, however, simply wanted to see more action, so they deliberately selected later working hours. Apparently, it was even more common for the 11 P.M.–7 A.M. shift to have younger officers, and a greater number of women as well.

In the briefings, the sergeant in charge told the assembled officers what they needed to know for that shift; for example, which citizens had warrants outstanding, what trouble areas or persons they might encounter, if extra patrolling was needed for some school property that was "tagged" by graffiti artists the night before, and, in this case, how preparations were going for the upcoming Fourth of July extravaganza. For this citywide event, an officer outlined the traffic and crowd control plan on maps. Many of those being briefed seemed to only half listen as they talked with their friends. (We learned later that the officers probably heard and absorbed everything. They had perfected the ability to be in a group having a conversation, or talking with us, and yet still easily listen to everything that went over the police radio, even when we observers missed it entirely.)

At one point during the briefing, a white man asked if officers would be assigned to traffic duty for the Independence Day celebration or would walk among the crowd. The sergeant answered that all police would be walking. One woman quipped, "Then we'll be doing 'community policing.' " She said it with a touch of sarcasm, and everybody mock-groaned and laughed. Poking fun at the neighborhood program was common, and the gibes were fully understood and appreciated by all those present, including any NPOs.

Toward the end of the briefing, several examples of "good" arrests or solid policework were relayed; the officers responsible were congratulated and everyone applauded them. We noted that these examples revolved around traditional kinds of crimefighting and law enforcement and that there was no mention of social service styles or accomplishments. Basically, during briefings the high-spirited officers seemed eager to finish and get on with their "real work" of fighting crime.

Typically, the sergeant in charge mentioned who we were and which NPO and patrol officer we would accompany for the shifts. In fact, as soon as the female sergeant called the meeting to order, she told the officers that they had two visitors and that we would introduce ourselves. Thus, everyone was aware that our research team would be doing walk-alongs with the NPOs and ride-alongs with the patrol officers for some months. Judging from some of the reactions, it was clear that a number of NPOs had established reputations, and that not all of these were good ones. For instance, whenever Curtis's name would come up as the assigned NPO for our research shift, the officers laughed and indicated there was something funny or not quite right with him. Later, when we headed to pick up a squad car for the shift, we asked if any current NPOs had a specific car assigned to them. The patrol officer said no, the cars were all up for grabs on each shift. Then he laughed and remarked that one or two community officers used their private cars while on duty. One of them was Curtis. The patrol officers believed that he often did this deliberately to get out of doing work. If Curtis did not have a radio, then he could not be called for backup. And Curtis could always claim to be too busy, since there was no effective way to monitor him. From the tone of the officer's comments, he viewed Curtis as a "skater," lazy and a shirker. Patrol officers believed that such shirking was easy for NPOs, because no one checked up on them, no one evaluated them, and they set their own hours.

It was clear that one woman or man could spoil the reputation for all NPOs. The widespread misunderstanding of the neighborhood position did not need further reinforcement. Within the jovial atmosphere of the briefing room, officers readily participated in making in-group and out-group distinctions; from the nature of the discussions and jokes, it was clear that neighborhood officers bore the brunt of their humor. With this in mind, I now examine what individual patrol officers said about community policing and NPOs.

Ride-Alongs with Patrol Officers

As with most call-driven policing in this country, patrol officers cruise their assigned beat, looking for things or people that seem out of place, always waiting to be sent to a call by radio dispatchers. Riding with them afforded us the opportunity to observe their work routine and the area under their control, and permitted ample time for conversation about policework. Most ride-alongs began with the patrol officer showing the researcher the "hot spots" in the beat and recounting success stories. These usually involved crimes cleared by arrests, or somehow turning a neighborhood problem or a problematic person in a more positive direction. The discussions that follow are based on six significant themes raised by every patrol officer. They tell an important part of the story of how cooperation and understanding between neighborhood officers on foot and their colleagues in squad cars could be enhanced or diminished. Patrol officers also admitted that they did not like dealing with ongoing problems, preferring their job's quick pace and limited citizen contact.

Interactions Between Patrol and Neighborhood Officers

Contacts between the two groups of officers were extremely limited. Only twice during the course of many hours spent riding in the field did a patrol officer leave the squad car to walk with an NPO. Much of this separation can be explained by the nature of a call-driven police force whose primary goal was rapid reaction. At the same time, however, patrol officers were quick to offer their own reasons for the limited interaction. Most claimed to have walked around with the community officers at least once in the past year. But they also felt that the NPOs were often absent from the neighborhood, probably attending a meeting. They never knew when NPOs were around due to their scheduling flexibility.

In the months of our ride-alongs, we observed only two occasions when patrol officers left their squad cars to "do policing" with NPOs. Both occurred in the most troubled and criminally active neighborhoods. The two patrol officers said they were bored, and they knew the NPOs well from serving together on the department's SWAT team. For the twenty minutes or less that they were on the street, the neighborhood activity consisted solely of meeting up with the NPO and talking with several uniformed private security employees. In one case, five white men stood in the middle of a mostly nonwhite neighborhood, talking informally. There was not even a nod at community policing; in fact, this grouping gave the appearance of heavy-duty surveillance. The police officers did not exchange information regarding the residents, crime, or community happenings. The patrol officer did not witness any "community policing" activities occurring. Joint operations involving patrol officers and NPOs were not discussed. The patrol officer even expressed some discomfort about being away from his "moving office," the squad car. This was consistent with comments by his colleagues. Some, for instance, revealed that they would never want to walk alone at night in a neighborhood, and that they would always wear bulletproof vests. They were emphatic about this, even though they admitted to not knowing a single officer who had ever been shot or shot at. In the same conversation, one of the patrol officers repeatedly apologized for how tame the ride-alongs were in Jackson City, asserting that if we were in larger cities we could have been dodging bullets. This apology reflected the crime control orientation that defined policing for patrol officers. Emphasizing crimefighting reinforced the oppositional image of social work, the "touchy-feely" component viewed as the NPOs' domain.

Patrol officers acknowledged some personal advantages that accrued from the department's neighborhood policing program. For instance, they believed that extensive interaction between NPOs and residents might have the residual effect of helping citizens improve their hostile attitudes toward patrol officers. They hoped that residents would no longer see the police as the enemy. Several patrol officers believed that the familiarity between residents and NPOs would help them by allowing them to check with NPOs to determine if a local person was lying.

However, the patrol officers also expressed negative thoughts about NPOs. Although they felt their colleagues were able to work more closely with residents, they believed that this could foster dependence, which would be the opposite of neighborhood policing's goal of community empowerment. And patrol officers were skeptical about the kinds of calls that NPOs answered. For instance, they had heard through the grapevine that NPOs received calls to help with household repairs, such as leaky toilets. Often, such inaccurate comments were quickly amended, and patrol officers would next suggest that their colleagues probably did do more than give plumbing advice.

Because of their limited interaction with it, neighborhood policing remained mysterious to patrol officers. They relied on stereotypes of the officer driven by social work, which fit in with "cop canteen culture." This phrase derives from Nigel Fielding's (1994, 47, 52) use of the term "canteen culture" to convey the masculine values of the police occupational culture. Such values include aggressiveness, unquestioning loyalty to each other among officers, physical action, competitiveness, preoccupation with the imagery of conflict, and an exaggerated heterosexuality often articulated through misogynistic attitudes. In Jackson City, this culture is in part established and reinforced by the humorous references to community policing made in the briefing room and in the field. These stereotypes were interrupted only when patrol officers had participated with NPOs in joint activities or when a well-respected, macho officer bid for an NPO position in a tough neighborhood. However, no patrol officer's change in thinking was publicly declared in the briefings. No one dared defend the neighborhood police officers.

Perceptions of Neighborhood Policing

The limited interactions just discussed have contributed to how patrol officers understand community policing. Within this broad theme, four specific issues were mentioned. Two of these subthemes reflected patrol officers' lack of knowledge about NPOs, and two more concerned the practical aspects of doing neighborhood policing. The first subtheme was *isolation*. Patrol officers viewed the neighborhood positions as undesirable since NPOs were confined to one place. They liked their own flexibility and the convenience of driving all over their beats. Patrol officers believed their colleagues spent too much time in meetings with landlords, social service agents, probation and parole officers, and business owners; this isolated them from the patrol officers and from the residents of the community. There was also an assumption that the "reliance" on meetings could be manipulated, thereby allowing some community officers to be lazy and get out of doing particular things, either by saying they had a meeting or by overscheduling their meetings so that they had less time for policing their neighborhoods.

Another subtheme, raised by all but one patrol officer, was that *NPOs do not do "real" policework*. Although some patrol officers acknowledged that there was a connection between NPOs and the ability to solve underlying problems, they all felt that NPOs responded to residents and political needs, not necessarily to crimefighting goals. This belief tied in to the third subtheme, that *NPOs had too much autonomy*. Such freedom, coupled with the absence of any formal evaluation or evidence of supervision, seemed to inflate patrol officers' cynicism about neighborhood policing. For instance, NPOs' paperwork did not get checked nightly, and they were typically not assigned to a sergeant who was in control of their shift; instead, NPOs had a regional supervising officer who looked in on them occasionally. Patrol officers continued to believe that no other structure of accountability for the NPOs' time existed, although they did acknowledge that it was left up to the individual NPO to determine what to do, when to do it, and what to let slide. Patrol officers seemed to be suspicious, if not resentful, of the lack of supervision of the men and women in the neighborhood positions, since their own work was more tightly controlled.

The last subtheme involved the issue of *backup*. In most police departments, it is common for more than one officer to respond to certain service calls. In

Jackson City, for example, two cars were always dispatched to handle incidents involving domestic violence. The patrol officers believed that they responded as backup to *all* neighborhood calls. However, they also believed that the NPOs rarely or never responded to *any* calls for service, even if the NPOs were in the neighborhood. Resentment that they could not count on their colleagues reinforced the patrol officers' belief that they were doing more work than the NPOs. Yet, the community officers garnered more rewards and professional recognition. This reward structure reinforced their belief that NPOs do not do "real" policework.

NPOs and Patrol Officers: Similarities and Differences

Earlier, I explored the NPOs' perceptions of their job expectations and duties in contrast to those of patrol officers. Now I explore the reverse. Despite patrol officers' belief that NPOs did less real policework than they, the patrol officers raised an almost equal number of similarities (four) and differences (three) in their work. The first similarity was a shared experience with the frequent need for police at certain addresses. Both groups of officers were very aware of problem people in their beats. All had been called back on multiple occasions either to the same address or in response to the same persons or problems. The patrol officers pointed out the same "hot spots" to the research team that the NPOs did. Given this recognition, a greater potential for better coordination of responses and services may exist. However, any efforts to realize it might clash with the organizational goals of patrol and neighborhood policing.

Second, both sets of officers used similar informal strategies. During our walk-alongs and ride-alongs, they gave out baseball cards to girls and boys. Both neighborhood and patrol officers focused on those they felt were "deserving." For instance, they did not mind if cute, well-behaved children asked for more cards, but they were less generous with impolite or greedy youngsters who never thanked them or seemed satisfied. Another example of similar informal strategies was that both the community and patrol officers aggressively ticketed cars that were parked where No Standing signs had been posted (the signs also gave police probable cause to ticket anyone who loitered). Moreover, some of the patrol officers, particularly the women, took part in a few of the outdoor events arranged by NPOs for children in the neighborhood. Since the patrol officers did this during their time off, their participation grew out of their friendships with the NPOs. Several female patrol officers also spoke about pet projects in their beats that had a social-work dimension, such as counseling an eight-year-old boy who pulls fire alarms and befriending a fourteen-year-old girl who runs away.

The third similarity involved what the patrol officers and NPOs said about policing programs. Ironically, the former group frequently spouted community policing rhetoric. For example, when one patrol officer, a black man, was asked how he felt about his work with residents, he said, "You take a bag of tools into each call. You may have to take out a different tool at each call, like helpfulness, humor, or control." Yet at the same time, patrol officers continued to draw a strong distinction between their law enforcement role and the NPOs' service-related role.

The fourth, and final, similarity involved follow-ups to earlier calls for providing service or dealing with problems. Although the neighborhood officers spent a huge amount of time in this fashion, overall, their colleagues in patrol did only limited follow-up, explaining that they did not have the luxury of time to do this regularly. A few officers did mention, however, that the department was moving in this new direction, since the chief's newsletters have begun to highlight problem-solving actions taken by patrol officers. Still, there are tighter limits on the amount of follow-up work that patrol officers can do. The following example described this kind of action.

During one shift, Jake, a white patrol officer, responded to a call about a child's stolen bike. Once at the home, he confiscated the screwdriver used to pry open the storage shed; the forensic lab would later check it for fingerprints. The residents were respectful, very eager to cooperate, and anxious to hear back from Jake about the evidence. As we left the house he told me, out of the residents' earshot, that it was very unlikely that fingerprints would be recovered, and he might never have the time to come back to tell them so. In fact, they would have to call in to the proper phone line at the department for this information. Jake mused that one nice thing about being an NPO was having the time to conduct follow-up activities. He speculated that this could be a valid reason for promotion if community officers acted like detectives. However, Jake remained unconvinced that NPOs spent much time doing "detective work."

The patrol officers also readily identified three major differences between their work and that of NPOs. The first of these involved pacing. The men and women were unanimous in stating they were not now personally interested in becoming community officers. More than half, however, did say that they would consider the neighborhood position sometime down the road because they saw it as a necessary stepping-stone for promotion. Most of the patrol officers described themselves as "adrenaline junkies" who were thrilled by the chase, the lights, and the sirens. They did not want to give up the rush. One woman commented: "The stress I feel from my job is *not* from adrenaline stuff like 'going lights and sirens' and not knowing what to expect on a call. That's the kick, that's the fun stuff. The stressful stuff is the everyday jerks and the frustration that there is not much you can do about it." A male officer remarked: "I am only twenty-seven years old. I might consider being an NPO when I turn fifty, since I could not see myself actively running around after people when I am that old. I'll need a slower job."

But for the moment, patrol officers found a slower pace to be less than exciting. During the ride-alongs, if they had not received a lot of calls, or if the calls were not crime related, the patrol officers, especially the white men, apologized to us about the lack of "action." They spoke of being bored themselves and of not liking to "make work" just to keep busy. Thus, the perceived lack of excitement in neighborhood policing was a disincentive; as one patrol officer stated, they were always on the edge, "waiting for something big to go down."

Career motivation constituted a second significant difference. Except when they saw NPO positions as an avenue to higher rank, the patrol officers simply were not interested. The reasons, expressed negatively, varied: in patrol, officers were not expected to follow up on calls; they did not have to attend regular, and multiple, meetings with constituency groups; they did not have to engage in continuing dialogues with "everyday jerks"; they did not have an extraordinary amount of paperwork, or feel there was always something left undone at the end of a shift; and they did not have to stay in an office, often without a squad car at their disposal.

The third, and last, difference patrol officers identified between themselves and typical NPOs was that they wanted to stay away from social work, mostly because community policing seemed too frustrating. They shared the feeling that residents should take control of their own lives, getting themselves out of bad situations or avoiding them in the first place. This applied even if persons could not be responsible for the situations they found themselves in, as in the case of a teenager with bad parents. The patrol officers felt that maybe NPOs "enable" citizens too much. They also believed that their own view of things was more realistic: being called to a horrible situation does not mean being able to fix it. The patrol officers liked their freedom to intervene in chronically bad situations without having to continue to confront them day after day. In fact, regardless of their position on the force, all police ultimately have the power to haul lawbreakers off to jail. Patrol officers, though, believed they exercised this power far more quickly than did NPOs. At the same time, however, some of them recognized that community police officers might understand more about the residents' life circumstances because of their greater involvement with them. As one patrol officer, Patricia, said,

> The scary thing is that you become quickly aware of the fact that in [a]
> city, a lot of people are marginal, and maybe one hundred years ago

would have had the trade skills and life skills to manage, but today there just isn't a lot they can do: they are functional, but barely, not educated, not skilled, and borderline in social skills. These are the forgotten folks, who come into the most contact with the police.

Neighborhood officers were seen as having the desire and time to deal with such marginalized populations.

Thus, patrol officers pointed to both similarities and differences between themselves and NPOs. These issues did not necessarily involve contradictions, but arose out of the different goals and strategies with which the two kinds of officers were involved. The patrol officers' unexamined, erroneous beliefs also particularly contributed to negative stereotypes about NPOs.

Departmental Politics

A fourth theme that emerged from the fieldwork revolved around the political dynamics within the Jackson City Police Department. As mentioned above, all of the patrol officers believed that neighborhood positions were used as a mechanism to get promoted. This aroused some resentment, since they saw the promotions as being more tied to politics than related to job or skill competence. All of the patrol officers noted that the new chief's last promotion slate heavily favored NPOs. One of the patrol officers, Kurt, a white man, summarized their views:

> I believe that the former chief made every decision based on politics, and he loved the idea of community policing and would only have followers and true believers in his inner circle. Whenever a group of business owners screamed loudly enough, he responded to them. He did not respond as quickly or as well if plain old people asked for an NPO.

There was consensus that several neighborhoods assigned full-time officers might not need them. But, owing to political pressures from merchant associations and from the university (which was concerned about off-campus properties where students lived), they kept their NPOs, even without proof of extensive criminal activity. Many of the officers, regardless of how long they had been on the force, explained this state of affairs by saying, "The chief brought in a lot of outside grant money." As noted in Chapter 1, this kind of dissatisfaction and lowered morale often results when a chief introduces policies without getting "buy-in" from the rank and file. The second and third waves of NPOs held similar views about departmental politics.

During the political discussions, patrol officers also mentioned their pride in being members of such a diverse department. Many attributed the large number of women to the former chief's commitment to diversity and his belief that they bring more finely developed communication skills to the job. The patrol officers tended to state they thought many women were physically aggressive, and those who were not so aggressive compensated with better developed interpersonal negotiating abilities. They also maintained that they were not aware of any tension between male and female officers, probably because they were all so used to working together. Women were not tokens in the department, although they were less well represented in higher management. The officers did acknowledge a number of personality quirks and conflicts on the force, but they believed these did not have much to do with gender. One patrolman, echoing many others, suggested:

> From the time you join the force, you are developing your reputation, and we just want to know if you are a team player, if you keep your mouth shut, if you don't tattle to the brass, and if you can be counted on for backup.

From these conversations, it was clear that although the patrol officers welcomed the diversity wrought by "political correctness," they harbored some negative feelings about the political influence they believed was tied to neighborhood policing. One development that may lessen this antagonism is that the NPO selection criteria now dictate that candidates must already be known and tested as patrol officers before moving into neighborhood positions. Thus, NPOs' new credibility may militate against patrol officers' distaste for political manipulation.

Masculinity Confirmation and Alternatives

Perhaps the most visible display of male camaraderie and macho talk occurred during the impromptu, yet frequent, meetings of several patrol officers in their squad cars. It was customary to gather during the shift, either at a predetermined place for dinner or in an uncrowded parking lot. Most of the time the officers never left their cars, pulling alongside each other so that the windows on the driver's side were adjacent. Meetings like these involved both women and men. Whenever the patrol officers got together, the conversation revolved around "guy stuff," such as joking about guns or other weapons, talking about surveillance work, and pretending to pull out one's gun. Their language was full of expletives, with some version of "f——k" being the most common. Information about suspicious persons or addresses was exchanged, all done with humor at the expense of citizens. Common topics of conversation were upcoming shooting competitions, physical training, qualifications, and similar physical activities. The men tended to tell us, the researchers, what kind of exercise regimens they followed, and which officers helped with running, training, and weight lifting at the police academy. These topics reinforced the tough, masculine, crimefighting image of policing.

Patrolwomen who were part of these "jawing" sessions engaged in the conversation with equal heartiness. At one point, a white lesbian officer claimed that an advantage of patrol was its paramilitary structure, because at least it did not allow for the "endless processing" one finds with some feminist groups. All of the officers commented on how much they loved "going lights and sirens"; one woman said it made her unable to get to sleep until three or four in the morning. However, away from their male counterparts, many women used their "downtime" to focus on activities that were less macho. For instance, they gave out McDonald's food coupons to girls and boys, and asked older children and teenagers about homework or why they were not at school. This showed a different side of the patrolwomen, although clearly they also loved the crimefighter image.

Even though the patrolwomen joined in the banter and told their share of crimefighting war stories, it became clear during one-on-one conversations with them that they dropped their aggressive facade when their actions were less visible to other patrol officers. The women were more than superficially involved in some of the local people's lives, particularly with the children. They said that their work was not always respected by female residents. These local women tended to respect the male officers more; in fact, a number of female patrol officers, African American and white, said that women, particularly black women, yelled at them a lot for hassling them, for stopping their patrol cars in the middle of a street or parking lot so children could pass by safely, and so forth. It seemed easier for female residents to be harsh with other women than for them to challenge male officers' power and authority.

The officers seemed at ease and talkative whenever gender or diversity issues arose. All of them mentioned at some point that the city and its police department were the only bastions of progressivism left in their state. They believed that officers from other forces knew the liberal reputation of Jackson City and even how progressive the department was, since they were always saying such things as "Don't bend over in front of a Jackson City cop." This and similar jokes were used to question the masculinity of the city's policemen, insinuating that they were homosexual or effeminate. What is interesting here is that outsiders lump all Jackson City policemen together as "sissies," not distinguishing between NPOs and patrol officers. At least on the surface, the patrol officers laughed these kinds of slurs off. In fact, several of the patrolwomen independently related a story with great pride. Six members of the force were selected to represent the department at a statewide Department of Justice conference. Jackson City reflected its diversity by sending five female officers (three of whom were lesbians) and one black man. The other departments' representatives were all white men. One of the women who told the story said, "You could see that the conference presenters had to work quickly to change their jokes so they wouldn't offend the audience."

None of the male officers mentioned this conference, despite their declared pride in the department's diversity. Only one patrol officer, a man, described himself as a conservative. He said that he was uncomfortable with Jackson City's liberal reputation, and went on to state, with great pride, that he was proud to be a conservative in a liberal community. He seemed to be an anomaly.

Several of the male officers, but none of their female colleagues, bragged about the recent publication in a national beauty magazine of a story featuring policewomen. Jackson City was highlighted because the department is one of the top five in the country in female officers per capita. Just a few of the men admitted that women were still privately classified as "bitch," "whore," "dyke," or "prude," and never seen as just another officer. Similar stereotypes or categories did not exist for men, who evaluated other male officers on performance: either they worked hard or they did not. Only the patrolmen raised this issue of women's images; the neighborhood officers tended to talk about all other NPOs in terms of work competency, not gender.

Several female patrol officers acknowledged variations in how men and women do their jobs. They believed the difference was not specifically related to gender per se, but to physical size. They knew that as 130-pound, five-foot six-inch women (or even smaller) they would be spending more time talking an agitated citizen down than using physical force. By contrast, a six-foot four-inch male officer under similar circumstances might move forward with more physicality. The women believed that the biggest gender difference came with male suspects. They did not seem to feel that women threatened their masculinity in quite the same way as a male officer did when he asserted his power. According to the patrol officers, male suspects appeared calmer and more cooperative with female officers. The women also noted that they themselves did not have a preference about having women or men to work with, but they did care a lot about individuals' reputations. Yet, the women acknowledged the likelihood that when they were with male officers, and already had a situation under control, the men would often walk in and upset the fragile balance they had achieved.

Although officers' gender was not explicitly identified as a divisive issue among the members of the Jackson City force, beneath the surface such differences permeated the ranks of patrol officers. Camaraderie dominated their public gatherings, but another picture emerged in the more private police-community encounters and in the one-on-one conversations with the research team.

Race

The sixth, and last, theme that was raised by every patrol officer touches on several issues concerning race: the factors that increased prejudice and social distance between communities and police, how residents responded to officers from different races, and how masculinity interacted with race. The first issue involves prejudice reinforcement. The patrol officers repeatedly said that in their rapid response, call-driven jobs they were overexposed to "bad people, dirt and stench, and disorganized families, or uncaring, crack-dependent mothers." One officer, a white man, summed up the consequences:

> It could make someone very prejudiced unless they have some other examples to contradict these images. For instance . . . I have a really close black friend who I went through the academy with. I need my friend in order to counteract the bad stuff we see on patrol: the constant lying, hostility, and uncooperativeness. If an officer didn't have any black friends, the job would confirm all his stereotypes.

Not one of the patrol officers speculated that a neighborhood policing position creates opportunities to see people at their best, not just when they are immersed in a crisis. According to white officers, the race of an officer would not make a difference in improving community-police relations. They seemed to feel that people just did not always trust the police, regardless of their race. Several of the white patrolmen felt that although white officers did not have a problem in predominantly African American neighborhoods, "black officers take more shit, mostly about being 'Oreos' and enforcing the white man's rule." Both white and black officers believed that African American citizens loved black officers until they enforced the laws. But basically the patrol officers, as one of them said, felt that "the citizens see blue uniforms as the enemy, and they do not see the person behind the uniform." At the same time, however, white officers felt that when there were tensions citizens frequently used race as an excuse to avoid taking responsibility for their own behavior. Several white patrol officers suggested that, as white persons, they were less likely to challenge black men verbally when they were "talking shit." But the white officers said they liked to work with aggressive African American officers who would not stand for hostile treatment and disrespect from other black women and men.

They believed these officers were able to get to the heart of a situation, properly challenge a black man's attitude, and make him back away from possible confrontation.

Regardless of race or gender, the patrol officers talked casually about racial matters. They all pointed out hot spots during the shifts, and seemed especially eager to pinpoint any cars with white drivers. The drivers and their white passengers were obviously nonresidents; they were there to try to purchase drugs. Such sales to white persons in nonwhite neighborhoods became a recurring theme. The joke among the patrol officers: Since the crackdown on drug sales in white residential areas, there had never been so many white people getting lost in black neighborhoods and asking police officers for directions. (Asking directions was the lame excuse given by the white drivers to explain away their presence.) The officers found this very funny and passed the story on to us many times during shifts.

The patrol officers also suggested some advantages to the social distance that their method of operating created between them and citizens. The officers said they did not get to know the residents very well, and, frankly, they did not necessarily want to. Donna, a white officer, remarked:

> Ninety-five percent of the people we come into contact with on calls are either jerks or nice people at their worst. Only close friends and other police officers understand this. Also, *everybody* lies to the police, everybody, even upstanding citizens, not just those who are most problematic or in trouble.

The patrol officers felt caught in a particularly vicious circle because the percentage of middle-class blacks in Jackson City was very small, and these were not the people whom the police regularly encountered. Instead, officers were overexposed to those African Americans who had the most problems, which reinforced (or initiated) patrol officers' racism or prejudice. Many officers found this very frustrating because they thought that, in general, they held nonracist values. The white and black officers believed this experience was the same regardless of race, since they were "seen by uniform, not by color."

What was striking about these comments was that the patrol officers seemed oblivious to the philosophical tenets of Jackson City's community policing program, which stressed informal contact with citizens and problem solving. A key to the city's idea of neighborhood policing was to confront underlying problems before neighborhoods deteriorated and chaos erupted. One patrol officer repeated a story that touched her. A teacher asked her second grade class to write down the first thing that popped into their minds when they heard a police siren. "Someone's gonna get it" and "I wonder who got shot" were the leading answers. The teacher told the girls and boys that her own first thought was "Help is on the way." This story epitomized the department's community policing philosophy, yet patrol officers failed to make such vital connections; instead, they viewed neighborhood policing as merely a vehicle for promotion. Their perspective contrasted sharply with that of the NPOs, who often saw their work as providing opportunities to educate and to embrace racial and cultural diversity.

To summarize, the six themes that grew out of the fieldwork reveal the complicated understandings and misunderstandings that patrol officers hold about the image and practical activities of NPOs. On the one hand, the patrol officers resist being labeled as service oriented and enthusiastically embrace the role and behavior of crimefighters. As they see things, their emphasis on law enforcement contrasts sharply with community policing. Yet, on the other hand—without their intent or realization—the patrol officers' conversations demonstrated some strong similarities between their actions and those of NPOs, especially when patrol officers were not being scrutinized by their peers or the public. This overlapping behavior is not too surprising, since police in Jackson City know of the community policing emphasis when they are recruited and all attend the same academy. Both NPOs and patrol officers exhibited race and gender differences in how they interpreted community problems, among other things, yet they wanted to highlight their own unique skills for their particular position on the force. Despite the similarities, patrol officers remain dismissive of NPOs. Their derision is initially framed in the "canteen culture" of the briefing room, and their repetition of derogatory comments in other settings reflects their resistance to challenging received opinions or misunderstandings. I now turn to the more specific issue of domestic violence, and explore whether officers' positions on the force influence how they may respond to it.

Dealing with Domestic Violence in the Neighborhoods

One of the most enduring and complicated social problems in any community is domestic violence. Police departments have been plagued by confusion and inertia in trying to figure out how best to respond to calls for help. Since many departments, including Jackson City's, now follow policies that favor arrest or make it mandatory for domestic violence offenders, it is possible to examine the ways in which responses to battering may vary across different kinds of police positions. For example, traditional patrol officers responding in squad cars to crisis calls may not react in the same way as do neighborhood foot patrol officers. Given the nature of their job, NPOs may have a greater background knowledge of the couple or family in question, and they may know these citizens far better than do their colleagues. In our research, there were very few opportunities for any of the investigators to observe a domestic violence call directly, since we shadowed the shifts of the NPOs; typically, they did not work late at night, when such incidents were more likely to occur. But part of the richness of the data set is that it allowed collecting officers' perceptions about domestic violence in other ways: questionnaires and in-depth interviews conducted with a variety of current and former neighborhood police officers.

As discussed earlier, current national police reforms stress a more community-oriented role for officers, emphasizing increased interaction with local citizens and greater overall accountability to them. Neighborhood officers are the perfect subjects to use to examine how a formal policy (mandatory arrest) plays out in an informal context (the work of NPOs). Considered together, these two changes in policy and policing introduce seemingly contradictory goals and strategies. On the one hand, community policing stresses informality, wide discretion, selective enforcement, and conciliation. On the other hand, mandatory arrest policies for domestic violence direct police officers to invoke formal, non-negotiable law enforcement powers that emphasize uniformity and decrease officer discretion and flexibility. What we do *not* know is whether a more personalized approach, such as neighborhood policing, can be more efficacious in dealing with interpersonal violence. To date, no research has been conducted to clarify the appropriateness of the two seemingly divergent philosophies.

My own evaluation of these conflicting goals and strategies began from three specific starting points. First, as I have already shown, the NPOs facilitated a greater familiarity and responsiveness in regard to the delivery of police services because they were more personally invested in their communities. Furthermore, such ongoing contact meant that residents appeared to trust them more. This raised two specific questions: (1) What advantages, if any, do neighborhood officers have over traditional patrol officers in dealing with domestic violence? (2) How could the NPOs maintain their informality and familiarity with residents, yet still comply with the formal law enforcement responses to domestic violence required by mandatory arrest laws?

My second starting point was to explore the previous research on police responses to domestic violence. This revealed two general themes. First, police hate answering such calls for a variety of reasons, among them lack of sufficient training, cynicism as to the efficacy of arrest, a belief that domestic calls were not part of "real" policing, and exaggerated worries over personal safety (Buzawa and Buzawa 1993, 552). For years, battered women faced police officers who routinely supported the offender's position, challenged their credibility, often blamed them for their own victimization, and trivialized their fears (Karmen

1982; Stanko 1985; Gil 1986). Police training manuals reinforced officers' behavior by stressing the use of family crisis intervention or separation tactics (International Association of Chiefs of Police 1967; Parnas 1967). These policies sent the message that it was a waste of police time to initiate criminal justice proceedings when a reconciliation might occur and make the matter moot (Field and Field 1973; Lerman 1986). The second general theme relating to responses to domestic violence indicates that police typically did not arrest batterers. This was true even of those officers who worked in jurisdictions that had mandatory or pro-arrest policies. When police had the discretion to make arrests in domestic assault incidents, they largely chose not to. For example, three different studies indicated that police arrest rates in domestic violence incidents were 10 percent, 7 percent, and 3 percent (see Buel 1988). In Milwaukee, although 82 percent of battered women wanted their abusers arrested, police took only 14 percent of the offenders into custody (Bowker 1982). In Ohio, officers again arrested only in 14 percent of the cases, even though in 38 percent of them victims had been injured or killed (Bell 1984). Additionally, until new legislation was enacted between 1977 and 1991, in virtually all states, "[d]omestic violence has . . . been characterized as simple assault, a misdemeanor, unless accompanied by aggravating circumstances such as use of a weapon, intent to commit murder or to inflict grievous bodily harm, or a sexual assault . . . police officers were legally unable to make warrantless arrests unless the violence continued in their presence or a previously existing warrant had been issued" (Buzawa and Buzawa 1990, 34).

My third point, the last, relates to procedural issues concerning the Jackson City Police Department. First, the NPO assignments were based on officer seniority. This procedure had advantages and disadvantages. In particular, the advantage for my study was that the NPOs have had many years of experience as traditional patrol officers in squad cars, and they were thus able to compare and contrast the two positions. The average length of service before becoming a neighborhood officer was ten and a half years (the range of actual experience in patrol ran from three to twenty years). As mentioned in an earlier chapter, one of the disadvantages of the seniority system was that some officers who applied each year to become NPOs might have wanted the position for the wrong reasons. For example, among the grounds the officers gave for applying were flexibility in scheduling so that they could pursue other opportunities, such as advanced schooling or a second job. In addition, since the chief, the department's management team, and the mayor were all strong advocates of community policing, there was an expectation that officers would be promoted more quickly ("get on the fast track") if they had been NPOs. Even though there appeared to be some correlation between advancement and neighborhood experience, in fact promotions were tied to the innovation, enthusiasm, and energy displayed by NPOs. It was not a "given" that the position was a free ticket to higher rank.

In another procedural issue, most of the NPOs in my sample reported that, as traditional patrol officers, they had burned out from overexposure to the bad sides of people or to people in crisis. They were tired of call-driven, "Band-Aid" fixes to larger issues, and they wanted the opportunity to see the good side of individuals and families. The officers also wanted to play a role in identifying and solving problems, with community input and support, before the difficulties became overwhelming. They wanted to be able to follow up on calls and be more proactive. They wanted to be seen as some of the "good guys." Although this may sound as though the NPOs were parroting the community policing line, the daily routines tracked during hundreds of hours of field observations suggested that the commitment of many officers went well beyond rhetoric.

What follows is a summary of the consistent patterns and themes revealed by the qualitative survey data and interviews with the current and former NPOs. First, I explore how the officers' familiarity with the residents had a direct impact on policing domestic violence. Second, I look at informal strategies NPOs used to resolve conflict and at how they balanced their informal styles with their law enforcement role. Finally, I explore several issues specific to the uniqueness of the neighborhood policing position in dealing with domestic violence.

Familiarity

The nature of the neighborhood position in Jackson City encouraged officers to become actively involved with the community they served: in prevention programs, case follow-ups, working on continuing problems, and acting as liaisons with residents, businesses, city services, and the criminal justice system. Such an extensive knowledge base broadened the range of options and responses for the police when there was a crisis in the neighborhood. Officers' choices were guided by a great deal of background information about the residents, and the NPOs had greater access to referral information. Having seen residents under normal conditions helped the officers to understand and communicate when these same persons found themselves in bad situations. Neighborhood officers could follow up after an arrest or other incident by better explaining things to children, victims, offenders, and probation officers, and they had the luxury of more time to do so. In contrast, patrol officers did not have the same detailed knowledge or the time to pursue neighborhood problems in the same way.

Community officers had stronger connections to a range of persons residing in the neighborhood. This familiarity meant that when managing a problem the

NPOs could talk with many different players. This had a positive effect on victims' willingness to divulge personal information. Neighborhood officers identified a reciprocal relationship that developed out of their familiarity and rapport with citizens. They believed that victims' reporting of incidents increased as the residents grew to trust their NPO and how she or he would respond. More importantly, the officers no longer dreaded answering domestic calls because they could feel the trust the residents placed in them. This trust also led NPOs to feel they were better equipped to handle interpersonal conflict. The officers had background information at their disposal, as well as impressions of the disputants formed on their "better" days. For their part, the residents saw NPOs track cases and listen to their feelings, fears, and concerns about safety, and knew as well that they could provide them with information about charges and the steps of the criminal justice or civil processes. Because the officers were responsive to all neighborhood residents, they made time for victims, offenders, and interested family members and friends. Much of this was possible because the NPOs sought out the residents after an incident; most of them also periodically checked back in with the persons involved. Neighborhood officers believed that this effort demonstrated that they would go the extra mile and that this, in turn, would ensure better citizen compliance. For example, one current NPO pointed out that the very nature of domestic violence could change because the residents trusted the officer:

> There are couples who have ties to me so I feel we have more success in changing behaviors. These few cases are much more encouraging than any other domestic abuse program I've encountered or been a part of. (Helen)

Another serving officer, Theresa, stressed that they were able to provide information for offenders as well as victims: "[We try] to counsel and advise all parties involved. To help work on underlying problems such as drugs, alcohol, or prior abuse." Some NPOs, such as Patrick, believed they were able to "give the victim some much-needed support and the courage to report the suspect" once the process was demystified.

By default, establishing and maintaining closer ties with residents meant that the arm of social control was further extended into people's lives. Neighborhood police officers felt they were able to monitor residents' problems more effectively, they could inform victims of their rights, and they could both encourage victims to seek help and encourage abusers to seek treatment. Terry, a former neighborhood officer, believed that "NPOs have a more intimate knowledge of what goes on behind the doors of [the] residents, [and] that knowledge makes the NPOs more effective." Another former officer, William, suggested that although he did not "know the role in stopping domestic violence, we have the luxury to spend more time with people and get to know them in nonpolice situations. With positive contacts and education we hope to decrease violence." If there were a lot of calls for police help involving domestic violence, the NPO worked to create ways of disseminating information to victims and neighbors:

> We gave information classes to women on a couple of occasions. We had literature in the office and the community center. Because we were there, known, and not distant, victims, families, and neighbors would make us aware of problems. (Wendy, former NPO)

Informal Styles of Law Enforcement

Because of increased familiarity with residents and their own decreased anonymity, neighborhood officers carried out their law enforcement obligations in a more informal way than did the detached, less well-known patrol officers. This section looks at several issues raised in the data, such as how the community officers balanced law enforcement with their informal style of policing. The section also examines how the unique responses of NPOs differ from patrol officers, such as the actions they take following arrests, the difficulties involved in these arrests, and their ability to spot potential trouble early.

Although, ultimately, arrest of domestic violence offenders was mandatory in Jackson City, the neighborhood officers turned more frequently to mediation and crisis intervention than did patrol officers because they knew the citizens. Based on their experience, all of the current NPOs felt that this more personal approach worked best. It was much easier to handle conflict between citizens because officers and residents knew each other well. As Hugh said, "[T]he nature of the conflict changes when the residents know they can trust me." Another officer echoed this sentiment:

> I know who is lying, everyone's history, prior conflicts, everything going on in their houses. I know the "real" story to begin with, so I am able to mediate with more knowledge and to a better end. (Patrick)

They felt that if the residents knew their NPO, he or she was granted more credibility, even if the resident(s) ended up arrested. The NPOs believed that local people were more likely to listen to an officer they knew.

All of the current and former NPOs explained that things went more smoothly after they had demonstrated that their job was still to enforce the law. The words of Garth, a former officer, are typical: "Because I have already established certain rules and they have had a chance to see the other side of police work, . . . when conflict arises they know that I will listen to them. They will expect me to do something and usually they won't even argue with me." Maintaining this position was not always easy, as another former NPO suggests.

[I]t was very difficult to take enforcement action against people I knew so well. In my new position [back on traditional patrol], it is easier now for me to make those kinds of decisions and not be so worried about making everyone happy, because you just can't. (Charlie)

Some officers saw this ongoing familiarity as creating more difficulties:

It affects your decision, but I don't know that making a decision is any more difficult. Writing a citation can have a long-lasting impact on relationships. You develop a different standard for enforcement action. And you learn to develop consensus for your decisions.

Other NPOs felt pressure from the residents. According to Karen, "They expect you to make the right decision." In Greg's view, "[R]esidents that know you expect different treatment in law enforcement matters, unless you let them know you enforce the law equally among the community." Most of the neighborhood officers believed things were more difficult when children were involved. And some of them believed that the problem was related to specific citizens: "Residents who are sensible do understand that, as a police officer, you are responsible for upholding the laws. If you then *have* to arrest them, they are *more* understanding" (Terry).

The NPOs saw no difference between how they and patrol officers handled domestic violence because of the state's mandatory arrest statute. Even so, they believed the two groups' responses before and after the arrest were different. For instance, investigations were easier for community officers because they knew the victim and the offender; as one of them, Helen, stated, "NPOs can check the welfare of participants after the fact, [and] become a liaison for all involved during follow-up concerns such as counseling, rehabilitation, and children." The NPOs could also do more with early conflict resolution programs. A former officer suggested that, because of mandatory arrest, the ultimate result was the same. But, the family *perceived* the result as being different because they trusted the officer to treat them with greater fairness.

The former NPOs specifically highlighted the "after-the-fact" options they were able to exercise.

There is a definite difference. As a patrol officer, I was a Band-Aid, responding to a crisis. I had little time or ability to follow up and see what was happening. As an NPO, it was part of my responsibility to follow up on all reported domestic violence calls whether or not I had been the initial responding officer. I could see restraining orders were enforced and that people were making court-ordered interventions. I could make further referrals, such as Narcotics Anonymous, Alcoholics Anonymous, Al-Anon, battered-women's shelters, and so on. (Karen)

Another former officer explained that initially with mandatory arrest domestic calls were "cut and dried." But circumstances grew more personal due to the follow-up the NPOs were able to do with the families, which built trust and support between them: "It made future problems easier and clearer since you have the background history" (William). A colleague, Francine, said that being recognized in the neighborhood as the residents' "personal representative or ambassador" helped with building trust. She linked this to race relations:

There are certain cultural issues that come up in neighborhoods that are very racially or ethnically mixed. For example, in one of the neighborhoods I worked there was a large Southeast Asian population. I attempted to work with residents on educating them to our laws relating to domestic violence, because domestic violence was accepted in the Hmong culture.

The structural reality of having a permanent neighborhood officer meant that she or he saw the victims, offenders, their children, and their neighbors more regularly. Policing was no longer anonymous. Thus, when NPOs were asked if it was more difficult to make a law enforcement decision knowing that they would see the residents again and again, there was no clear consensus: of the thirteen current NPOs, five said it was harder, five said it was not, and three said sometimes. The former NPOs displayed far less ambivalence, but they also believed the ambivalence they did feel helped them develop more effective and creative ways to make decisions. In fact, several of them were emphatic about how much *more* difficult it was to make an arrest once they had been associated more informally and personally with the victims and the offenders and the family. It may be that, now having achieved greater career success, the former NPOs felt more secure in noting any problems they struggled with in their earlier positions. Thus, it is possible that, for career reasons, the current neighborhood officers did not want to suggest having experienced any conflict that they could not manage or negotiate.

Those NPOs who did not see ongoing familiarity as creating more difficulties when formal action was taken generally agreed with Theresa: "When I make a decision, I know it's for the long-term betterment of the situation. And if I make a bad decision, I *should* be reminded of it." Another NPO explained:

> It became obvious that no single decision works equally well in every case. The people let you know if things were not working! But it also became apparent that one was not stuck with a decision forever in many cases. It was OK to try something else. It also often became important to present alternatives and let people pick one. Decisions such as arrest did not become harder. If anything, they were often easier, as you knew the results of arrest, good or bad. It is often a very positive choice. (Helen)

Former community officers felt that familiarity increased cooperation under these circumstances: "There is more chance for listening and compliance than escalation to crisis. Of course, that depends on officers' relationship with citizens" (Terry). Bill, another former NPO, said, "You have more information to make a decision, and people usually understand that even though you try to be an advocate, you are a law enforcer first." Only one former officer, Barbara, dissented from this consensus, and she did so quite vehemently: "It is absolutely harder! When you must take enforcement action against the people you see nearly daily, it's like you're doing this to your own neighbor."

Consistently, the neighborhood police officers found that increased familiarity with residents shifted the dynamics of domestic violence calls, even if their ultimate outcomes were the same whether NPOs or patrol officers were involved.

Unique Issues

Most current and former NPOs in Jackson City believed their job was made easier by knowing a community's residents more fully. This was particularly true with both the victims and the offenders in domestic violence cases. The officers gave a variety of reasons: "[T]hey know you so they don't try to cover up as much" (Patrick), and

> [K]nowing the participants and their histories seems to help sort out disputes and aids in making better arrest decisions. Some residents that know me and have regular [domestic incidents] seem more willing to call for intervention sooner. Community support and involvement is easier [i.e., other residents are more willing to get involved]. And it is less

likely that participants in domestic violence will be able to manipulate the system. (Helen)

The NPOs were also more aware of the need to identify brewing conflict early:

> Once trust is developed, family members may be able to reach out to us prior to violence if they recognize their own "breaking point." We can help with respite care for children, and sometimes, just our police presence in standing by helps to preserve the peace. (Terry)

Similarly, a former officer, Christine, remarked: "You are able to provide a consistent approach to helping stop the violence by providing follow-up contacts, and giving some consistent message to parties involved that violence is not an appropriate way to resolve disagreement."

Even when arrest was the ultimate outcome, the NPOs believed that residents perceived they got a "fair deal" as a result of their personal connection with the community officer. The NPOs capitalized on the relationship that they had developed, or were developing, in order to establish trust, rapport, and credibility. The background knowledge of residents' underlying problems and personal strengths provided more tools for NPOs to use proactively in identifying trouble spots, or later in conducting follow-ups after a domestic violence incident. Officers were more personally invested in and committed to their neighborhoods, and they had greater access to the daily lives of the residents. As mentioned earlier, this closeness aided in providing information, referrals, and explanations to all parties involved, whether victims, offenders, neighbors, or other professionals in the criminal justice system. In a formal, social control sense, NPOs were more effective at monitoring civil protection orders, temporary restraining orders, and other court-mandated interventions such as participation in treatment programs. This insider knowledge and the officers' often daily presence in the neighborhood helped victims and offenders more. The greater ability of NPOs to keep track of protection orders was especially important, since research has demonstrated that the routine monitoring of civil protection orders or restraining orders is often a low priority for traditional police officers. In fact, workers in battered women's shelters typically view these "pieces of paper" as placebos for victims, since often patrol officers do not have the time or inclination to take them as seriously as they should.

The success of "before-the-arrest" and "after-the-arrest" assistance rested on the strength of the connections between NPOs and residents. "Shaming" or "losing face" were consistently cited as reasons why local people were more cooperative with NPOs and did not turn against them when the officers had to invoke their formal law enforcement powers. Police felt that residents viewed them as the "conscience" of the community. As one former NPO explained,

> By being visible in the neighborhood, the NPO becomes a sort of "conscience" for the neighborhood. By going in and talking to participants in domestic violence after the fact, I believe there is a better chance for more permanent resolution of the problem. Or at the very least, people feel "watched" and less likely to act out again! (Andrea)

Other officers suggested that violence lessened because of the familiarity between residents and NPOs:

> Knowing someone personally makes it easier to deal with them during times of conflict. People are less likely to be physically or verbally abusive when they know you and are also aware that you know who they are—they are no longer anonymous. (William)

Yet another officer said,

> If you have cordial relationships with people and you suddenly must deal with conflict involving them, most people will try to behave a little better. I think they see an NPO as a person to whom they are accountable, and they often don't want to look bad in front of them.

The consensus could be summarized in these words from another NPO: "They know I am fair, and they know they'll see me again." In fact, as we were conducting hundreds of hours of fieldwork, many residents joked with the research team that their NPOs would be "all over them" and not let them rest if they, the residents, did not handle some matter still outstanding. Shaming thus became a significant mechanism of informal social control within the visible context of neighborhood policing, although the importance of this tool varies by the community and the individual officer's commitment.

The NPOs' conversations also revealed that an evaluation process existed, with feedback from citizens. The officers used this information from the community to change their strategies or to become more creative in handling situations. Confidence, trust, and respect were further reinforced by this indication that officers really *did* care about the residents' realities and experiences.

Ultimately, given their flexible schedules, most NPOs chose to work primarily during the day. In most cases this was because the bulk of their duties involved such daytime activities as foot patrol, youth events, attending neighborhood and business meetings, school-related activities, follow-up contacts, and meeting with landlords, city officials, and probation officers. Furthermore, in order to cultivate and sustain more intensely meaningful and friendly relationships with local citizens, community officers needed to be around when a good number of them were at home and not embroiled in some crisis. Most of the NPOs in the sample mentioned the many times they had been invited into homes for coffee, or something to eat, or to meet visiting relatives. This potential informal mechanism of social control would not exist if the local people had not already established trust and rapport with their community police officers.

With regard to domestic violence, their daytime schedules meant that NPOs would be the officers least likely to respond first to a crisis call. Most domestic violence incidents happened late at night or in the early morning hours, precisely the times when the known and trusted NPO was least likely to be on duty. Therefore, the disputants faced unknown officers, who probably were less aware (or totally unaware) of their history and complicated relationships. Interviews with traditional patrol officers suggested that if the police officer was unknown to the residents, the victims of domestic violence tried to manipulate the system by using the threat of calling the police against their partners (*before* any violence occurred) because it was so well known that arrest of a batterer was mandatory. For their part, the NPOs believed that citizens would be less likely to try manipulating officers they trusted, but it was easier to attempt it with officers they did not know.

NPOs became involved during the important period following the violence, since they read reports of all incidents that had occurred in their neighborhood at the time they were off duty. If the community officers had been the first responders, it might have been difficult for the residents to manipulate the system, since the NPOs would know their background. Moreover, a known and trusted neighborhood officer often could defuse the violence. When arrests were made by impersonal patrol officers, however, NPOs retained their "good guy" status (at least with the offender), which could help down the road in dealings with the victim and the batterer. Then, the residents' anger and hostility would be directed at the arresting patrol officers.

Citizens, in fact, often asked for their "own" NPO during a dispute when the responding officer was not known to them. Such requests had both good and bad implications. On the one hand, they showed the residents had some faith that their NPO would give them a fair shake. On the other hand, they revealed that some residents believed that *all* other police officers, except for the one they personally knew, were not as fair. As one former NPO said, although it was good to have one officer who was known to all residents and permanently assigned to one neighborhood, a *better* scenario would be to have all of the patrol officers so involved in and connected to a neighborhood that people feel comfortable calling any officer. Then, the "bad guys" would identify this as a neighborhood [where] citizens and police *in general* will not allow crime to occur. (Bill)

Thus, the multiple data sources revealed that, overall, the formal social control aspects of mandatory arrest of domestic violence offenders were accomplished through a dance with multiple steps between traditional patrol officers and neighborhood officers. Mandatory arrest was non-negotiable, yet the "personal touch" of community policing smoothed the process. The NPOs felt that domestic violence arrests were ultimately more effective because of follow-ups and opportunities for them to monitor the needs of both victims and offenders. The community officers believed that both sets of persons appreciated the extra efforts they made to carry out their law enforcement duties.

What this analysis also suggested was that gender, as an important variable, did not appear in the conversations with the NPOs. This omission was interesting, given the gendered dynamics of domestic violence itself and the historical legacy of insensitive (usually male) officers who have responded inappropriately to domestic violence calls. But in this analysis of the NPOs in Jackson City, the gender of the individual neighborhood officer was not the attribute that gave meaning to the social control of domestic violence within a community policing context. Rather, it was the *relationship* that developed between the NPO, male or female, and the residents that offered hope of a more efficacious tool for police to use in responding to interpersonal violence.

In this chapter I have looked at the other side of the story—at how patrol officers view neighborhood policing. Despite the hostility that patrol officers frequently displayed toward community officers, significant similarities emerged across the two styles of policing and practice of policework. These findings may reflect a department moving toward a comprehensive emphasis on community- and problem-oriented policing, where patrol officers grow to incorporate this philosophy into their reactive, rapid response roles. I have also looked at the complicated issue of police response to domestic violence, and the various ways in which the informal nature of neighborhood policing enhances formal police thought and action. Both of these themes have important policy implications for police departments, and I explore these and others in Chapter 7.

7

Summary

The Findings and Their Policy Implications

This final chapter considers relevant findings from the analysis, addressing the multiple audiences who have an interest in community policing: makers of public policy, scholars of gender in criminology and sociology, police officers, and police administrators. I begin by placing the issue of neighborhood policing in a larger context in order to reflect the national discourse on new crime control strategies. Across the country, enthusiasm continues to surround community policing, despite the paucity of program evaluations and the absence of any clear-cut evidence that it works to reduce crime. There are many reasons for this high level of support, some well-founded, some idealistic, and some misguided. The chapter opens with a summary of the forces that motivated the dramatic movement from traditional reactive policing toward community policing, including an examination of the many promises the new approach makes and their implications. Such a dramatic shift in law enforcement models suggests questions about general policy and about issues specific to the Jackson City Police Department. By raising and evaluating the major issues surrounding the community approach against the backdrop of this city's experience, I illuminate the new brand of law enforcement in a more realistic way, separate from the rhetoric surrounding it. Ten policy recommendations are presented where they logically follow from the text. The final section of the chapter explores issues of gender, race, and sexuality that emerged in the analysis.

The neighborhood approach marks a dramatic transformation of policing models and constitutes a move away from the "just the facts" aloofness of the detached police professional. In contrast, an emotional, informal link is forged between the officer and the community that she or he serves. This more personal approach did not appear out of thin air. The limitations of the professional policing model were legion, as were research findings demonstrating its gross ineffectiveness: saturated car patrol, rapid response, routine crime investigation, and traditional crime scene analyses have all failed to help detect and reduce crime (Rosenbaum and Lurigio 1994, 300). Citizen involvement came to be recognized as the key factor that could improve crimefighting, since good policework often depends upon men and women, as victims and witnesses, coming forward and providing information about crime. Once such involvement was acknowledged as the essential ingredient of successful policing, ways of involving citizens with law enforcement needed to be developed. The community policing model was the result.

Part of the philosophy behind this approach rests on the assumption that citizens and police jointly produce strategies to combat neighborhood disorder and crime. This teamwork holds an advantage for the police. Once "the community" has been identified as a key tool in crimefighting, police "success" does not rest solely on officers' efforts; it is shared. The residents' contribution can be praised or blamed as community policing works or fails to work, thus alleviating the pressure on officers to assume full responsibility. Consequently, the police must somehow encourage residents to view them as teammates, not the opposition. Since this change also affects the image of officers, there must be concomitant strategies to encourage them to become fully invested in community policing.

In order to attract citizens' interest, the "talk" of neighborhood policing evokes a more conciliatory, friendly style, rather than an authoritarian, law-and-order orientation. Community policing programs often adopt the language of the business world, which entails seeing the residents as "customers" who are "invested" in the joint production of community stability. Such a linguistic change can be persuasive to both sides, for it capitalizes on the entrepreneurial spirit. Effective officers are described as having a solid work ethic, creativity, and an innovative view of things. Participatory management is one example of a new administrative style that goes hand in hand with community policing. In Jackson City, for example, the political administration, as well as the police department, adopted several models of leadership that reflected a strongly business-minded organizational culture and spirit, rather than the paramilitary style of the older policing philosophy. (Using business standards to evaluate officers' performance, however, does vary by gender; I will discuss this issue below.)

Some critics of community policing feel the subject itself has become too politicized, with departments that have not latched on to the rhetoric being characterized as nonprogressive, stagnating, and backward. Typically, however, such criticisms remain unvoiced; departments have grown to rely on federal grants to fund additional officers and programs, and chiefs are reluctant to go public with negative views. Too much is at stake for them or administrators to denounce the neighborhood approach, despite their private reservations.

Another, often unexamined, consequence of community policing efforts has been a shift in the boundaries of state power. The traditional scope of police activity is extended into more personal public space, through introducing ministations and frequent foot patrols into residential areas. Community policing is made up of multiple strategies that link residents to resources and bring the police back to the people—it is not just one program, but a collection of them. No longer is most police activity a matter of reactive responses by detached strangers in uniform to citizen requests for service. Rather, neighborhood policing extends state power and the reach of the law to a more intimate level. This could be viewed as an attractive proactive stance, safeguarding neighborhoods from a downward spiral of neglect and decay. Critics of the expansion of state power, however, may feel that Big Brother (and Big Sister) have, simply by knowing the residents and their comings and goings in a far more familiar way, slipped into contested space under the guise of offering community help.[1] However, in June 1999, the Supreme Court ruled as unconstitutional the new laws against loitering that have sprung up in many cities to enable police to order suspected gang members off the streets. Critics of these ordinances argued that they are too vague and give officers too much discretion, allowing them to make arbitrary and discriminatory arrests and to unfairly target members of minority groups. Yet supporters of the ordinances (numerous community groups, as well as more than thirty states and municipalities) believed that these laws reflect a progressive, innovative form of community policing.

Other critics of the neighborhood approach believe that, although departments have embraced broad mission statements, no changes have been wrought that are structural and long-lasting. Even many of the supposedly new tactics— among them saturation patrolling, directed investigations, and strong enforcement of statutory laws such as those governing curfew violations and truancy—call to mind earlier police efforts, leading some critics to suggest that "the emperor *still* has no clothes" (Taylor, Fritsch, and Caeti 1998).

Obstacles

Community policing has now existed for over a decade. As the popularity of adopting such programs, and of qualifying for research grants and additional police officers, increases, so does the awareness of the obstacles to putting them into practice. There are three categories of impediments. The first involves assumptions about community members' desires: Do residents really want more of a police presence in their neighborhoods? The second group of hurdles entails "selling" the community policing position to the officers themselves. This requires reducing the emphasis on traditional crimefighting, as well as finding ways to erase the stigma associated with moving from traditionally masculine policing activities into "social work." The third obstacle comprises procedural concerns, among them such questions as matching officer style and neighborhood needs, as well as more fundamental issues surrounding selection and training, scheduling, rewarding and promoting, setting goals, and the dynamics and interactions between NPOs and traditional patrol officers. All of these obstacles become more complicated when differences in gender, race, and sexual orientation on the force are acknowledged.

The first obstacle identified above entails negotiating a convergence between the interests and expectations of the community and the police. The neighborhood approach rests on a powerful assumption that "the community" is on board and indeed desires closer contact with the police. Yet, problems develop in impoverished neighborhoods, where women and men have no interest in, and little time and energy for, helping with policework. Additionally, when there exists a legacy of racial discord and distrust between citizens and police, community liaisons and teamwork are at best problematic, and often impossible. For instance, the brutal beating of Rodney King by officers of the Los Angeles Police Department in 1991 reinforced a perception of institutionalized racism existing among law enforcers. Similarly, recent court cases challenging traffic stops of African American motorists for no apparent reason other than race—stops for "DWB," or Driving while Black—have done little to relieve black citizens of their distrust of police procedures and motivations. Public exposure and private experience of these racist abuses of power increase antagonism between nonwhite residents and police officers, and they may have an adverse effect on the cooperation that is being sought through officers' heightened involvement in community policing.

Some residents simply avoid the police because they fear retaliation by drug dealers or gangs (Rosenbaum and Lurigio 1994, 303). Often, interest and involvement vary; in Houston, for example, researchers found that the residents most in need were also the ones least likely to use or know about community policing (Skogan and Wycoff 1986). Michael E. Buerger (1994, 428–429) claims that community policing is most effective at the tipping point, and is not effective in inner-city neighborhoods characterized by tremendous, enduring social and economic neglect. Additionally, it should be borne in mind that when something is fun to do and free, everyone shows up, but when something requires work or expending time and energy, no one comes; thus, there are problems in maintaining community involvement once the "fun" subsides (Grinc 1994). Herein lies the threat to the success of community policing: officers cannot do much to reduce fear and crime if the community does not wish to get involved. Furthermore, whose community interests should be reflected? Some researchers contend that neighborhood policing works best in districts that do not need it, and that the persons who might benefit the most live in the poorest urban areas, where political factionalization, poverty, and crime are rampant (Taylor, Fritsch, and Caeti 1998).

The second obstacle to instituting neighborhood policing involves re-creating the *image* of policing for officers who are often characterized as rigid bureaucrats resistant to change. Departments that move to community policing need to achieve "buy-in" from their members. Given that the neighborhood approach is a far cry from the style of Dirty Harry, its image must be reconstituted so that community policing loses its stigma and comes to be seen as an attractive position within the department. This question of image is particularly crucial in an occupation that is so associated with all that is quintessentially masculine and macho. The very success of community policing rests upon developing and using "women's" roles and traits, such as creating and sustaining intimate connections and practicing a more conciliatory, nonaggressive style of policing. Thus, macho police officers who disdain such traits must be convinced to appropriate them in such a way that the stigma is dissolved.

A related personnel concern involves addressing the grumblings of the officers. Too often, departments that have moved to community policing are described as having a "split force," where the veterans, resistant to change, no longer believe in departmental philosophy (see Pate and Shtull 1994). Officers typically take this ideological shift as indicating the "break-up of the family" (see Wycoff and Skogan 1994, 381). Such a split can cause substantial strain and can lead to an "us versus them" culture, particularly if men and women in patrol complain that neighborhood officers do not do their share of "real" policework (Pate and Shtull 1994). In fact, many patrol officers "expressed resentment at what they perceived to be a lack of recognition and support for what they believed to be the mainstay of police work" (Pate and Shtull 1994, 410). Others on the force will show little interest in wanting a community policing position, such as foot patrol, because of the physical discomfort in bad weather, increased vulnerability of working without a partner, inability to take emergency calls without a car, preference for the cachet of lights and sirens, and perception that walking the beat is boring (Pate and Shtull 1994, 408). Officers are not monolithic, however, and they do not all acquiesce in dividing their colleagues into traditional patrol officers ("us") and neighborhood officers ("them"). Strategies need to be created that will strengthen and maintain connections between the two groups so that these potential divisions do not become real ones. For example, Houston's Neighborhood-Oriented Policing program was ridiculed by many in the department as "Nobody on Patrol," since patrol officers had not been involved in the concept or endorsed it. This indicates how crucial it is for men and women on the force to be consulted about and supportive of new policing practices if their help is to be expected (Taylor, Fritsch, and Caeti 1998).

Resentment deepens when officers feel policies are being thrust on them by politicians or "desk cops," who are seen as having no knowledge of or experience with street-level policing. To counteract this, the department in Jackson City tried participatory management as a way of fostering links that would convince those on the force to support the neighborhood approach. Survey data from officers questioned in an earlier study there conducted by a different author indicated higher degrees of satisfaction with work and the working environment, but officers' attitudes toward community-oriented policing or problem solving were unaffected by participatory management. The researchers argue, however, that officers' satisfaction with the organization made them far more open to change.

Third, and finally, procedural obstacles endure and remain plentiful. In many troubled residential areas, community policing strategies have initially targeted the "hot spots" with increased enforcement efforts. Only after these "hot spots" (high-crime zones) calm down or disappear will the more "community"-oriented aspects of neighborhood policing be introduced, and have any hope of meeting with success. The challenge of fighting hot spots tends to attract the more aggressive, law-enforcement-minded men and women on the force. Yet once the hot spots are extinguished, officers must assume a less forceful posture and develop more intimate ways of connecting with the residents. Persons who may be drawn to intensive police activity in some high-crime neighborhoods may not be the same ones who would do well, or even enjoy, working in more stable, less criminally active residential areas. In addition, a program development neighborhood or a maintenance neighborhood may be viewed as an unattractive assignment by the more macho officers.

Even before developing appropriate policing strategies, however, departments must recognize that their recruiting efforts should be geared toward developing a very different kind of officer. Since the community policing role does not require the same kind of men and women that the established police culture has sought and attracted for a century, selection and training must change. This means that the department has to take the lead in imparting new skills and knowledge so that officers can perform effectively (Rosenbaum, Yeh, and Wilkinson 1994, 333). Women and men need to be recruited in ways that make clear their expanded roles, and departments must stress that candidates need to be open to learning and developing new skills. Recruits are now selected with different criteria in mind. In Jackson City, for instance, administrators closely evaluate a candidate's thinking in a test essay that deals with community policing.

Recruitment in general can become difficult, especially if candidates were initially attracted to policing by a department's promise of the excitement of special squads. New recruits are not placed in these units initially, however; this kind of "bait and switch" tactic should be downplayed, and the new, community approach should be reflected in entrance tests. Departments should highlight the "challenge of working in a collaborative environment to address quality-of-life issues, and resolve substantive community crime and disorder problems," which are more realistic descriptions of the job (Oettmeier 1997, 1). In the same article, Oettmeier also cautions police administrators against calling NPOs a "new breed," which rankles veteran officers.

In Jackson City, training and selecting community officers were related issues; obtaining the position came through a selection process that operated on seniority, not on demonstrable skills. Men and women are attracted to the new neighborhood positions for a variety of reasons, although some of their motivations have little to do with embracing the community policing philosophy, at least in Jackson City. Since becoming an NPO is a matter of seniority there, it is likely that most candidates joined the department when its philosophy reflected more traditional policing values. Thus, as is true on many forces, the longest-serving officers may be the least supportive of the community approach. Another issue related to training involves the traits or skills that are emphasized at the police academy. There needs to be a move away from a concentration on physical factors toward an emphasis on different professional orientations, such as ethics, character, law, emotional as well as physical fitness, and moral decision making (Lebowitz 1997, 2). Then, there is the matter of getting rid of incompetent neighborhood officers. For instance, the NPOs in Jackson City were given some general guidelines to follow, but they were left to devise neighborhood policing strategies on their own, with no criteria or mechanism by which supervisors could evaluate their work. Because the job descriptions were so broad and vague ("respond to your neighborhood's needs"), firing an incompetent officer was difficult and time consuming. Without performance assessment tools of some sort, departments will be unable to measure the effectiveness of either skillful or inept persons.

Community policing introduces another unique procedural dilemma, the scheduling of NPOs' shifts. Since neighborhood policing is inextricably tied to community needs, officers must be able to set their own schedules to respond to these needs. Such flexibility can be both a blessing and a curse. The match is simpatico when the hours the officer wants to work are compatible with the neighborhood's requirements. Such scheduling can also help officers to re-arrange their hours of work to meet family or personal needs, or to allow them to attend important community or police meetings. The downside is that women and men may become overinvolved with an "easy" group, such as merchants (Trojanowicz 1986). Beyond this, in some neighborhoods police tend to avoid working nights or weekends, an absence that might be at odds with local needs. And there is often some decrease in pay associated with taking the new community policing position, although some jurisdictions allow for overtime pay (see Wilson and Bennett 1994). The frustrations of scheduling and reduced income can convince some potential officers that they really do not want to become NPOs.

Very few empirical evaluations of community policing exist, so it is difficult to know its actual effect on the crime rate. Although some politicians and police administrators credit it with driving crime down, others contend that community policing has little to do with such fluctuations, arguing that rates are more tied to the economy or to the number of juveniles and young adults in the population.

One reason for the dearth of evaluations of community policing is the lack of goal setting. There are few benchmarks from which to measure "success." One department (Brooklyn) used "beat books" to set monthly priorities and thus was able to see if various goals had been met (McElroy, Cosgrove, and Sadd 1993). In Jackson City there was a lot of posturing about "problem-oriented policing," after Herman Goldstein's model; however, very little was done to follow through using the principles of problem solving called SARA (scanning, analysis, response, and assessment) (Goldstein 1990). Without clear goals and objectives, evaluations become elusive and may end up consisting predominantly of impressions and anecdotal evidence. For example, in Jackson City no formal assessments are conducted of the neighborhood (or any other) officers once they pass their eighteen-month probation. Without any consistent, empirical way to measure effectiveness, however, the efficacy of community policing remains largely unknown.

Many NPOs feel marginalized and isolated from the rest of the force. Although some departments require community officers to attend at least one of three daily roll calls (see Marzulli 1994), being by yourself, on your feet, and devising your own agenda often results in a loss of connection with patrol. Officers are generally reluctant to embrace new policies and they resist change. Police are creatures of habit. They are wary about the role of politics or community pressure in their internal business, they remember failed past ideas, and they are suspicious of attempts at empowerment and changes in management (Lurigio and Skogan 1994, 317).

Police culture is negative overall about developing partnerships with citizens and the ability of bureaucratic structures to encourage problem solving (Rosenbaum, Yeh, and Wilkinson 1994). Yet, some of the few evaluations done of community policing efforts suggest the importance of partnerships with the community. In Tulsa, Oklahoma, for example, bus drivers take residents of public housing to jobs, grocery stores, and job-training sites at no charge (*Community Policing Exchange* 1997, 2). This idea developed from a SARA problem-solving method used by a community police officer.

A high burnout level is often associated with neighborhood policing positions, if, that is, the person is doing his or her specific job. In Jackson City, for example, the absence of a written job description meant that the responsibilities were endless, or at least were often perceived that way, a situation that contributes to officer burnout. Becoming overly stressed may be especially prevalent among women, since they often bring more emotional worries home with them. Men tend to delegate responsibilities; they also usually choose to handle the more instrumental tasks themselves and pass the expressive ones on to others, thus minimizing emotional involvement. And in a broader context, if burnout or job dissatisfaction causes the neighborhood officer to leave the position prematurely the residents feel betrayed, taking the situation to signify a lack of commitment by the police to their community.

Although many of the problems and issues identified above were relevant to and have been demonstrated by the Jackson City Police Department, they are also of concern to community policing efforts across the nation. I will now look in more detail at the dilemmas that emerged within the department in Jackson City. These more specific findings can provide insight and guidelines for other police forces that may be struggling with similar issues.

Specific Local Policies

Jackson City launched its community policing program over a decade ago, and since then many plans and procedures have been introduced and modified. Lessons have been learned that will be valuable to other departments and makers of public policy. The ramifications of the city's program, often involving unintended outcomes, have been revealed by the passage of time as well as by research projects, this one included. This section examines significant findings that can inform planning decisions for community policing, as well as our understandings of some of the gendered dynamics implicitly structuring the neighborhood policing program in Jackson City.

Due to the seniority requirement for becoming a neighborhood officer, virtually all of the serving and former NPOs had spent at least several years in patrol. The seniority requirement, which was negotiated and supported by the police union, replaced any other meaningful eligibility criteria for selecting officers who would perform well in the neighborhood position. This raises a paradox: many current and former NPOs believed that community policing allows for an expansion of the police role, in which officers are encouraged to be creative and take risks. However, since anyone can be an NPO by virtue of the number of years she or he has on the force, the more significant qualification, an individual's genuine interest in the position, is pushed to one side. Thus, as one current officer contended, "[T]here could be a lazy NPO or a goofy NPO or even a lazy and goofy NPO, and believe me, Jackson City already has one of these in the neighborhoods."

• *Policy Recommendation 1:* Although this would be difficult to implement in Jackson City due to union regulations, departments should strive to have officers meet minimum selection criteria. One tool might be a written statement from candidates clearly articulating their reasons for wanting the job of NPO and outlining what skills they would bring to it and what others they hope to develop.

Since NPOs were patrol officers at one point in their careers, it is not surprising that many of the issues that arose were related to these previous roles and responsibilities. For example, all of the men and women wanted to keep in contact with their friends from patrol, yet they were not sure how to do so because they felt cut off in their new neighborhood positions. This isolation remained a source of regret, perhaps sharpened by some officers' memories that they were initially attracted to the neighborhood position by a positive encounter with an NPO while they themselves were on patrol. No longer did the community officers share in the informal camaraderie of the briefings. Moreover, their schedules often made it difficult to see other officers for weeks at a time. Although some men and women were drawn to neighborhood policing because of its flexible scheduling, they soon found the loneliness of the position to be a significant drawback. In Jackson City, the isolation was lessened for those officers assigned to the smaller police station, since patrol, detectives, and management all attended briefings there, rather than at the main station downtown.

This seeming invisibility could, in turn, create or reinforce the impression among patrol officers that NPOs did not do "real" policework. In fact, despite over ten years' exposure to a community policing program, many in patrol continue to dismiss neighborhood policing as mere "social work" and to cast this aspect of the program in an extremely negative light. This dismissal is consistent with evaluations conducted of other community policing endeavors, such as the one in Detroit. There, the officers not themselves involved with the program "expressed unfavorable opinions about the assignments, labeling it *social work* rather than real police work" (Skolnick and Bayley 1988, 306).

Although some neighborhood police officers are overcommitted and work many hours beyond their expected shifts, this hardworking image is not universally accepted by either NPOs or patrol officers. Both frequently share the perception that some community officers "skate" (i.e., shirk their duties). And, occasionally, women and men decide to become NPOs for *precisely* this reason. Moreover, since supervision is limited, some members of the force believe that officers can use the NPO position when they want to hide from doing work, particularly if they already have a reputation as a "skater," or if they are close to retirement and view being a neighborhood officer as an easy way to finish their last few working years. As one officer said, "I could have fooled the powers that be at the station; I could have gone and checked in for five minutes, and then gone home."

Integrating community and patrol officers will increase the latter's understanding of NPOs, and make for more effective policing generally. In Jackson City, some community officers sought out their patrol colleagues and encouraged them to leave their squad cars so that they could walk the neighborhood together for a while. The NPOs' motivations were to stave off loneliness and to enhance their own safety. Some community officers also made use of the "enforcement muscle" of patrol officers, preferring that they arrest a resident so that the "bad guy" image would not fall on the NPO and hurt his relations with the residents. Only men said they used this strategy; women did not want to give credence to the stereotype that they were too "soft" or emotionally attached to make an arrest involving persons they knew. Despite this difference between men and women in making arrests, there were many similarities between NPOs and patrol officers in how they went about their jobs. Regardless of assignment, all officers knew the same "hot spots." Both groups used informal strategies and decisions, such as determining which children were "bad" and which children were merely "mischievous." All of the men, and many of the women, in the two groups mentioned the social work stigma of the neighborhood position; they also felt residents needed to take more personal responsibility for their problems and not rely on police so much. Finally, both patrol and community officers agreed that patrol arrested citizens far more quickly, regardless of the officer's gender.

• *Policy Recommendation 2:* Devise more ways to integrate NPOs with patrol officers. Generate better-coordinated responses based on shared interests and priorities, perhaps by creating opportunities for teamwork. Undertaking joint activities is very important so that the patrol officers can be "educated" about the work that the NPOs are performing. More knowledge will mean less mocking.[2] Stigma will decrease if patrol officers are more aware of or actively engaged in crimefighting activities with the NPOs.

Regardless of what strategies are used to better integrate the two groups, the patrol officers on the graveyard shift will rarely, if ever, encounter their colleagues. Thus, because they have the least exposure to NPOs, these patrol officers may be the most cynical about the NPO position, even though they know the least about its requirements. And owing to lack of contact, this attitude would be reinforced daily. In particular, one "bad" community officer could spoil the reputation of the whole bunch. Note that the interviews in the Jackson City research project targeted only those patrol officers *most* likely to be exposed to and interact with NPOs. Even these officers, who were assigned to patrol the perimeter of the NPOs' beat, were not cognizant of their work.

• *Policy Recommendation 3:* Develop strategies for publicizing the work of NPOs to the patrol officers who are the least familiar with neighborhood policing. Highlight chronic hot spots and NPOs' efforts to tackle problems, so that patrol officers may notice changes over the long run and attribute some of the success to their colleagues.

Another issue of isolation involved the community officers' experience with their supervisors, particularly when NPOs needed help in addressing issues using problem-solving techniques. When the NPOs were still in patrol, they knew who supervised them; their supervisor attended briefings and did "checks" during and at the end of the shifts. In fact, the presence of supervisors is usually very noticeable in the routine patrol world. The former and current neighborhood officers in Jackson City, however, lamented being "on their own," without adequate support from administrators and supervisors. The only exceptions were the few NPOs who had been "assigned" to a supervising sergeant or other higher-ranking officer. *If* the supervisors took their positions seriously, and only some did, the NPOs felt that both enforcement and community activities were better coordinated, more goal oriented, and more smoothly run. In fact, the current sergeants and lieutenants who had been community officers believed that they better understood the pushes and pulls experienced by NPOs. These supervisors also felt that they could more easily counter patrol officers' criticism of NPOs for not answering dispatch calls in their neighborhoods.

The lack of accountability in the community policing position could be addressed by assigning supervisors to a subset of NPOs. One police administrator, who supervised four neighborhood officers from the first wave, believed that when more women were NPOs there were additional meetings in which officers could troubleshoot issues with their peers. As more men entered the neighborhood program, the meetings grew fewer and the conversation turned to law enforcement concerns, not social issues. This administrator was the only female supervisor, which seemed to offer increased validation of female NPOs' concerns, before men began to dominate the community policing positions, and subsequently the conversations at meetings.

• *Policy Recommendation 4:* Encourage more troubleshooting strategy meetings with NPOs from adjacent neighborhoods and their supervisors; have each officer identify problems and then set goals together, using SARA problem-solving techniques as well as collective efforts. Have experienced community officers serve as mentors for newer ones.

Unhappiness about the reward structures and promotions linked to neighborhood policing has been a consistent theme in the empirical literature, and it was also part of the strong discontent voiced by police officers in Jackson City. This problem also appeared in Brooklyn's community policing experiment, where officers became disgruntled about promotions once the different sections of the city all changed to community policing. So sweeping a change meant that there was no longer anything NPOs did that was unique, thus foreclosing any promotions to special units (see Pate and Shtull 1994, 400). Yet, if a community police officer carries out the expectations of the neighborhood and the police department, the demands of the job and the time and energy invested in it far exceed what a patrol officer is accustomed to doing. It is thus easy to see why committed, hardworking NPOs think their promotions are totally justified. In fact, many former community officers believed that the NPO position should be a "promotable" one for a patrol officer because of the extra time it usually demanded and the loss in overtime and holiday pay. On the other hand, if the commitment and energy necessary to be a good NPO were fully understood, many persons would be deterred from selecting the position. Patrol officers often prefer the routine and predictability of their flat eight-hour shifts. Thus, for a man or woman in patrol who already holds the community policing philosophy in disdain, the NPO position is seen as "punishment." Some departments have therefore created incentives to attract greater numbers of NPO candidates, often by creating a rewards structure that could include such things as promotion and authorizing overtime pay.

• *Policy Recommendation 5:* Encourage NPOs to keep track of their work, listing their weekly or monthly agendas and accomplishments. This will do four things: it will provide individual neighborhood officers with a sense of accomplishment; it will provide a way for supervisors to measure effectiveness in reaching goals; it will inform patrol officers about the NPOs' workload and the projects that are ongoing or recently completed; and it will be possible, using the workload lists, to educate future applicants about the range of the community policing position.

As captured in the interviews with patrol officers and NPOs in Jackson

City, it was the topic of promotions that aroused the most heated controversy. Ironically, when community policing was introduced it was greeted with suspicion and a lack of interest, and dismissed as one of the former chief's latest harebrained ideas. Women and people of color constituted the first wave of neighborhood officers, and no one envied them; in fact, they were mocked and ridiculed. The chief, however, remained steadfast in his commitment to the concept. He was so adamant that NPOs seemed to hold almost an anointed place in the department. The chief demonstrated his commitment with public statements, published articles, and promotions that favored neighborhood officers. Others on the force quickly realized the program's significance to him and, naturally, began to rethink their opposition. Many of them began to look on the community position as the "promotion elevator." All of the second- and third-wave NPOs mentioned that the expectation of promotion was one of the key motivations for their interest in neighborhood policing. Perhaps if the positions had not come to be thought of as synonymous with career advancement there would be far fewer women and men competing for them. In their research on community policing in Brooklyn, for example, Pate and Shtull (1994, 408–409) found that many persons stayed away from such jobs because of the lack of a clear rewards structure, even though many other officers perceived that they "had to do it" to get promoted.

In Jackson City, two major problems were identified that relate directly to promotion, the rewards structure, or both. Each problem has implications for the entire force. First, it was common knowledge among NPOs and patrol officers alike that accepting the neighborhood position meant that they would no longer receive overtime pay for working on holidays, making court appearances, and the like. This is a function of the very structure of the community policing position; it is deliberately flexible so that a court appearance could be incorporated within an NPO's work day, just like any other scheduled meeting. Most of the women and men interviewed mentioned that they took a cut in annual pay of two to three thousand dollars upon joining the neighborhood program. At the same time, however, because of their union contract, they *did* have all holidays off with pay (although no one mentioned this as a benefit). It appeared that low morale about the cut in pay was unmitigated by the fact that the NPOs did not have to work on holidays. As the NPOs saw it, they actually worked longer and harder than patrol officers, yet were financially penalized for doing so.

• *Policy Recommendation 6:* To counteract reluctance to become a community police officer because of financial concerns, the chief could devise a policy to make being an NPO more lucrative. One way to achieve this could be to make the position a promotable one, perhaps to the equivalent of detective. In

Jackson City, being promoted to detective was not the same as advancing to the rank of sergeant; rather, it offered additional financial compensation in recognition of the job's specialized duties.

The second problem involving promotion is the perception that NPOs "rapidly rise" to higher ranks. Like most police departments, Jackson City's uses promotion boards—and although many persons apply, few are chosen. Advancement is based on ability, performance, and special efforts made or projects undertaken. All officers in the sample noted a well-known phenomenon: NPOs were overrepresented, disproportionately, in the promotion lists. For many patrol officers this smacked of favoritism, reinforcing the belief that anyone who mouthed the rhetoric and put in some time in community policing would be promoted. Only a few persons who were not NPOs believed that the neighborhood officers actually worked enough to deserve promotion. By the time of the second and third wave of NPOs, their members acknowledged that advancement was one of the main reasons they had competed for the position. This perception of a "fast track to promotion" for the NPOs caused resentment among patrol officers and deepened their scorn for the neighborhood position. The NPOs maintained, however, that the uniqueness of their work afforded them more frequent and more visible opportunities to "shine," such that their efforts were justifiably recognized at promotion time. Patrol officers' work, by contrast, was less public, and they tended to be less distinguishable from each other due to the nature of their rapid response, call-driven work.

• *Policy Recommendation 7:* Create opportunities for patrol officers to display their skills, and honor them when they make extra efforts to fulfill their ordinary work assignments. The officers' activities need to be recognized publicly so that their innovations are not downplayed.

Successful community policing is made easier by having good supporting players. In Jackson City, the more effective NPOs were the more actively visible ones, who were able to enlist the help and support of those who had power in the neighborhood. At least three combined factors lay behind a successful outcome for a community officer in Jackson City. First, the NPOs were no doubt greatly aided by the information passed on by the managers of the local rental properties. Often, they knew details about each family member, what the residential and family problems were, and who did not belong in the neighborhood. Such information provided invaluable insight into the dynamics of the neighborhood. In fact, the NPOs often relied on the property managers to help deter "losers and bad guys" from entering their neighborhoods by aggressively screening rental applicants. This made the officers' job easier by allowing them to make an initial sweep of the known criminals and then by helping them to remain aware of who to keep out or throw out. To place this relationship in a larger context, evaluations conducted in Milwaukee and in Aurora, Colorado, showed that community police officers worked well with property owners to secure the help of the managers of rental properties; this aid included screening applicants and designing strategies to gain control over drug dealing and other problems. The landlords gave lists of residents and building keys to the officers, put up No Trespassing signs, and shared lists of evicted tenants. The two studies found that such coordinated efforts between resident managers and police resulted in a significant drop in drug-related arrests and calls for service (*Community Policing Exchange* 1996, 6–7).

Second, the NPOs' foot patrol was strengthened by the ubiquitous presence of a private security company's armed employees. Not only did the neighborhood officers simply enjoy walking the beat with other professionals, but they were also more likely to venture onto the streets (without any compelling reasons) later at night because they felt safer. And finally, the third factor underlying success in community policing was the coordinated effort between NPOs and the city to enact statutes against loitering and trespassing. The signs announcing these ordinances were strategically placed in neighborhoods with a high degree of drug trafficking. By establishing substantial penalties for violators, the statutes provided officers with a tool to control the flow of outsiders into the neighborhood. The hefty fine attached to a ticket for loitering or trespassing was a big deterrent. Even though the NPOs often took full credit for cleaning up "hot spots," on many occasions they played only a small role, which depended on help from property managers, private security guards, and city government.

There are a number of downsides to this increase in aggressive police surveillance and presence, of course. First, teaming up with the private security guards in what was intended as a show of force became a massive display of police authority. Often the neighborhoods resembled occupied zones, which certainly did not endear the police to the residents, although a few of them did express their gratitude. This issue relates to the dissolution of citizens' trust in the police, as addressed at the beginning of this chapter. In Louisville, Kentucky, for example, enforcement around "hot spots" and the stronger police presence near public housing in the evenings "aroused some opposition in the community and may have contributed to officers' perceptions of lower support for their community policing efforts compared to other districts" (Wilson and Bennett 1994, 368). Other residential areas, however, have seen more positive links forged between officers and citizens. Some NPOs who had gained the residents' confidence began to be viewed as the "conscience of the community." Local people began to trust them with their private lives, turning to these NPOs for help even before a criminal matter exploded. In Jackson City, some community officers played this role with respect to domestic violence incidents. Yet the NPOs' "shaming potential" is viable only in some neighborhoods, and not necessarily the most troubled ones. Residents' trust also rests on the individual officers' personalities, on who they are perceived to be.

Not all law enforcement was viewed as unnecessary, either by the police or by the citizens. For instance, an evaluation of eight community policing sites nationwide revealed that officers believe the first act in taking back a neighborhood is to step up enforcement efforts and promote "zero tolerance," even if this increases hostility from the "bad" residents:

> Our initial step was . . . to show them that we are doing something. . . . [A] lot of these people are scared and they are not going to go out there just because you tell them to go—"Hey, let's start a march against drugs or a neighborhood crime watch!" . . . We have to go into their neighborhoods and show them that we actually do care . . . and make lock-ups! (Grinc 1994, 448).

Aggressive enforcement action sometimes increased satisfaction on the part of the "good" residents, who liked to see a heightened police presence. However, this could be a short-lived effect that would disappear once police backed away from their newly aggressive stance (Grinc 1994, 449); in Norfolk, Portland, and Houston that was precisely what happened (Grinc 1994, 453). As the police researcher Peter Manning (1984) and others have observed, "[S]o long as the police exercise violence in the name of the state, they will be despised by many in poor communities and will always represent the potential for violence to all (even those the police define as good) community residents" (quoted in Grinc 1994, 450). After the initial period of aggressive enforcement, if the residents do not get involved in community development, officers' enthusiasm may turn to disillusionment and demoralization. This result is not surprising, given that the research reported in Grinc in eight other sites has found that most officers believed that police departments are not the appropriate agency to do community organizing (Grinc 1994, 456). Both neighborhood and patrol officers in Jackson City echoed this belief. It is important to remember, however, that residents have been conditioned for a hundred years to see police as crimefighters who did not welcome their help. So, citizens' lack of involvement does not necessarily reflect laziness or apathy; it is, rather, the historical fruit of the professional police model and the conflict and distance it created (see Grinc 1994).

• *Policy Recommendation 8:* Police need to be aware of the negative consequences of aggressive law enforcement action conducted by NPOs, particularly the lasting impact of some of the strategies. Efforts such as issuing citations for loitering and going on nightly foot patrol in groups may further alienate residents who already feel disenfranchised and do not trust the police.

Despite some of the negative effects or controversies arising from neighborhood policing in Jackson City, there were a number of positive elements as well. With only one exception, all of the former and current NPOs mentioned having higher morale and greater job satisfaction when they were community officers. Most of them craved a change from the routine of patrol. They were happy to find that they could be innovative and that this trait was encouraged. Many had not previously had the opportunity to be creative, and the responsibility of carrying out new ideas made them feel personally satisfied. For the most part, women and men loved the job's flexibility and the fact that every day was different. However, a few former community officers mentioned that the position eventually *did* become routine over time, since they were assigned to just one area. The problems in the neighborhood remained the same, even if the composition of the population changed.

Consistent with evaluations of community police done elsewhere, the Jackson City NPOs enjoyed not being a "slave to the radio" (see also Pate and Shtull 1994, 406). Having a permanent assignment in one district allowed them to follow-up on calls and handle them all the way through to their resolution. Community police officers could also play integral roles in addressing ongoing local issues. Most importantly, they were glad to be free of the constant exposure to the more base, hostile, and sad parts of humanity. By interacting with the residents every day and walking around in the neighborhoods at all hours, the NPOs were able to see people at their best, not just at their worst. Such contact also enabled the officers to step in before minor issues became major problems. These continual encounters and the positive reinforcement of seeing the good side of citizens buoyed the NPOs' spirits and helped them sustain their emotional investment in the community and their commitment to their own position within it. All of the men and women maintained that they "loved" being thought of as part of the "good team."

Another benefit of neighborhood policing noted by the officers in Jackson City was that it made it easier to enforce the law. This was especially true of conducting follow-ups with victims and issuing warrants. Since the NPOs worked hard to establish personal connections with citizens, in the residents' eyes their role often changed over time, from "police officer" to such identities as the neighborhood's ambassador, the helper, and the liaison between families and the criminal justice system or social service agencies. Community officers were able to demystify the process of criminal justice, and they helped young people learn not to fear the police. The NPOs could be especially helpful if they were aware of a family's financial hardship and of the need to find baby-sitters if primary caregivers were arrested. Overall, simply knowing the residents better made it easier for NPOs to make arrests and otherwise enforce the law. The situation in Jackson City is in line with the findings in other research conducted by Paternoster and his colleagues (1997), which indicated that, if citizens believed police were fair and treated them in a procedurally just manner, recidivism was reduced and people's support for the legal system was enhanced (see also Casper, Tyler, and Fisher 1988).

Another positive consequence of some NPO efforts was that increased police attention to a neighborhood stimulated citizens toward increased community involvement. Although the neighborhood police officers cannot take the full credit, they were part of a team founded to resuscitate failing areas and help them become healthier residential environments. Establishing a community center and having it offer various activities for children and adults (such as after-school mentoring and tutoring programs, community gardens, visiting nurses, probation and parole officers, and social workers) blended with the efforts of the neighborhood officer to create a sense of community. Some NPOs were very closely involved with the community centers, others less so. In a number of neighborhoods, police officers played key roles in facilitating involvement by the social service providers and the residents alike. The bottom line for successful neighborhood work is that officers must encourage citizens to become invested in their community; having done so, they will be more likely to help the police prevent and solve crimes and will feel less intimidated by or distrustful of them. Policy priorities should reflect the importance of such coordinated programs that encourage interaction between police and citizens in noncriminal situations.

Still other benefits of community policing became clear from the research in Jackson City and could inform similar efforts elsewhere. A major strength of the neighborhood program was its lasting effect on officers. Virtually all of the former NPOs indicated that they were able to use the skills they had learned and refined in their next jobs. Both men and women mentioned that they began to look at crime as part of a larger constellation of social issues, often related to poverty, poor schooling, and blocked opportunities. This emphasis on issues "bigger" than simple law enforcement increased the NPOs' job satisfaction once they were out of the neighborhoods. More than half of the former officers were surprised to discover the lingering transformative effect of their neighborhood experience. In their present positions, these women and men found that they were less cynical about people, more willing to look behind the immediate crisis to the larger picture, and better able to comprehend situations by using a problem-solving approach. They found themselves looking for the "broken window." The creativity and innovation they had used in their neighborhoods became part of their current approach to policing. Many of the men said that they had learned new skills, such as enhancing the ways in which they communicated with others, and in particular had improved their verbal abilities.

In a similar vein, many officers felt that the neighborhood experience had expanded their general fund of skills. They felt better able to identify community resources and better equipped to link residents with an area's liaisons or social service providers. Without the stint as an NPO, they contended, this familiarity with programs and willingness to help citizens make use of them would not have been part of their modus operandi when dealing with the community.

Former neighborhood officers can also play a substantial role in winning the hearts and minds of those on the force who are unfamiliar with community policing, or even antagonistic toward it. Continuing contact with former NPOs can do much to reduce patrol officers' resistance to and ridicule of the neighborhood approach and those involved in it.

• *Policy Recommendation 9:* Have former NPOs act as ambassadors to other members of the force. By drawing on their experiences and individual reputations, they can help foster a better understanding of what community policing entails. This would provide other officers with a larger, more solid and realistic base of information from which to draw their conclusions and might, in fact, challenge some of the uninformed, incorrect, and sometimes derogatory assumptions that are made about neighborhood policing.

The importance of integrating NPOs and patrol officers cannot be emphasized too much. Mechanisms need to be in place to discourage mockery and derision of foot patrol by those who work in traditional patrol.

• *Policy Recommendation 10:* The department should encourage and create opportunities for more cross-training of patrol officers and NPOs. Neighborhood officers could also receive additional in-service training on community development or activism. Involving patrol officers with the law enforcement *and* social-work elements that underlie solid community policing efforts will challenge their negative stereotypes about the new model. It will also provide an atmosphere conducive to reeducating police about their new roles. In fact, research conducted in Britain by Nigel Fielding reveals that the "canteen culture" referred to in Chapter 6 can be interrupted with cross-training.

In carrying out the community policing mission, departments can utilize the language of problem solving and stress that activity. This approach raises a few additional policy-related issues. Rewards should accrue to those who actively practice the new methods. As in Jackson City, departments can encourage both foot patrol and traditional patrol officers to "do community policing" by distributing information throughout the force and by publicizing the efforts of patrol officers in community policing so that accolades do not always go only to the NPOs. For the latter group in particular, using goal-setting techniques may eliminate any temptation for self-aggrandizement and also the receipt of any unfair rewards (those based on the loudest boasting), since there would be a benchmark from which to measure officers' effectiveness. Evaluations based upon goals set and reached could also level the playing field for NPOs stationed in the less criminally active neighborhoods where law enforcement activity is not highly visible and for those officers, particularly women, who are reticent about publicizing their accomplishments. By writing up problem-oriented policing reports or regularly evaluating their efforts to meet the unique goals developed for their own districts, NPOs in the less troubled communities can receive roughly as much attention and credit as those making many arrests in the criminally active neighborhoods. Publicizing the NPOs' efforts may help to reduce the tension that exists between community and patrol officers concerning the "mysteries" of neighborhood policing.

To summarize, my research with the Jackson City Police Department revealed a number of problems faced by both neighborhood and patrol officers. When departments are transformed in ways that challenge their traditional philosophy and operation, they need to become dynamic, alert, and responsive to the consequences and unintended problems that result. The policy recommendations offered thus far have addressed the major professional struggles confronting the officers interviewed and observed in Jackson City, and have reflected as well some general policy issues being discussed in the policing literature. The next section of this chapter explores the complications facing neighborhood officers that arise from issues of gender, race, and sexual orientation.

Questions of Gender, Race, and Sexual Orientation

Who is drawn to community policing, and why? In Jackson City, the motivations of the different waves of community officers varied. At first only women or people of color took the risk. And it *was* a risk, due to the lukewarm, sometimes even hostile reception they faced from other officers. Perhaps the early NPOs felt they had less to lose, given their already low status (based on rank, gender, and race) in the masculine police occupation. The "founders" also indicated that they had become disillusioned with aggressive, after-the-fact policing and desired an approach oriented more toward prevention and the community. As the rhetoric and philosophy of neighborhood policing became increasingly prominent in the former chief's memorandums, public statements, and promotion lists, more men were drawn to these positions, as was a new group of women and people of color. The second- and third-wave NPOs often did not share the goals of the original neighborhood officers, but saw the position as an opportunity to distinguish themselves and get promoted more quickly.

The evolution of community policing in Jackson City, as is perhaps the case in *any* jurisdiction that is changing (or has changed) from a crime control to a neighborhood model, reflects a subtly articulated construction of masculinity and femininity. A crucial issue for community policing involves how best to attract "masculine" men to perform "women's work" in a masculinist police subculture. It is important not to essentialize either women or men here; not *all* women possess stereotypical "women's traits," nor do all men *not* possess them. But the general tendency is to associate women more with social service; such an aptitude is often seen as being linked to women by their gender, regardless of where it may actually be found, and thus as being undesirable for "masculine" men to possess. At the same time, it is important not to perpetuate stereotypes about "feminine" tasks in policework in a way that would cast any doubt on women's ability to be competent law enforcers. One way to avoid gender-role stereotyping is to recast the stigmatized aspects of community policing so that they no longer have any semantic or perceptual connection to femininity or to womanly ways of "doing policing." This suggestion builds on related work in the gender field: to be masculine means being not-female, being detached, aloof, and independent. Inappropriate behavior, such as expressions of intimacy or warm feelings, is stigmatized. "Emotional detachment is one way in which gender hierarchies are maintained. Expressing emotions signifies weakness and is devalued, whereas emotional detachment signifies strength and is valued" (Cancian 1987, 125). Ostensibly in Jackson City, neighborhood policing skills had to become gender neutral so that the new positions would attract both male and female candidates.

Although the paragon of the community officer is nurturing, expressive, and empathetic, the informal job descriptions in Jackson City of the ideal neighborhood officer included traits such as good leadership skills, the ability to communicate with merchants and property managers, innovation, autonomy, and self-direction. These characteristics are more typically associated with the business world and with the work ethic of rugged individualism, in other words, with "manly" pursuits. Once nurturing skills are recast in a gender-neutral context, men become more willing to "try them on." Such skill transformation seems to be the case in Jackson City; men were more drawn to community policing once the job description reflected qualities that were more likely to be perceived as masculine. Women's involvement, on the other hand, was more likely to be interpreted as natural caregiving activities, rather than entrepreneurial in a (manly) business sense. Studies by Joan Acker (1990) and others (Acker and Ask 1989; Baran 1990; Cockburn 1988, 1991; and Hacker 1990) have found that whereas computerization and other new technologies upgraded women's skills across a variety of occupations, such as engineering, banking, and insurance, men remained in charge. Male workers were perceived as having more skills than their female counterparts, and women's skills were undervalued; consequently, female workers remained at lower levels of status within an organization's hierarchy.

To stay with the business language metaphor, in Jackson City residents were viewed as the department's "external" customers, whereas the police themselves were seen as the department's "internal" customers. In this way, the illusion that the NPOs would "serve" the customers was challenged, in that officers, too, were thought of as customers who had a stake in the work environment. This clever labeling reinforced the gender-neutral or even masculine language of the business world, rather than permitting the use of more feminized words such as "serve" and "service."

Men, in particular, had to establish their masculinity in order not to feel threatened or challenged when accepting the less macho role inherent in community policing. Virtually all of the male former and current neighborhood officers had confirmed their masculine status in alternative ways before becoming NPOs. Since selection rested upon seniority, the men chosen had ample years of experience as participants in special law enforcement units or activities, such as SWAT teams, hostage negotiation units, and shooting contests. Many were veterans of the military, and some had prior law enforcement experience with other cities or states, or with the federal government. Female officers, too, were concerned about their image. They were reluctant to be essentialized as "perfect" for neighborhood policing since, as women, they were already seen as nurturers and stereotyped as more emotional and intimacy oriented. Those who were single and had no childcare responsibilities followed "macho" career paths similar to the ones of the "career-motivated" men in the department, including having reputations for their past experiences with "tough crimefighting units." These past activities were well known and a constant point of reference in conversations, although women did not speak of them as frequently as did men. Women's participation in aggressive crimefighting assignments calls to mind Jennifer Hunt's work with police, which demonstrated that acceptance of women in the male subculture rested upon displays of toughness and verve. Many of the NPOs, both male and female, continued their involvement with the special crimefighting units while they were neighborhood officers.

When it was to their advantage to do so, and in different ways, both the men and the women capitalized on public acceptance of stereotypically male and female roles. For example, the women, both current and former NPOs, when speaking about their part in the community and the acceptance they felt from the residents often mentioned how being a woman helped to facilitate some of their outreach efforts. In particular, being female seemed to help bridge general differences between them and the citizens and helped in connecting with different racial and ethnic groups. Women who were mothers found that mentioning their children to a resident helped to break down barriers of suspicion and mistrust through the common ground of parenting. This was most helpful in the Southeast Asian community. Although the residents feared the male police, who reminded them of the war and the harsh regime they had fled, they brought with them a patriarchal tradition of not respecting women in positions of authority. Motherhood became an avenue through which such differences could be overcome while alternative connections were being forged. This success held true for all female NPOs with children, whether they were heterosexual or lesbian (many of the lesbian officers had children or were coparenting those of their partners). The public declaration of the common bond of motherhood between community officers and residents is something rather distinctive in the neighborhood policing context; it would not, for example, be done by female officers on patrol.

Over time, women gained more informal social control in the neighborhoods because they strengthened their role as confidante; this aided them in carrying out crimefighting later on. Although the path may have been smoothed by the "essentializing" of women's roles (as mother, caretaker, nurturer), it was very clear from what the female officers said that this mechanism for gaining acceptance was far more than a simple matter of bridging differences through gender commonality. The women seemed *very* clear about how they were manipulating stereotypes to their advantage to achieve a greater goal. (As I will illustrate in another section, men acted similarly.)

Stereotypes about the "feminine nature" of community policing seemed to be interrupted only when a "macho," well-respected officer of either gender was placed in a very tough, criminally active neighborhood. Thus, issues of masculinity influenced the choice of assignment. Some officers were drawn to high-crime, high-activity districts. These areas needed more aggressive law enforcement action, so there were greater opportunities to display traditional masculine crime control efforts, such as intensive surveillance, undercover investigations, and buy-and-bust operations. Because of ongoing or endemic crime problems, the neighborhood's reputation was well known to all of the other officers in the department. Enforcement activity in these more troublesome neighborhoods often involved a coordinated effort between the neighborhood officer, regular patrol officers, and special task forces geared to combat drugs or gangs. Thus, these criminal neighborhoods provided a site for officers to demonstrate their masculinity within the marginalized feminine setting of community policing.

For their part, women who were attracted to these districts could also preserve, reinforce, or enhance their reputations as tough and able cops. In the rougher, criminally active neighborhoods, there were more "Dirty Harriets" because law enforcement, rather than an approach like bonding through shared parenthood, was necessary. Since these high-crime areas were familiar to the entire police force, women may have felt the need to use such assignments to "prove" themselves to the patrol officers and their supervisors to show that they could handle rough neighborhoods with competence. In the less dangerous program development and maintenance neighborhoods, female NPOs had more freedom to play a nurturing role. For those women who already possessed finely developed interpersonal communication abilities, being assigned to a criminally active neighborhood provided an opportunity to fine-tune their aggressive, crimefighting skills during incidents when words failed to prevent conflict.

Regardless of the type of neighborhood, the kinds of activities that were organized and performed there also afforded officers opportunities to confirm their masculinity, or "do gender." Many men gravitated toward visible, street-level crimefighting and patrolled more often in squad cars, when available. Some male officers, though, wanted to coast until retirement, or only deal with local merchants and other business owners, or use their flexible schedules for their own ends, such as going to law school. Overall, the men were less concerned with enhancing links with the on-site health workers and social workers. Many of the women were much more involved with these social service providers, especially in coordinating efforts to fight truancy, in developing mentoring programs, and in starting projects to educate female residents about domestic violence. In contrast, many of the men joined forces with the male private security guards and walked or rode around the neighborhood together. This difference may indicate that women tend to be more accustomed to reaching out and forming networks, whereas men stick with the familiarity of the old boys' club (e.g., other male police officers and male private security guards), rather than reaching out to embrace strangers (i.e., female social service providers).

Once enforcement efforts had stabilized the tougher, criminally active neighborhoods, the male officers poured their energies into activities for the local children and teenagers. This is not a new focus for police, nor a bad one. For much of the past century, police athletic leagues and similar activities for youngsters have been a mainstay of crime prevention. They fill in unsupervised time in the children's lives, diverting them from delinquent pranks that could lead to more serious criminal involvement, and they help to build self-esteem. There was also the hope that young people would come to see police as role models and friends. Bonding with officers might deter crime in that youngsters would not want to jeopardize the positive relationship.

Male officers developed "all-American" sports programs, such as baseball, football, and basketball, and other rugged recreational activities, such as hiking, camping, and fishing. It is not unusual that men would turn to things that they had loved as children. Essentially, however, these programs attracted boys but did little to involve girls. The efforts also generated media attention, since the police sought corporate sponsorship for uniforms, equipment, and transportation assistance and often enlisted journalists to help spread the word. This resulted in a lot of positive stories in the newspapers as well as recognition from police supervisors. The programs' popularity also made it easier to get male patrol officers to participate.

Competitive sports programs, especially those easily identified as manly, provided another avenue for confirming masculinity, since many neighborhood officers felt that they were expected to work with children as part of their job. By contrast, the female NPOs who developed athletic programs tended to introduce soccer to the children. They viewed it as a more cooperative game and one that both girls and boys could play and enjoy. The women also mentioned that soccer could be used to integrate children from different racial and ethnic backgrounds in an environment that stressed teamwork and cooperation. (This was one of the few deliberate efforts at integration.) Other activities for boys and girls that were more often spearheaded by the female NPOs were after-school tutoring and computer skills programs, although as fancier equipment became available more male officers became interested in the computer projects. However, the men often admitted, rather sheepishly, that they became involved to develop their own computer expertise.

As noted earlier, the topic of "rewards" received considerable negative attention from NPOs and patrol officers. The perception was that serving in the community position correlated with promotion. Thus, in order to demonstrate their worthiness, some officers may have felt that their neighborhood activities needed to be highlighted so as to attract the attention of outsiders, particularly their supervisors. From the interviews, it was clear that the men were more likely to publicize their efforts and achievements. The women seemed to simply do their work, without highlighting their activities. This finding may reflect the ease with which men brag to each other, particularly if (as in Jackson City) most supervisors are men. Although the absence of women who supervise NPOs may reflect the reality that they have not attained many upper-level positions within police departments, it may also be the case that men, especially those doing "unmanly" tasks, may be more comfortable being supervised by other men. With same-sex supervision, an already existent perception of femininity in assignment will not be further reinforced by female supervision of men doing "women's work." Despite the large numbers of women serving as patrol officers, all but one of the supervisors for the NPOs have been men.

A number of the officers in Jackson City believed that the supervisors greatly contributed to their carrying the neighborhood workload. Supervisors were believed to encourage the NPOs toward greater esprit de corps and sense of common purpose. Since all of them save one were men, part of this level of comfort could be attributed to the fact that the men (and women) who had chosen to be in the lower-status position of NPO found that having their actions evaluated by men gave them some needed credibility. This was particularly true when the officer and the supervisor were both men. The one female supervisor had never "tainted" her reputation by being a neighborhood officer, so she did not have to "prove" her masculinity in the same way as did male supervisors who had once been NPOs. Any community officer who has been promoted may have accomplished this simply by virtue of having left the neighborhood; it reconfirms that, man or woman, one's "masculinity" was not blemished there, or else that it has been regained. In fact, it was the former NPOs in Jackson City who most readily admitted the large role that social work played in being a neighborhood police officer; the current officers downplayed this aspect of the job.

In her gender and occupational research, Christine Williams (1992) found that subtle tracking systems exist and that they favor men. Since men typically run systems, they "kick [other] men upstairs in the process," pushing them into administration (Williams 1992, 256). And these "upstairs" positions, of course, are "more legitimate [and] tend to be the most prestigious, better paying ones" (Williams 1992, 256). This is quite the opposite of the so-called glass-ceiling effect encountered by women. Typically, female workers experience invisible fences, caused primarily by the sexist attitudes of men with power in organizations (Freeman 1990).[3] Williams found that many men embraced subtle tracking, and that "leaving the most female identified areas of their professions helped them resolve internal conflicts involving their masculinity" (Williams 1992, 257). Their career advancement may be smoother because they are far more likely to be supervised by another man. The two establish an atmosphere of good rapport, closeness, mentorship, and encouragement for one another, and their interactions are not sexually based. So, for men, "[G]ender is construed as a *positive* difference. Therefore, they have an incentive to bond together and emphasize their distinctiveness" (Williams 1992, 259). The consequences for women are to be excluded from informal decision-making networks and, perhaps, to be evaluated by men using different standards than they would apply to other men.

Traditional gender-role expectations play a part in how men's and women's job performance may be perceived and evaluated in many community policing situations. Typically, men engaged with children's activities were highly praised for their work. Residents, particularly mothers, were very impressed by their interest in and commitment to youth programs. Women carrying out the same activities, however, were merely accepted without fanfare. After all, the activities led by the female NPOs were part and parcel of women's "natural" roles. Thus, female officers who worked with youth programs were seen as simply extending women's accepted role in the community. The men, however, became "Super Men" in the eyes of the community for their efforts. So it is easy to see how the men came to receive more accolades and rewards for doing this "feminine" work. Williams (1992, 260) also discovered that women often welcome men into "their" professions, although they *do not* like how easily men advance once they have been included. As more men became neighborhood officers in Jackson City and were then promoted to supervise other NPOs, the community policing program came to be viewed as more legitimate. A relatively young cohort of men occupy high-ranking positions within this police department, reflecting promotions made by the former chief, who valued neighborhood policing and rewarded those men who, early on, risked their careers to become NPOs.

Thus it is that, given traditional gender-role expectations, in many community policing situations women do not get any or enough credit and men get too much. This is the strongest policy message related to gender and neighborhood policing, because it has tangible consequences for the promotion process. Unfair standards of evaluation are manifested in the assumptions made about gender roles and about who is "working" versus who is "doing what comes naturally." In Marian Swerdlow's (1989) examination of women who entered the traditionally male field of rapid-transit operator, she found that some men adjusted to women's presence by relating to them as friends, which interrupted seeing women as sexual beings whom they could dominate. Some of the female rapid-transit operators noticed that their male coworkers were surprised when they performed the job as well as men could. Swerdlow (1989, 382) and others (see Nivea and Gutek 1981) have remarked on the "talking platypus phenomenon," in which women are given lavish praise for routine competence. In Jackson City, though, it was the *men* in the neighborhood policing program who were the beneficiaries.

Race was also related to why officers wanted to be a part of the community policing program in Jackson City. Persons of color in the first wave of NPOs were motivated by such altruistic reasons as "taking back the street" and helping communities. Officers of color from the next two waves did not express the same sentiments. Rather, they focused on issues of career development and advancement. This change may also reflect the presence of more black *men* in the second and third waves. The perceptions gleaned from interviews with some of the former and current second- and third-wave *white* officers raised an interesting point. They believed that because there were so few African American men who could serve as role models in the troubled neighborhoods, the black men who were positioned there could do far less, but would be seen as doing more, simply because their presence was so welcomed by the residents. Although there may be some truth in this belief, the white NPOs could also be expressing some resentment about what, to them, were unjust promotions.

White officers, both men and women, adamantly asserted that race did not matter in successful community policing. They believed that success reflected an officer's personal style, and that it had nothing to do with one's race or gender. Black men, though, believed their race *did* make a difference in establishing rapport with residents, especially in that children needed to be able to look up to an employed man of color. The African American male NPOs overwhelmingly emphasized law enforcement above race relations, as did their white counterparts. This finding is consistent with Susan Martin's (1994) research on race and gender alliances within police departments; she found that men of color are more likely to align themselves with the existing power structure (in other words, white men) and that they are less race loyal than black women. This alliance suggests that the men of color "fit in" better with other (white) men than they do with women of color on the force, since all the men are still seen as "masculine."

Neighborhood policing, and the alternative methods that it introduces, challenge the masculinist ethos of the policing profession. Within the Jackson City Police Department, as the reward structure began to reflect a strong commitment to the social service style of NPOs, the administration transformed the feminized aspects of community policing in order to attract men, and men began to seek these jobs. Challenged to demonstrate their masculinity in new ways, they pointed to earlier and current crimefighting activities, selected tougher neighborhoods, and favored a more visible law enforcement stance in their everyday work (even the men who excelled in interpersonal skills continued to emphasize law enforcement). Not all of the men were go-getters, however; some sought the NPO position as a way to serve at a slower pace until their retirement. Women's responses as community officers, on the other hand, took several different paths. Some exaggerated their masculinity, following the more "male" career advancement model. Others emphasized their femininity as a means to an end, which allowed them to connect more easily with residents, and in particular afforded them some success in interrupting the uneasy relationship and calming the tensions between police and minority populations.

Still other female officers adapted both masculine and feminine dimensions, paralleling women who assume a more androgynous style as correctional officers in male settings (Zimmer 1986; Jurik 1988).

In part, male NPOs construct an exaggerated masculinity so that they are not seen as feminine as they carry out the social-work functions of policing. Related to this is the almost defiant expression of heterosexuality, so that the men's sexual orientation can *never* truly be doubted even if their gender roles are contested. Male patrol officers' language—such as their use of terms like "pansy police" to connote neighborhood police officers—served to affirm their own heterosexuality. This defensiveness could even be heightened, since there were so many women on the force as well as in the neighborhood positions and since a relatively large number of them were openly lesbian. Male community police officers, too, used sexualized language to talk about their jobs. For example, men spoke of new NPOs as "virgins," thus clearly and negatively referring to newcomers from foot patrol by casting them in a feminized, passive, naive light. Such traits are antithetical to the quintessential macho, aggressive, crime-fighter image. Other examples include the male NPOs' use of the word "prophylactic" to describe their role as neighborhood officers and the paternalistic manner in which the men say they will "take care of" the residents. In addition, the male officers, but not the women, deliberately wove their heterosexual status into conversations, explicitly mentioning their female domestic partner or spouse and their children. This finding is consistent with research conducted in the occupational field. The studies reveal that men in female-dominated occupations, such as teachers, librarians, and pediatricians, over-reference their heterosexual status to ensure that others will not think they are gay.

At first glance, there seem to be a disproportionate number of lesbians in community policing in Jackson City. There are several possible explanations for this. The high number may simply mirror the distribution of lesbians in the full department. It may also be that persons from socially oppressed groups are more keen to confront the issues and problems facing members of marginal groups, and hence are more apt to become NPOs. Or, the looseness of the neighborhood position may provide "outsiders" more flexibility to meander away from the norms of social dominants and the established macho heterosexual police culture. Given the receptivity the Jackson City Police Department has shown to homosexual officers, it may also be that the force accepts "different" officers, in line with the "good cop syndrome." Coined by a chief inspector of the Metropolitan Police in England, the term indicates that as long as "odd" individuals are seen as effective officers by others, they will be accepted and even respected (Burke 1993). Respect may be enhanced because the lesbian or gay NPO is already a known quantity from her or his past years of work as a patrol officer or in some other capacity.

Change of any kind generates anxiety. The feeling may be worse for police officers, who are accustomed to following similar daily routines with fairly predictable kinds of disruptions. Adjusting to change in police roles and expectations, such as the movement away from patrol to the neighborhood position, is further complicated by the "feminine" stigma of the new concept and the uncertainties involved in carrying out the new style. Officers adapt and act in ways that reflect enduring cultural images of masculine policework, images that must be balanced with their own gender, race, and sexual orientation.

This being the case, it is difficult to formulate either explicit policy recommendations that are not so specific as to reduce officers' variations by gender, race, and sexual orientation to caricatures, or policy recommendations so general as to be meaningless and impossible to implement. On the one hand, social assumptions about gender and the ways that, without reflection, we "do gender" are deeply embedded in our culture. On the other hand, however, issues of gender, race, and sexual orientation have very real implications for policing styles, job satisfaction, and perceptions of success. The use of three independent data sources (surveys, in-depth interviews, and field observations) in Jackson City to gather the data maximized the opportunity to uncover the meaning of the community policing experience for nontraditional officers and to understand the nuances of their behavior as compared to that of traditional officers.

Challenging police departments to be proactive and introspective seems compatible with their drive to be dynamic institutions that possess a mandate for a new kind of policing. It is clear, however, that departments need to be aware that gendered assumptions, interpretations, and consequences *do* exist. Police administrators need to anticipate that benefits accrue differently for different officers because of gender, race, and sexual orientation and that the process of advantaging and disadvantaging is layered. For example, assessing skills has been made more complicated by the introduction of gender-neutral skill and competency language, which masks gendered nuances in evaluations. At the same time, however, until a more androgynous policing style is fully embraced, accommodations must be made in order to attract masculine men into roles perceived as feminine. The Jackson City neighborhood policing program has attracted male and female officers with stellar qualities; most do the job extremely well. By raising here the complexities associated with gender, race, and sexual orientation, I am asking police departments, scholars, and students to seriously consider the complex issues associated with negotiating masculine space, as well as to seriously consider the solutions.

Conclusion

Although Jackson City is a fairly progressive community, it is not so distinctive that the findings presented here are anomalous. As other researchers (who are not cited in order to preserve the city's anonymity) have pointed out, there are 125 municipalities in this country that are roughly the same size (100,000–249,000), and Jackson City has been compared to such similarly situated localities as Austin, Texas, and Portland, Oregon.[4] What Jackson City *did* have, though, was "organizational readiness." In their study of Joliet, Illinois, Dennis Rosenbaum, Sandy Yeh, and Deanna Wilkinson identified this as necessary for reform—in fact, it is viewed as essential in order to succeed in community policing efforts. Only when "an organization has in place the structure, policies, procedures, knowledge, and officer skills needed to deliver a new set of police services and a new approach to crime prevention and control [is it] prepared to make a lasting difference, both internally and externally" (Rosenbaum, Yeh, and Wilkinson 1994, 350). Jackson City had such a commitment, beginning with the former chief, who served twenty years, and continuing with the efforts of the new chief.

What is also important in Jackson City is that the community policing concept was conceived and carried out using both top-down and bottom-up strategies and involvement by personnel. The former chief was intrigued by neighborhood policing, and he was thus more receptive to the push from several patrol officers who wanted to try it. With supportive leadership and well-designed plans, police departments can ease the change from being a masculinist, crimefighting organization to being a strong force that plays an active role in establishing community stability and a better quality of life. This does not mean that there will be no growing pains or clashes between the macho old guard and the more androgynous new community police officers. In fact, this chapter has offered various policy recommendations that address such points of contention. And this change in orientation does not mean that all the residents or officers are clamoring for increased police involvement in the neighborhoods. But the department's administrators must play a leading role in creating a more accepting rank and file and a more dynamic environment for reforms like neighborhood policing. For example, in Joliet the chief publicly recognized the need for officer "buy-in" and knew how important it was; he rewarded good community policing skills so that the behavioral changes would be positively reinforced (Rosenbaum, Yeh, and Wilkinson 1994, 333). In Jackson City, there was also an attempt to involve all officers with all levels of decision making. Earlier research showed that it was important for the rank and file to participate: "perceptions, ideas, and needs of officers are as important to the decision-making process as are those of managers" (Wycoff and Skogan 1994, 371).

As the police scholars Robert Taylor, Eric Fritsch, and Tony Caeti (1998) suggest, however, without the direct involvement of the city government and political infrastructure to coordinate cooperative programs, community policing is doomed to be a fad. Police can not carry the burden of change in isolation. If the force's mission is broadened to include addressing enduring social problems, the mission will fail without the resources and commitment of the city. Despite the seemingly unstoppable enthusiasm for community policing across the country, curricula in training academies nationwide and personnel evaluation standards have been slow to reflect these significant changes in officers' roles. If the long-term root causes of social problems are not addressed collectively, police will bear the brunt of the failure of neighborhood policing. This is an unfair gamble for departments to take, since community policing is "sold" to the public with the expectation that citizens can rely on officers to solve social problems. Even well-designed neighborhood programs that are held up as national prototypes, as in the case of Jackson City, must work in tandem with the larger structures of social service agencies and government to accomplish such massive tasks.

To conclude, in this book I have explored how the police in Jackson City worked to "redefine" feminine tasks associated with community policing in order to allow the neighborhood officers to undertake impression (or "image") management and negotiate a previously stigmatized identity. Beginning in the 1800s, policewomen carved out a place for themselves by focusing on gender-appropriate "feminine" skills, such as interpersonal communication, prevention, and informal conflict negotiation. For a century, men denigrated these skills as not being part of "real" policework. But now, with community policing, such "feminine skills" are recognized as essential to success, and men must be enticed to embrace them. In Jackson City, it is obvious that some men excel at such work, just as some women excel at work more commonly associated with masculinity. "Women's work" today is being reconceptualized and reframed as a new approach to policework involving gender-neutral job skills; in this way, their peers on patrol and supervisors (both mostly male) can continue to think of NPOs as masculine crimefighters. Within the community policing setting, there existed ample opportunities to engage in masculine pursuits. However, the NPOs in Jackson City still exhibited *more* androgynous police behavior than what is typical of traditional officers. Even the NPOs most oriented toward law enforcement performed various human relations tasks and nurturing social efforts that lay beyond what patrol officers could or would embrace. In Jackson City, though, despite the existence of subtle ways of projecting masculinity, it was necessary to "upgrade" feminine skills so that they would be perceived as more highly valued masculine ones, as in the department's use of the concept of "problem solving." Skill assessment was interpreted differently for male and female officers who exhibited such aptitudes.

Human beings create social constructions of human behavior, among them the gender differences between men and women. As West and Zimmerman (1987) and Martin and Jurik (1996) point out, the meanings behind the concepts of masculinity and femininity are socially learned and reinforced, not biologically determined or reflective of natural differences. It is the social construction of gender roles that defines what behavior is considered appropriately feminine or masculine, and most persons accept such categorizations without reflection. This gender-role dichotomy is strikingly clear in the police officer's world.

The cultural image of the masculine crimefighter endures, despite the knowledge that most policing revolves around providing services and maintaining order. Such feminine skills as interpersonal communication, conflict negotiation, and human relations work in general continue to be devalued, whereas the myth that "real men" are the crimefighters in the trenches persists (Jurik 1985; Hunt 1984). In Jackson City, the neighborhood officers gave up some of the power and authority that typically belongs to "street cops" as a contribution to making a difference in their own lives and in the lives of citizens. Thus, the NPOs were willing to risk feeling overwhelmed by social conditions over which they had no control. Even if their sole motivation was career advancement, the very structure of neighborhood policing involved a temporary transformation in thinking and in doing the job. In contrast, patrol officers sought to *avoid* the frustrations of encountering the sorts of unfixable situations that confronted the NPOs every day. By avoiding becoming too familiar with people's struggles, and by not getting too close to the residents, patrol officers escaped feelings of powerlessness. The neighborhood officers' exaggerations of masculinity may be a defense against such feelings, which grew stronger as NPOs grew more intimately connected to the residents in their neighborhoods.

The structure of community policing capitalizes on the skills that have been culturally designated as feminine, and therefore undervalued. Coming to terms with the cognitive dissonance between the images of social worker and crimefighter is one component of the new approach, and learning to do the job while resolving tensions in the informal police subculture is another. The ultimate goal may be to convince all police officers to follow androgynous models, in which they, as professionals, recognize that the ideal repertoire of skills includes a range of both masculine and feminine ones. Many departments already recognize this, and officers strive to manifest such flexibility in their policework. The importance of understanding the enduring effects of gender and consequent interpretations of masculinity and femininity cannot be overestimated. Both

NPOs and patrol officers need to realize that relying on a larger range of behavior and emotions does not "feminize" their occupation, nor does it prevent policework from being accomplished. In fact, as shown in this research, it can enhance job performance. As I discovered in my time with the Jackson City police, however, "talking the talk" did not always mean that one was truly "walking the talk." The police environment must foster acceptance of alternative ways of defining "real" policework. Jackson City's open-ended community policing mandate, which asks neighborhood officers to respond to neighborhood needs, empowers NPOs to experiment with a range of roles and skills without relinquishing their masculinity. The benefits of building a relationship with residents can be conveyed by NPOs to their colleagues in patrol to demonstrate successful outcomes of the neighborhood policing approach. Strengthening alliances between the two groups of officers should be made a priority before the ruptures between them grow too big to close.

Traditional patrol officers and the neighborhood officers are not as far apart as their dual images and work expectations might suggest. This research revealed some common ground and shared perspectives. In negotiating masculine police space, especially when today's forces attract officers of different races, genders, and sexual orientations, finding a blend of compatible styles is paramount. Increased unity based on the recognition of mutual struggles, and on respect for each other's knowledge, could create departments that are more democratic among the members and more responsive to the community. Without such acknowledgment and reciprocity in sharing ideas, the strength, character, and potential of the whole force are compromised.

Notes

1. The intensive "surveillance" aspect of community policing can be seen as a technique for optimizing social control in the neighborhoods, in some ways similar to Jeremy Bentham's panoptical prison design of the late eighteenth century. In the panopticon, the guards are located in the center of the structure so that all activity is visible, yet the prisoners do not know when they are being observed. Neighborhood surveillance, where an NPO's presence is continuous and sporadically visible, creates the impression among residents that, since they never know exactly when they are being watched, they are always being watched. And, as Michel Foucault pointed out, individual behavior can be regulated without explicit controls. In this case, simply knowing the NPO is around may encourage residents to internalize societal norms and "police" their own actions.

2. There are both negative and positive kinds of mockery. Positively, mocking and sarcasm are well understood and frequently a part of the camaraderie in the police sub-

culture; humor is also used as a coping mechanism, and to rally officers and boost their esprit de corps (Pogrebin and Poole 1988). Negatively, humor in connection with neighborhood policing involves targeting NPOs for scorn and ridicule.

3. Sometimes affirmative action includes the glass-escalator effect for some men, especially in higher education (Williams 1992, 257).

4. In fact, "[M]any cities . . . share qualities of relative stability, low industrialization, the presence of a college or university, and political support for community policing. Add the elements of being midwestern and a state capital and having a relatively homogeneous population with growing minority communities, and you still will find a large number of similar cities. The exaggerated liberal reputation of the town may be based more on highly publicized activities on campus in the 1960s and 1970s than on the broader orientation of the citizenry. . . . [T]here are many more police departments the size of the [Jackson City] Police Department than the size of the departments in New York or Los Angeles, cities to which we pay considerable attention but which may not be the best models for the 'average' police department." (The source is not cited to preserve confidentiality; please contact the author for additional information.)

Appendix: Methodology

Sampling

At the time of data collection, the Jackson City Police Department had designated 13 officers to work in 12 different neighborhood positions (one neighborhood was assigned 2 officers). This program began a decade earlier; thus, there are 32 persons who had previously served as neighborhood officers, creating the total of 45 present and former NPOs. The sample consisted of 13 current neighborhood police officers, 6 key administrators (chief of police, inspector, and 4 past NPO supervisors), 27 of the 32 former neighborhood officers, and 19 corresponding patrol officers in each designated neighborhood (there are more than 13 patrol officers because shifts overlapped).

Since the respondents cover all aspects, phases, and periods of the program in Jackson City, the data reflect a range of views on how community policing operates. A small number of former neighborhood police officers had left the department for reasons unrelated to neighborhood policing. I diligently pursued all those who had worked as NPOs in the past decade, including tracking down two of the six officers who had subsequently retired or left due to disabilities. Five former neighborhood police officers whom I was unable to find were not included in the sample: three had retired or left on disability and moved away, one was not available for an interview, and one was suspended while undergoing a criminal investigation related to his alleged drug use. No respondents in my sample indicated that the missing officers were key persons in the community policing program in Jackson City. Thus, their absence does not affect the findings.

Sixty-five is a robust sample, and several factors involving access contributed to achieving it. First, the chief of police was extremely open to research and strongly supported my efforts. The second factor was my personal connection with two female officers in the department. My two friends used their personal contacts to connect me with the people I needed to interview, facilitating my exploration of their "hearts and minds." One of these police contact-friends was a neighborhood officer at the time I proposed the research project. She has since been promoted to detective. The other was a sergeant and had served as the female supervisor of neighborhood officers. She is now one of a handful of women in the department who rank above sergeant. Both of my friends were well liked on the force and had great credibility with their colleagues. They vouched for me to others, tracked down retired officers for me to interview, helped with scheduling, answered my questions, and provided clarification and other assistance as the need arose. Third, and finally, the Jackson City department as a whole was very accustomed to being the subject of various outside research projects. The officers' familiarity with academic probing enhanced their receptivity to my project. In fact, they told me and members of my research team repeatedly that they much preferred our method (i.e., asking them questions face-to-face and spending time with them in the field) to dealing with "yet another pen-and-paper" survey.

Data Collection

The gathering of information was triangulated (Denzin and Lincoln 1994; Denzin 1997), using questionnaires, in-depth interviews, and field observations.

1. *Questionnaires* were administered to all thirteen current neighborhood police officers and to the twenty-seven available former NPOs. There was a 100 percent completion rate for the current officers and one of approximately 75 percent for the former NPOs (seven of them indicated that they would rather be interviewed face-to-face).

The majority of the survey questions were open-ended. They covered a range of attitudinal measures and policy-related issues, among them job satisfaction and morale, role conflict, perceptions of effectiveness, evaluation criteria, attitudes about community and neighborhood strengths and weaknesses, policing goals, strategies of deterrence and social control, police subculture, and domestic violence issues.

In order to become acquainted with the current NPOs, I attended a neighborhood officer meeting with the inspector. As second in command of the department, he publicly endorsed my project there; this legitimated my work in the eyes of the neighborhood officers. I was permitted to introduce the entire project and to distribute the questionnaires, which officers were given three weeks to complete. My two police contact-friends were instrumental in prodding their colleagues to finish and in retrieving the surveys. Interviews with current and former neighborhood officers were then scheduled; these were carried out over the next sixteen months.

2. *In-depth interviews* were conducted with the thirteen current neighborhood police officers and with all twenty-seven of the located former NPOs. Simi-

lar qualitative interviews were also undertaken with nineteen rapid response patrol officers in order to assess their differences and similarities (compared to NPOs) in occupational philosophy, goals, and styles and to allow for comparisons between groups. The rapid response officers patrol the perimeter of the designated "community policing" neighborhoods and provide quick assistance and backup to the neighborhood officers on foot patrol there.

In constructing and administering the interview instrument, I followed Lofland and Lofland's (1995, 78–88) interview preparation guidelines: I initially explained who I was and gave a broad outline of the project; I adopted the language of the respondents and tried to be sensitive to what made sense to them; I structured the questions around general clusters and topics, beginning with less-sensitive material in order to build trust and rapport; and I developed probes that took into account both what the respondents mentioned and what they did not mention. After the interview, I jotted down on a comment sheet any leads or issues that I wanted to follow up on, noted the emotional tone of the interview, including any difficulty encountered at the time (methodologically or personally), and added any reflections I had about the interview. Although for consistency I followed an overall checklist with each interview, I also followed a flexible format and stayed open to pursuing other issues of merit. Respondents were free to interrupt, clarify my questions or their responses, and challenge my questions (e.g., on grounds of style or content); they were also free to turn off the tape recorder at any point or ask me to erase any of their comments. I took sparse notes (limiting myself to key words and issues) so as not to be conspicuous or obstruct the flow of the interview.

In the face-to-face interviews with neighborhood police officers it was my sense that being a woman facilitated the conversation. In fact, other investigators who have considered how the researcher's gender could impede or enhance rapport with respondents have found that women interviewing men may facilitate the subjects' ability to talk openly about their feelings (Williams and Heikes 1993). Men may be more comfortable speaking of intimate topics with women than with other men (Williams and Heikes 1993, 281). This is reminiscent of Rubin's (1976) study of working-class families, where she found that men had more experience expressing their feelings to women: "To the degree that the American culture approves of male expression of closeness or intimacy, it is between a man and woman, not between two men" (Rubin 1976, 21). Similarly, in Diana Scully's (1990, 12) interviews with convicted rapists, she discovered that "men seemed to find it easier and more natural to talk to a woman" than to her male colleague. Interviews, like any other interaction between people, "take place in a 'gendered context'—the context of either gender similarity or gender difference" (Williams and Heikes 1993, 282). It made sense to the police that a female researcher would ask them about gender issues and that, as a criminologist, I would ask these questions in the context of community policing. Thus, I was able to examine gendered behavior and assumptions of masculinity and femininity within community policing with greater ease.

3. *Field observations* were also conducted. These entailed a member of the research team accompanying police officers on their daily shifts in their neighborhoods and observing and recording their actions and comments. Both neighborhood and patrol officers' shifts were observed, either on foot with neighborhood officers, or in squad cars with patrol officers. This component of the project also permitted gathering some observational information about citizens' reactions to police delivery of services.

The fieldwork took place in the summers of 1995 and 1996, with the most intense activity in the first year. Three professors and three advanced graduate students were involved; two were men and four were women. Before beginning, the researchers were trained to follow Lofland and Lofland's fieldwork steps (1995, 89–98): during the period of observation, take notes to aid memory and to let respondents know that they are being taken seriously; convert these to full fieldnotes at the end of each shift to minimize the time between observation and writing so that crucial material is not lost; write up observations fully before the next trip to the field; and, when additional information is recalled, add it to the written notes. For the research team, fieldnotes were a "running description of events, people, things heard and overheard, conversations among people, conversations with people. Each new physical setting and person encountered merit[ed] a description" (Lofland and Lofland 1995, 93). Investigators distinguished between the respondents' verbatim accounts and their own paraphrasing and general recall. The researchers also recorded their private emotional responses, based on Lofland and Lofland's admonition (1995, 95) that their "emotional experience, even if not shared by others in the setting, may still suggest important analytical leads."

The fieldwork was conducted in the summer months for several reasons. First, it was important to observe how the neighborhood officers interacted with residents in each district, and the warmer months offered increased opportunities for community social contact, with more available out-of-doors activities and city-sponsored programs for children. Second, in nicer weather, neighborhood officers might be more willing to be outside for longer periods. Third, because of the increase in social activities, including drinking, there would be a greater potential for crime and a greater need for social control, thus creating a wider range of police operations to observe. And finally, since our home university was not in session, summertime allowed greater flexibility in scheduling fieldwork. Overall, several hundred hours' worth of interviews and field observation data were collected.

Typically, we tried to work the same shifts as the neighborhood police officers, and we shadowed the NPO and each corresponding patrol officer during the same shift. Eight-hour shifts were evenly divided into four-hour blocks of walking in the neighborhood with the neighborhood officer and four-hour blocks of riding in the squad car with the patrol officer assigned to the same neighborhood. Shadowing both permitted a cross-check of how neighborhood officers perceived the role of patrol officers and of how patrol officers saw their role in conjunction with, or opposition to, the neighborhood policing concept. We could also observe any joint operations or interactions between the two groups. Unfortunately, shadowing the neighborhood officers' daily schedule involved a trade-off. The patrol officers who might demonstrate the least respect and support for NPOs—those who served on the fourth detail, from 11 P.M. until 7 A.M.—were also the ones who had the least contact with them. On the other hand, since daytime and early evening shifts were typically slower, patrol officers had more time to answer our questions and we had a better chance to observe their interactions with NPOs.

Each observer carried a tiny notebook on shift, and transcribed notes from it into longer, more descriptive typed versions within twenty-four hours of the shift's completion. I reviewed these and maintained an ongoing dialogue with members of the research team to resolve any points of confusion. The fieldwork team met weekly to talk about situations that were unclear and to troubleshoot any problems. We also made use of peer-debriefing techniques. Here, multiple colleagues, who were familiar with qualitative data analysis but not involved in our research, participated in preliminary analysis of our findings (Lincoln and Guba 1985).

Reliability and Validity

All researchers need to address these key concepts. Reliability concerns the extent to which findings can be replicated. Validity concerns the extent to which data actually reflect what investigators set out to measure. The chief concerns about the reliability of the data for this project are stability and consistency and how the findings may be affected by mood and memory. We addressed stability during the fieldwork observations. As for consistency, discrepancies were explored during the interviews and covered across interviewees, since the researchers met and talked about the data collection together.

Measurement issues relating to validity were well covered. Given the high response rate, the sample virtually mirrors the population. In addition to the robust sample, I had access to archival information from the police department and to the files of a number of individual officers who were instrumental in the neighborhood policing program. The department also let me review internal memos, printed documents, and video tapes of training sessions and meetings. I did not use any themes that were not discussed at length by at least three officers.

The fieldwork component allowed for observing officer activity directly, thus providing a "reality check" to determine if officers' accounts match what they actually do on the job. Investigator triangulation was achieved by involving both male and female members of the research team (Lincoln and Guba 1985). Every neighborhood with an NPO was observed at least twice, always by fresh researchers. Different shifts on different days were covered throughout the field observations. Whenever possible, the gender of the observer was also switched.

In order to validate the findings further and clear up discrepancies related to the police department, questions and issues gleaned from data collection and interpretations were presented to some of the officers interviewed, as well as to members of the department who were not part of the neighborhood policing program (see Kingry, Tiedje, and Friedman 1990; Krueger 1994; Lincoln and Guba 1985).

The veracity of respondents' answers, particularly when the subject matter might be controversial or make them feel uncomfortable, is a major component of the problem of validity. I was particularly concerned about the issue of social desirability, the tendency to play with the truth so that respondents' answers sound "nicer" and more acceptable to a researcher. Since I was implicitly and explicitly exploring issues related to gender, work, and notions of masculinity and femininity, I was very cognizant of the rapport established between me and my respondents. In other researchers' analyses of transcribed interviews, Williams and Heikes (1993) found that men talking to male interviewers were more direct and forceful in their responses. When male respondents were interviewed by women, their answers were less direct and less definite. This difference could reflect social desirability: the men could "be themselves" when speaking with other men who might innately understand their views, whereas they were more aware of how racist or sexist they might sound to an out-group member. In my project in Jackson City, even if male respondents had "toned down" their responses, consistent themes still emerged repeatedly and strongly across the sample—if not explicitly in words, then implicitly in the examples the respondents chose to illustrate their experiences. My being female may also have helped to encourage men to talk more openly about gender issues, since I was not a man asking other men about their masculinity; as a woman, I was a safer "confidante."

As Babbie (1983, 135) points out: "Whenever you ask people for information, they answer through a filter of what will make them look good. This is especially true if they are being interviewed in a face-to-face situation." Since I had spent so many hours over eighteen months with the Jackson City Police Department, I had grown to be a familiar face; this, I believe, decreased respondents' tendencies toward social desirability. Officers took my presence for granted in the briefing room, the hallways, the interview rooms, and in the field, including me in jokes and informal conversation in the coffee shop. It also helped that respected members of the force vouched for me. Whenever I encountered scheduling snafus or any reluctance by a police officer to schedule an interview or a walk-along (since not everyone remembered me), my friends on the force would make a call and easily arrange the time I needed with other officers. In addition, triangulating the data provided important cross-checks to minimize answers based on social desirability. Mishler (1986) found that successful interviews involve active participation of both researcher and respondent in a joint construction of meaning. In this regard, I always asked officers to explain or rephrase points for greater accuracy and to raise any issues or add any explanations that they felt I had not covered in my own questions.

Analysis

The data were examined using coding techniques described by Strauss (1987). Each transcript was read several times and analyzed into emergent conceptual categories. Once no new conceptual categories were unearthed, saturation was believed to have been achieved (Krueger 1994).

Feminist Research

As a feminist woman conducting a study of policing, a topic that is typically cast as "men's work," I want to make explicit how who I am affects the research process. Community policing, in particular, has not been explored from a feminist perspective. How *does* such a standpoint differ? In general, feminist research has been characterized by four major themes: topic selection, process of methodology, interruption of power and control hierarchies, and acknowledgment of researcher subjectivity (see Gelsthorpe 1990).

With regard to the first theme, the argument is that the topic should be relevant to women, with the hope that the research will have some kind of political and practical significance (Gelsthorpe 1990, 90). Another feminist researcher, Maureen Cain (1990), argues that this does not mean that feminist research has to be solely on, by, and for women; rather, it seeks to explore relationships. Within criminology and criminal justice areas especially, it would be difficult to exclude men from research on the system. Because my study is ultimately concerned with how social constructions of men's and women's work (and, concomitantly, their masculinity and femininity) influence the social control aspects of both the "job" and gender politics, my questions and topic clearly reflect a feminist approach. Whether the findings will have practical or political significance for women raises another recurring theme. Research findings should speak to audiences beyond academia. I believe that my analysis will be useful to persons outside the world of scholarship, including police and administrators as well as interested citizens who know little about community policing. Since law enforcement officers represent the ultimate formal source of protection, social control, and apprehension in our society, strategies such as community policing have the potential to touch all of us.

The second theme involves selecting and using a methodology. Typically, feminist research employs qualitative methods. For their part, quantitative methods have been criticized for being narrowly objective and for often reflecting only male experiences, thereby excluding in-depth coverage of the experiences of women. Social status, gender differences, and their implications are often masked in quantitative studies. Feminist research encourages interviewing techniques that emerge as more of a two-way process, so that respondents are not objectified and interviews do not lose "personal meaning" (Gelsthorpe 1990, 91). As I have stressed, I followed a two-way, interactive style in my interviews and fieldwork. My questions were phrased so as to convey to respondents that I was not an expert, and that I did not believe there was one objective "truth" to uncover. Rather, there could be multiple truths, and part of the research process was to uncover and untangle them by recognizing that my respondents have expert, intimate knowledge of the events, issues, and situations of their own lives.

The third theme explores ways to interrupt conventional relations of power and control between the observer and the observed. Feminist researchers tend to adopt a more interactive method so as not to reproduce hierarchical relationships between interviewer and interviewee. Once it is recognized that "the researched have power and knowledge which researchers need, and the power to withhold it," a more collaborative process evolves. By using an interactive style of communication, I became more than a body holding a tape recorder who asked scripted questions from printed pages. I remained engaged in the conversation, probing issues raised by the respondents and actively challenging both them and myself to push beyond simple surface responses. As this was taking place, I indicated my intense engagement with the subject and with the respondent by introducing relevant information from prior knowledge, research, or my own experiences. In addition, my willingness to be involved in the interview and fieldwork process was illustrated by the many occasions on which I was able to reciprocate favors—for example, by bringing in articles for officers or by helping to locate social science citations or research for some among them who were going to graduate school.

Because of my own middle-class, educated, white, female status, I was cognizant of the nexus of issues involving gender, race, social class, and sexual orientation. I made connections to the social and personal lives of my respondents by asking them about their families or relationships and how these affected their views on community policing and gender. I did not consider respondents as outside their contexts, but rather saw them as belonging to many affiliations beyond being a police officer. Moreover, I asked them what other questions I should ask, thereby creating an interactive exchange with the officers. I also sought their interpretation of data collected from other patrol and neighborhood officers. Finally, I used my friends in the department to verify, clarify, and dispute findings.

The fourth, and last, theme concerns the acknowledgment of researcher subjectivity—that "feminist research is characterized by a concern to record the subjective experiences of doing research" (Gelsthorpe 1990, 93). As Stanley and Wise point out (1983, 157):

> Whether we like it or not, researchers remain human beings complete with all the usual assembly of feelings, failings, and moods. And all of these things influence how we feel and understand what is going on. Our consciousness is always the medium through which the research occurs; there is no method or technique of doing research other than through the medium of the researcher.

No research is ever value-free. My analysis, like that of any other investigator, is conducted through my own eyes and interpretations. However, as Dubois (1983) asserts, "A rejection of the notion of 'objectivity' does not mean a rejection of a concern for being accurate."

In sum, I looked at the world of community policing in Jackson City from the standpoint of the officers who performed the roles. I sought their words, their knowledge, and their experiences. I did not let one point of view create the "truth," but I listened and watched for how the officers made sense of their world. All research should seek to uncover the standpoint of those researched. To paraphrase Loraine Gelsthorpe (1990): Is this feminist research, or just good research?

References

Acker, Joan. 1989. *Doing Comparable Worth*. Philadelphia: Temple University Press.

———. 1990. "Hierarchies, Jobs, and Bodies: A Theory of Gendered Organizations." *Gender and Society* 4:139–158.

———. 1992. "The Future of Women and Work: Ending the Twentieth Century." *Sociological Perspectives* 35:53–68.

Acker, Joan, and A. M. Ask. 1989. *Wage Difference between Women and Men and the Structure of Work and Wage Setting in Swedish Banks*. Stockholm: Arbetslivscentrum.

Anleu, S. L. 1995. "Women in Law: Theory, Research, and Practice." In *The Criminal Justice System and Women: Offenders, Victims, and Workers*, 2d ed., edited by Barbara Raffel Price and Natalie J. Sokoloff. New York: McGraw-Hill.

Appier, Janis. 1998. *Policing Women: The Sexual Politics of Law Enforcement and the LAPD*. Philadelphia: Temple University Press.

Babbie, Earl. 1983. *The Practice of Social Research*. 3d ed. Belmont, Calif.: Wadsworth.

Baran, B. 1990. "The New Economy: Female Labor and the Office of the Future." In *Women, Class, and the Feminist Imagination*, edited by K. V. Hansen and I. J. Philipson. Philadelphia: Temple University Press.

Bayley, David H. 1991. "Community Policing: A Report from the Devil's Advocate." In *Community Policing: Rhetoric or Reality*, edited by Jack R. Greene and Stephen D. Mastrofski. New York: Praeger.

———. 1994. *Police for the Future*. New York: Oxford University Press.

Bell, D. J. 1984. "The Police Response to Domestic Violence: An Exploratory Study." *Police Studies* 7(1):23–30.

Bem, Sandra Lipsitz. 1974. "The Measurement of Psychological Androgyny." *Journal of Consulting and Clinical Psychology* 42(2):155–162.

———. 1993. *The Lenses of Gender: Transforming the Debate on Sexual Inequality*. New Haven: Yale University Press.

Berheide, C. 1988. "Women in Sales and Service Occupations." In *Women Working: Theories and Facts in Perspective*, edited by A. Stromberg and S. Harkess. Mountain View, Calif.: Mayfield.

Bianchi, S. M., and N. Rytina. 1986. "The Decline in Occupational Sex Segregation during the 1970s: Census and CPS Comparisons." *Demography* 23:79–86.

Biecke, Witt. 1980. "Response Time Analysis." Manuscript. Kansas City, Mo.: Kansas City Police Department.

Bird, Sharon R. 1996. "Welcome to the Men's Club: Homosociality and the Maintenance of Hegemonic Masculinity." *Gender and Society* 10(2):120–132.

Black, Donald J. 1976. *The Behavior of Law.* New York: Academic Press.

———. 1980. *The Manners and Customs of the Police.* San Diego: Academic Press.

Blumenfield, Warren J. 1992. *Homophobia: How We All Pay the Price.* Boston: Beacon Press.

Bowker, L. H. 1982. "Police Service to Battered Women: Bad or Not So Bad?" *Criminal Justice and Behavior* 9:476–486.

Buel, S. M. 1988. "Recent Developments: Mandatory Arrest for Domestic Violence." *Harvard Women's Law Journal* 11:213–226.

Buerger, Michael E. 1994. "A Tale of Two Targets: Limitations of Community Anticrime Actions." *Crime and Delinquency* 40:411–436.

Burke, Marc E. 1993. *Coming Out of the Blue: British Police Officers Talk about Their Lives in 'The Job' as Lesbians, Gays, and Bisexuals.* London: Cassell.

———. 1994. "Homosexuality as Deviance: The Case of the Gay Police Officer." *British Journal of Criminology* 34:192–203.

Buzawa, Eve S., and Carl G. Buzawa. 1993. *Domestic Violence: The Criminal Justice Response.* Newbury Park, Calif.: Sage.

Cain, Maureen. 1990. "Realist Philosophy and Standpoint Epistemologies, or Feminist Criminology as a Successor Science." In *Feminist Perspectives in Criminology,* edited by L. Gelsthorpe and A. Morris. Philadelphia: Open University Press.

Cancian, Francesca M. 1987. *Love in America: Gender and Self-Development.* Cambridge: Cambridge University Press.

Casper, Jonathan D., Tom R. Tyler, and Bonnie Fisher. 1988. "Procedural Justice in Felony Cases." *Law and Society Review* 22:483–507.

Cockburn, Cynthia. 1988. *Machinery of Dominance: Women, Men, and Technical Know-How.* Boston: Northeastern University Press.

———. 1991. *In the Way of Women: Men's Resistance to Sex Equality in Organizations.* Ithaca, N.Y.: ILR Press.

Cockburn, Cynthia, and S. Ormrod. 1993. *Gender and Technology in the Making.* London: Sage.

Code, L. B. 1983. "Responsibility and the Epistemic Community: Woman's Place." *Social Research* 50:537–555.

Cohn, Samuel. 1985. *The Process of Occupational Sex-Typing.* Philadelphia: Temple University Press.

Collins, Patricia Hill. 1990. *Black Feminist Thought: Knowledge, Consciousness, and the Politics of Empowerment.* New York: Routledge.

Community Policing Exchange. 1996. "Landlords Use Compact to Strike Back at Criminals," September–October, 6–7.

———. 1997. "The Ingredients of Effective Partnering," July–August, 2.

Connell, Robert W. 1987. *Gender and Power: Society, the Person, and Sexual Politics.* Stanford: Stanford University Press.

———. 1992. *Gender and Power.* Palo Alto: Stanford University Press.

Cotter, David A., JoAnn M. DeFiore, Joan M. Hermsen, Brenda Marsteller Kowaleski, and Reeve Vanneman. 1995. "Occupational Gender Desegregation in the 1980s." *Work and Occupation* 22(1):3–21.

Daly, Kathleen. 1989. "Criminal Justice Ideologies and Practices in Different Voices: Some Feminist Questions about Justice." *International Journal of the Sociology of Law* 17:1–18.

———. 1994. *Gender, Crime, and Punishment.* New Haven: Yale University Press.

Delgado, Julie Rees, and Madeleine Kornfein Rose. 1994. "Caregiver Constellations: Caring for Persons with AIDS." *Journal of Gay and Lesbian Social Services* 1(1):1–14.

Denzin, Norman K. 1997. *Interpretive Ethnography: Ethnographic Practices for the 21st Century.* Thousand Oaks, Calif.: Sage.

Denzin, Norman K., and Yvonna S. Lincoln. 1994. *Handbook of Qualitative Research.* Thousand Oaks, Calif.: Sage.

Dubois, B. 1983. "Passionate Scholarship: Notes on Values, Knowing, and Method in Feminist Social Science." In *Theories for Women's Studies,* edited by G. Bowles and Duellie R. Klein. London: Routledge and Kegan Paul.

Dunn, D. 1995. "Sociological Dimensions of Economic Conversion." In *The Socio-Economics of Conversion from War to Peace,* edited by L. J. Dumas. Armonk, N.Y.: M. E. Sharp.

Ehrenreich, Barbara, and Deirdre English. 1978. *For Her Own Good: 100 Years of Expert Advice to Women.* Garden City, N.Y.: Anchor Books.

Encyclopedia of Social Work. 1933. "Policewomen," 360–362.

Epstein, Cynthia Fuchs. 1988. *Deceptive Distinctions: Sex, Gender, and the Social Order.* New Haven: Yale University Press.

Field, M. H., and H. F. Field. 1973. "Marital Violence and the Criminal Process: Neither Justice nor Peace." *Social Science Review* 47:221–240.

Fielding, Nigel. 1994. "Cop Canteen Culture." In *Just Boys Doing Business? Men, Masculinities and Crime,* edited by Tim Newburn and Elizabeth A. Stanko. London and New York: Routledge.

Fogelson, Robert M. 1977. *Big-City Police.* Cambridge: Harvard University Press.

Freedman, Estelle B. 1979. "Separatism as Strategy: Female Institution Building and American Feminism, 1870–1930." *Feminist Studies* 5(3):512–529.

———. 1981. *Their Sisters' Keepers: Women Prison Reform in America, 1830–1930.* Ann Arbor: University of Michigan Press.

Freeman, Sue J. M. 1990. *Managing Lives: Corporate Women and Social Change.* Amherst: University of Massachusetts Press.

Gelsthorpe, Loraine. 1990. "Feminist Methodologies in Criminology." In *Feminist Perspectives in Criminology,* edited by L. Gelsthorpe and A. Morris. Philadelphia: Open University Press.

Gil, D. G. 1986. "Sociocultural Aspects of Domestic Violence." In *Violence in the Home: Interdisciplinary Perspectives,* edited by M. Lystad. New York: Brunner/Mazel.

Gilligan, Carol. 1982. *In a Different Voice: Psychological Theory and Women's Development.* Cambridge: Harvard University Press.

Gilloran, Alan. 1995. "Gender Differences in Care Delivery and Supervisory Relationships: The Case of Psychogeriatric Nursing." *Journal of Advanced Nursing* 21:652–658.

Goldstein, Herman. 1990. *Problem-Oriented Policing.* New York: McGraw-Hill.

Greene, Jack R., and Ralph B. Taylor. 1991. "Community Based Policing and Foot Patrol: Issues of Theory and Evaluation." In *Community Policing: Rhetoric or Reality?*, edited by Jack R. Greene and Stephen D. Mastrofski. New York: Praeger.

Grinc, Randolph M. 1994. "'Angels in Marble': Problems in Stimulating Community Involvement in Community Policing." *Crime and Delinquency* 40:437–468.

Guyot, Dorothy. 1979. "Bending Granite: Attempts to Change the Rank Structure of American Police Departments." *Journal of Police Science and Administration* 7(3):253–284.

Hacker, S. 1990. *Doing It the Hard Way.* Boston: Unwin Hyman.

Hall, Elaine J. 1993. "Smiling, Deferring, and Flirting: Doing Gender by Giving 'Good Service.'" *Work and Occupations* 20(4):452–471.

Haller, Mark H. 1976. "Historical Roots of Police Behavior: Chicago, 1890–1925." *Law and Society Review* 10(2):303–323.

Hamilton, Mary E. 1924. *The Policewoman: Her Services and Ideals.* Reprint. Police in America Series. New York: Arno Press, 1971.

Hirsch, Carl. 1996. "Understanding the Influence of Gender Role Identity on the Assumption of Family Caregiving Roles by Men." *International Journal of Aging and Human Development* 42(2):103–121.

Hochschild, Arlie Russell. 1983. *The Managed Heart: Commercialization of Human Feeling.* Berkeley and Los Angeles: University of California Press.

Hunt, Jennifer. 1984. "The Development of Rapport through the Negotiation of Gender in Field Work among Police." *Human Organization* 43:283–296.

———. 1990. "The Logic of Sexism among Police." *Women and Criminal Justice* 1:3–30.

Hutzel, Eleanor. 1926. "The Value of a Central Registration Bureau to the Women's Division." *International Association of Policewomen* 10:7–11.

———. 1933. *The Policewoman's Handbook.* New York: Columbia University Press.

IAP Bulletin. May 15, 1925. Albany, N.Y.: International Association of Policewomen.

International Association of Chiefs of Police. 1967. *Training Key 16: Handling Disturbance Calls.* Gaithersburg, Md.: International Association of Chiefs of Police.

Jacobs, Jerry. 1989. *Revolving Doors: Sex Segregation and Women's Careers.* Stanford: Stanford University Press.

Jurik, Nancy C. 1985. "An Officer and a Lady: Organizational Barriers to Women Working as Correctional Officers in Men's Prisons." *Social Problems* 32:375–388.

———. 1988. "Striking a Balance: Female Correctional Officers, Gender Role Stereotypes, and Male Prisons." *Sociological Inquiry* 58:291–305.

Jurik, Nancy C., and Susan Ehrlich Martin. 1999. "Femininities, Masculinities, and Organizational Conflict: Women in Policing and Corrections Occupations." In *Women, Crime, and Justice: Contemporary Perspectives*, edited by Lynne Goodstein and Claire Renzetti. Boston: Roxbury Press. Forthcoming.

Kanter, Rosabeth Moss. 1977. *Men and Women of the Corporation.* New York: Basic Books.

Karmen, A. 1982. "Women as Crime Victims: Problems and Solutions." In *The Criminal Justice System and Women,* edited by Barbara Raffel Price and Natalie J. Sokoloff. New York: Clark Boardman.

Kaye, Lenard W., and Jeffrey S. Applegate. 1990. "Men as Elder Caregivers: A Response to Changing Families." *American Journal of Orthopsychiatric* 60(1):86–95.

———. 1993. "Family Support Groups for Male Caregivers: Benefits of Participation." *Journal of Gerontological Social Work* 20(3–4):167–185.

Kelling, G. L., and Mark H. Moore. 1987. *From Political Reform to Community: The Evolving Strategy of Police.* Cambridge, Mass.: Harvard University JFK School of Government.

———. 1991. "From Political Reform to Community: The Evolving Strategy of Police." In *Community Policing: Rhetoric or Reality,* edited by Jack R. Greene and Stephen D. Mastrofski. New York: Praeger.

Kelly, Norma R., Mary Shoemaker, and Tim Steele. 1996. "The Experience of Being a Male Student Nurse." *Journal of Nursing Education* 35(4):170–174.

Kingry, M., L. Tiedje, and L. Friedman. 1990. "Focus Groups: A Research Technique for Nursing." *Nursing Research* 39(2):124–125.

Kohlberg, L. 1984. *The Psychology of Moral Development.* San Francisco: Harper and Row.

Krueger, R. 1994. *Focus Groups: A Practical Guide for Applied Research.* 2d ed. Newbury Park, Calif.: Sage.

LaFree, Gary, B. Reskin, and C. Vischer. 1985. "Jurors' Responses to Victims' Behavior and Legal Issues in Sexual Assault Trials." *Social Problems* 32:213–232.

Lebowitz, Howard. 1997. "Academy Training Curriculum Minimizes the Physical Factor, Emphasizes Moral Decision Making." *Community Policing Exchange* 13(March–April): 2.

Lerman, L. 1986. "Prosecution of Wife Beaters: Institutional Obstacles and Innovations." In *Violence in the Home: Interdisciplinary Perspectives,* edited by M. Lystad. New York: Brunner/Mazel.

Lincoln, Y., and E. Guba. 1985. *Naturalistic Inquiry.* Beverly Hills, Calif.: Sage.

Literary Digest. 1921. "The Policewomen of Indianapolis and Their New Methods," April 23, 41–43.

Lloyd, G. 1983. "Reason, Gender, and Morality in the History of Philosophy." *Social Research* 50:490–513.

Lofland, John, and Lyn H. Lofland. 1995. *Analyzing Social Settings: A Guide to Qualitative Observation and Analysis.* 3d ed. Belmont, Calif.: Wadsworth.

Lurigio, Arthur J., and Wesley G. Skogan. 1994. "Winning the Hearts and Minds of Police Officers: An Assessment of Staff Perceptions of Community Policing in Chicago." *Crime and Delinquency* 40:315–330.

Lurigio, Arthur J., and Dennis P. Rosenbaum. 1994. "The Impact of Community Policing on Police Personnel: A Review of the Literature." In *The Challenge of Community Policing: Testing the Promises,* edited by Dennis P. Rosenbaum. Thousand Oaks, Calif.: Sage.

MacKinnon, Catherine. 1984. "The 1984 James McCormick Mitchell Lecture: Feminist Discourse, Moral Values, and the Law—A Conversation." *Buffalo Law Review* 11:20.

———. 1989. *Toward a Feminist Theory of the State.* Cambridge: Harvard University Press.

Manning, Peter K. 1984. "Community Based Policing." *American Journal of Policing* 3:205–227.

Maquire, Kathleen, and Ann C. Pastore. 1997. *Sourcebook of Criminal Justice.* Publication of the Bureau of Justice Statistics, 1996. Washington: U.S. Government Printing Office.

Martin, Susan E. 1980. *Breaking and Entering: Policewomen on Patrol.* Berkeley and Los Angeles: University of California Press.

———. 1988. "Think Like a Man, Work Like a Dog, Act Like a Lady: Occupational Dilemmas of Policewomen." In *The Worth of a Woman's Work: A Qualitative Synthesis,* edited by Anne Stathan, Elenor Miller, and Hans O. Manksch. Albany: SUNY Press.

———. 1989. "Women on the Move? A Report on the Status of Women in Policing." *Women and Criminal Justice* 1:2–40.

———. 1994. " 'Outsider Within' the Station House: The Impact of Race and Gender on Black Women Police." *Social Problems* 41:383–400.

Martin, Susan E., and Nancy Jurik. 1996. *Doing Justice, Doing Gender: Women in Law and Criminal Justice Occupations.* Thousand Oaks, Calif.: Sage.

Marzulli, J. 1994. "Community Cop Program a Bust." *New York Daily News,* January 24.

McElroy, Jerome, Colleen Cosgrove, and Susan Sadd. 1993. *Community Policing: The CPOP in New York.* Newbury Park, Calif.: Sage.

Menkel-Meadow, C. 1985. "Portia in a Different Voice: Speculations on a Women's Lawyering Process." *Berkeley Women's Law Journal* 1:39–63.

———. 1989. "Exploring a Research Agenda of the Feminization of the Legal Profession: Theories of Gender and Social Change." *Law and Social Inquiry* 14:289–314.

Messerschmidt, James W. 1993. *Masculinities and Crime: Critique and Reconceptualization of Theory.* Lanham, Md.: Rowman and Littlefield.

Metchick, E., and A. Winton. 1995. "Community Policing and Its Implications for Alternative Models of Police Officer Selection." In *Issues in Community Policing,* edited by P. C. Kratcoski and D. Dukes. Cincinnati: Anderson Publishing.

Miller, Susan L. 1996a. " 'Real' Police Work or the Work of 'Pansies'?" Manuscript. Newark: University of Delaware.

———. 1996b. "Gender Paradoxes: Reconciling Informal and Formal Social Control of Battering in a Community Policing Context." Paper presented at the annual conference of the American Society of Criminology, Chicago.

———. 1998. "Rocking the Rank and File: Gender Issues and Community Policing." *Journal of Contemporary Criminal Justice* 14(2):156–172.

Miller, Susan L., Kay B. Forrest, and Nancy Jurik. 1997. "Diversity in Blue: Lesbian and Gay Police Officers in a Masculinist Profession." Paper presented at the annual conference of the American Society of Criminology, San Diego.

Milton, C. 1972. *Women in Policing.* Washington: Police Foundation.

Mishler, Elliot. 1986. *Research Interviewing: Context and Narrative.* Cambridge: Harvard University Press.

Monkkonen, Eric. 1981. *Police in Urban America, 1860–1920.* Cambridge: Cambridge University Press.

Montgomery, Brenda. 1994. "Caregiver Education: Feminist or Male Model?" *Health Care for Women International* 15:481–488.

Morash, Merry, and Jack Greene. 1986. "Evaluating Women on Patrol: A Critique of Contemporary Wisdom." *Evaluation Review* 10:230–255.

Morris, Allison. 1987. *Women, Crime, and Criminal Justice.* New York: Basil Blackwell.

Moyer, Imogene L. 1992. *The Changing Role of Women in the Criminal Justice System: Offenders, Victims, and Professionals.* Prospect Heights, Ill.: Waveland Press.

Murphy, P., and D. G. Caplan. 1993. "Fostering Integrity." In *Critical Issues in Policing: Contemporary Readings,* edited by R. G. Dunham and G. P. Alpert. Prospect Heights, Ill.: Waveland Press.

Myers, L. B., and C. Chiang. 1993. "Law Enforcement Officer and Peace Officer: Reconciliation Using the Feminine Approach." *Journal of Crime and Justice* 14:31–41.

Nivea, Veronica F., and Barbara Gutek. 1981. *Women and Work: A Psychological Perspective.* New York: Praeger.

Oettmeier, T. 1997. "Perspectives on Selection Procedures." *Community Policing Exchange* 13:1–8.

Owings, Chloe. 1925. *Women Police: A Study of the Development and Status of the Women Police Movement.* Publication of the Bureau of Social Hygiene. New York: Fredrick H. Hitchcock.

Parnas, R. E. 1967. "The Police Response to the Domestic Disturbance." *Wisconsin Law Review* 31:914–960.

Pate, Antony M., and Penny Shtull. 1994. "Community Policing Grows in Brooklyn: An Inside View of the New York Police Department's Model Precinct." *Crime and Delinquency* 40:384–410.

Paternoster, Raymond, Ronet Bachman, Robert Brame, and Lawrence W. Sherman. 1997. "Do Fair Procedures Matter? The Effect of Procedural Justice on Spouse Assault." *Law and Society Review* 31(1):163–204.

Pavalko, R. M. 1988. *Sociology of Occupations and Professions.* Itasca, Ill.: Peacock.

Perry, Beth. 1996. "Influence of Nurse Gender on the Use of Silence, Touch, and Humor." *International Journal of Palliative Nursing* 2(1):7–14.

Pharr, Suzanne. 1988. *Homophobia: A Weapon of Sexism.* Little Rock, Ark.: Chardon.

Pigeon, Helen. 1927. "Policewomen in the United States." *Journal of Criminal Law and Criminology* November:372–377.

Platt, Anthony M. 1977. *The Child Savers: The Invention of Delinquency.* Chicago: University of Chicago Press.

Pogrebin, M. R., and E. O. Poole. 1988. "Humor in the Briefing Room: A Study of the Strategic Uses of Humor among Police." *Journal of Contemporary Ethnography* 17:183–210.

Police Foundation. 1981. *The Newark Foot Patrol Experiment.* Washington: Police Foundation.

Police Journal. 1929. "Police Functions Best Performed by Men and by Women Police Officers," 20–22.

Policewomen's International Bulletin. August–September, 1927. Albany, N.Y.: International Association of Policewomen.

President's Commission on Law Enforcement and Administration of Justice. 1967. *Task Force Report: The Police.* Washington: U.S. Government Printing Office.

Rafter, Nicole Hahn. 1990. *Partial Justice: Women, Prisons, and Social Control.* New Brunswick, N.J.: Transaction Publishers.

Remmington, P. W. 1981. *Policing: The Occupation and the Introduction of Female Officers.* Washington: University Press of America.

Reskin, Barbara. 1988. "Bringing the Men Back In: Sex Differentiation and the Devaluation of Women's Work." *Gender and Society* 2:58–81.

Reskin, Barbara, and Heidi Hartman. 1986. *Women's Work, Men's Work: Sex Segregation on the Job.* Washington: National Academy Press.

Reskin, Barbara, and Patricia Roos. 1990. *Job Queues, Gender Queues: Exploring Women's Inroads into Male Occupations.* Philadelphia: Temple University Press.

Reuss-Ianni, E., and F. A. J. Ianni. 1983. "Street Cops and Management Cops: The Two Cultures of Policing." In *Control in the Police Organization,* edited by M. Punch. Cambridge: MIT Press.

Roos, Patricia A., and Katharine W. Jones. 1993. "Shifting Gender Boundaries: Women's Inroads into Academic Sociology." *Work and Occupations* 20(4):395–428.

Rosenbaum, Dennis P. 1988. "Community Crime Prevention: A Review and Synthesis of the Literature." *Justice Quarterly* 5:323–395.

Rosenbaum, Dennis P., and Arthur J. Lurigio. 1994. "An Inside Look at Community Policing Reform: Definitions, Organizational Changes, and Evaluation Findings." *Crime and Delinquency* 40:299–314.

Rosenbaum, Dennis P., Sandy Yeh, and Deanna L. Wilkinson. 1994. "Impact of Community Policing on Police Personnel: A Quasi-Experimental Test." *Crime and Delinquency* 40:331–353.

Rubin, Lillian B. 1976. *Worlds of Pain.* New York: Basic Books.

Schneider, Beth E. 1989. "Invisible and Independent: Lesbians' Experiences in the Workplace." In *Women Working,* edited by A. Stromberg and S. Harkess. Palo Alto, Calif.: Mayfield Publishing.

Schulz, D. M. 1995. *From Social Worker to Crimefighter: Women in United States Municipal Policing.* New York: Praeger.

Scully, Diana. 1990. *Understanding Sexual Violence.* Boston: Unwin Hyman.

Shusta, Robert M., Deena R. Levine, Philip R. Harris, and Herbert Z. Wong. 1995. *Multicultural Law Enforcement: Strategies for Peacekeeping in a Diverse Society.* Englewood Cliffs, N.J.: Prentice-Hall.

Skogan, Wesley G. 1990. *Disorder and Community Decline: Crime and the Spiral of Decay in American Neighborhoods.* New York: Free Press.

Skogan, Wesley G., and M. Maxfield. 1981. *Coping with Crime.* Beverly Hills, Calif.: Sage.

Skogan, Wesley G., and Mary Ann Wycoff. 1986. "Storefront Police Offices: The Houston Field Test." In *Community Crime Prevention: Does It Work?* edited by Dennis P. Rosenbaum. Beverly Hills, Calif.: Sage.

Skolnick, Jerome H. 1966. *Justice without Trial.* New York: Wiley.

———. 1994. *Justice without Trial: Law Enforcement in a Democratic Society.* New York: Macmillan.

Skolnick, Jerome H., and David H. Bayley. 1988. *The New Blue Line: Innovations in Six American Cities.* New York: Free Press.

Spelman, Elizabeth. 1988. *Inessential Women: Problems of Exclusion in Feminist Thought.* Boston: Beacon.

Stanko, Elizabeth. 1985. *Intimate Intrusions: Women's Experience of Male Violence.* London: Unwin Hyman.

Stanley, L., and S. Wise. 1983. *Breaking Out: Feminist Consciousness and Feminist Research.* London: Routledge and Kegan Paul.

Strauss, Anselm L. 1987. *Qualitative Analysis for Social Scientists.* New York: Cambridge University Press.

Sulton, Cynthia G., and Roi D. Townsey. 1981. *A Progress Report on Women in Policing.* Washington: Police Foundation.

Swerdlow, Marian. 1989. "Men's Accommodation to Women Entering Nontraditional Occupations: A Case of Rapid Transit Operators." *Gender and Society* 3(3):373–387.

Taylor, Robert W., Eric J. Fritsch, and Tony J. Caeti. 1998. "Core Challenges Facing Community Policing: The Emperor Still Has No Clothes." *ACJS Today* 17(1):1–5.

Townsey, Roi D. 1982. "Female Patrol Officers: A Review of the Physical Capability Issue." In *The Criminal Justice System and Women,* edited by Barbara Raffel Price and Natalie J. Sokoloff. New York: Clark Boardman.

Trojanowicz, Robert C. 1986. "Evaluating a Neighborhood Foot Patrol Program: The Flint, Michigan, Project." In *Community Crime Prevention: Does It Work?* edited by Dennis P. Rosenbaum. Beverly Hills, Calif.: Sage.

Trojanowicz, Robert C., and Bonnie Bucqueroux. 1990. *Community Policing: A Contemporary Perspective.* Cincinnati: Anderson Publishing.

U.S. Department of Labor. Bureau of Labor Statistics. 1991. *Employment and Earnings.* January. Washington: U.S. Government Printing Office.

Van Maanen, John. 1978. "The Asshole." In *Policing: A View from the Street,* edited by Peter K. Manning and John Van Maanen. Santa Monica, Calif.: Goodyear.

Walker, Samuel. 1977. *A Critical History of Police Reform.* Lexington, Mass.: D. C. Heath.

———. 1983. *The Police in America: An Introduction.* New York: McGraw-Hill.

Wasserman, R., and M. H. Moore. 1988. *Values in Policing: Perspectives on Policing.* National Institute of Justice and John F. Kennedy School of Government. Cambridge: Harvard University Press.

Weatheritt, Mollie. 1987. "Community Policing Now." In *Policing and the Community,* edited by P. Willmott. London: Policing Studies Institute.

West, C., and D. H. Zimmerman. 1987. "Doing Gender." *Gender and Society* 1:125–151.

West, R. 1988. "Jurisprudence and Gender." *University of Chicago Law Review* 55:1–72.

Williams, Christine. 1989. *Gender Difference at Work: Women and Men in Nontraditional Occupations.* Berkeley and Los Angeles: University of California Press.

———. 1992. "The Glass Escalator: Hidden Advances for Men in the 'Female' Professions." *Social Problems* 39(3):253–267.

Williams, Christine, and E. Joel Heikes. 1993. "The Importance of Researcher's Gender in the In-Depth Interview: Evidence from Two Case Studies of Male Nurses." *Gender and Society* 7(2):280–291.

Wilson, Deborah G., and Susan F. Bennett. 1994. "Officers' Response to Community Policing: Variations on a Theme." *Crime and Delinquency* 40:354–370.

Wilson, James Q., and George Kelling. 1982. "The Police and Neighborhood Safety: Broken Windows." *Atlantic Monthly* 12(7):29–38.

Wycoff, Mary Ann, and Wesley G. Skogan. 1994. "The Effect of a Community Policing Management Style on Officers' Attitudes." *Crime and Delinquency* 40:371–383.

Young, M. 1991. *An Inside Job: Policing and Police Culture in Britain.* London: Clarendon Press.

Zimmer, Lynn E. 1986. *Women Guarding Men.* Chicago: University of Chicago Press.

———. 1987. "How Women Reshape the Prison Guard Role." *Gender & Society* 1:415–431.

———. 1988. "Tokenism and Women in the Workplace." *Social Problems* 35:64–77.

Index

abuse of authority, 85, 196

accountability: of NPO, 26, 71, 108, 113, 181, 204; of police departments, 79; of residents, 190. *See also* responsibility

activities, neighborhood: bike rodeo, 112, 125–26; clubs/groups, 34–35, 44, 47, 91, 185; computer workshops, 22, 39, 49, 91, 129, 152, 161; cooperative garden, 47, 211; for holidays, 22, 47, 153; recreation, 34–35, 91, 128, 151, 161. *See also* gendered activities; meetings; sports programs

administrators, police: hiring policewomen, 75, 76, 78, 86; rebuilding police image, 196, 198–200; top-down policies, 79, 81, 108–9, 198; views on crime rate, 200

African Americans: body language, 155–56; and traffic stops ("DWBs"), 196

Aid to Families with Dependent Children (AFDC), 49–50

alcohol use, 22, 52, 87, 145, 184

arrest rates, 84, 93, 184

arrests: in crime control model, 5, 81, 100, 148, 167, 173; for drug violations, 30, 36, 208

arrests by NPOs, 145–50, 162–63; by appointment, 148–49; for domestic violence, 44, 180–82, 185–89, 192; patrol assistance with, 203

Asian immigrants, 57; cultural elements, 130, 155–56, 187; Hmong Laotians, 17, 50, 156, 157, 187; public housing for, 37, 42

Aurora (Colo.), tenant areas, 207–8

autonomy of officers: in history, 73; neighborhood officers, 170, 181; patrol officers, 79, 81, 85, 170

backup work, 133, 141, 171, 175

briefings: NPO attendance at, 49, 166–68; roll calls, 200. *See also* camaraderie

Brooklyn (N.Y.), 205–7

burnout, officer, 22, 102, 162, 183, 201

business associations, 100, 112, 174

calls for service: dispatch systems and, 79, 81, 101–2; for domestic violence, 161, 171, 185; emergency, 49, 81, 109, 146, 197; from high-crime areas, 32, 141; NPO response to, 110, 112, 116, 171, 204

camaraderie: during briefings, 166, 169–70, 180, 202; on patrol, 175–76, 178; with security employees, 41–42, 120

car patrol. *See* patrol officers

Chicago world's fair (1893), 75

chief of police: and community policing, 7, 148, 174, 182; Jackson City, 12–16, 62; top-down decision making, 14, 79, 108–9, 198

children: baseball cards for, 39, 40, 52, 171; handicapped, 34–35; Head Start for, 60, 130; informal counseling of, 171; as informants, 39, 45; respite care from, 47, 189; school attendance by, 48–49, 51–52; small gifts for, 50, 176; taught to distrust police, 38, 142; unsupervised or neglected, 132–33, 150. *See also* activities; teenagers

Children and Family Services, Department of (DCFS), 44

citations: long term impact of, 186; for ordinance violations, 22, 38, 171; for trespassing, 45, 46, 56, 64, 140; for underage driving, 42, 43

Civil Rights Act of 1964, 86

community centers: as activity center, 39, 53, 60, 211; external funding for, 56, 63, 152; health services at, 38, 39, 40, 56; as information center, 152, 185; social workers at, 58, 104, 156

community involvement, 125–26, 194, 195–97, 207–9. *See also* activities; connections

community partnerships: probation/parole with NPOs, 22, 32, 40, 120, 142; social workers with NPOs, 32–33, 34, 40, 51–52, 91; tech-